When Winning Was Everything

ALABAMA FOOTBALL PLAYERS IN WORLD WAR II

by DELBERT REED

Copyright 2010©

ISBN 978-0-615-38605-8

Published by

300 Paul W Bryant Drive
Tuscaloosa, AL 35487
(205) 348-4668 • bryant.ua.edu

When Winning Was Everything

ALABAMA FOOTBALL PLAYERS IN WORLD WAR II

Foreword by

PAUL W. BRYANT JR.

Published by

THE PAUL W. BRYANT MUSEUM

CONTENTS

Continued

DEDICATION

To the more than 300 members of the University of Alabama football family who courageously rushed into World War II to help rally the struggling free world in its must-win battle against brutal and fanatical opponents. They earned our cheers for victory on the football field and our enduring gratitude for victory in wartime.

FOREWORD

by Paul W. Bryant Jr.

The date was December 7, 1941, and my father—then an assistant coach at Vanderbilt—had been in Little Rock visiting with University of Arkansas officials about becoming the head football coach in Fayetteville.

Actually, he had accepted the job to be the next Razorbacks coach, but when he was en route back to Nashville, he heard about the bombing of Pearl Harbor on the radio. A few days later, he went to Washington, D.C., to enlist in the United States Navy. It wasn't a noble act but one of allegiance to his country and one made by virtually every able-bodied man in this country, including some 325 young men who had worn another uniform—that of the Crimson Tide football team.

During my formative years in Lexington, College Station and Tuscaloosa, I always listened with especial pride when friends of my father would visit and relate their own stories about a war that truly impacted the entire world. To Papa, who frankly always downplayed his own role in this fight for liberty, these men were the true heroes and the ones who enabled all of us to enjoy the freedom of watching football on autumn afternoons.

While these gentlemen's contributions to Alabama football can be determined by championship hardware, the only true way to measure their courage is by their valor on the battlefields of World War II.

A few years ago I was reading a book about major league baseball players who forfeited some of their most productive years to fight on foreign continents and distant islands. Really, that was the genesis of the idea for this historical look at the soldiers and sailors from the University of Alabama. I solicited the help of Delbert Reed, who intricately and masterfully weaves the stories of these true Crimson Tide heroes into *When Winning Was Everything,* a book that I consider essential reading for anyone with an interest in our nation's history or University of Alabama football history.

For those who gave their lives and didn't come home and to the others who risked their lives for our freedom and did return to the soils of Alabama, this book is a small tribute to you.

INTRODUCTION

"They came up during the Depression. They had a hard early life, but they were achievers—true Americans— symbols of what this country is. They lived it in words and deeds."

— *Bob Rast*

Opposite: U.S. ships explode at Pearl Harbor, Hawaii, on December 7, 1941, as Japanese dive bombers attack the Navy's Pacific Fleet. The attack drew the U.S. into World War II. (National Archives photograph)

The *SCENE*

War brought drastic change in America

War was raging in much of the world in 1941 as Germany and Japan expanded their empires by overrunning neighboring countries and islands.

America was still struggling to recover from the Great Depression and had been cautious—perhaps to a fault—about becoming involved in the war. It was becoming more evident each day, however, that the free world would not survive without U.S. assistance.

Japan, boldly and rapidly expanding its Pacific reach, attacked U.S. ships and installations in a surprise bombing raid at Pearl Harbor, Hawaii, on December 7, 1941, severely crippling America's naval fleet and killing nearly 2,400 U.S. servicemen and civilians.

Americans were gripped by anger and fear and life changed suddenly and drastically for every man, woman and child in the country. The U.S. officially declared war on Japan the next day and the Axis powers, led by Germany, Japan and Italy, declared war on the U.S. in return.

Japan pressed the war in the Pacific, attacking the Philippines on December 8, 1941, and eventually forcing the surrender of 100,000 American and Filipino troops there on May 8, 1942. University of Alabama graduate Bert Bank, an Army Air Forces captain from Tuscaloosa, was among those captured and forced to endure the infamous "Bataan Death March" during which 10,000 Filipinos and 3,000 Americans died.

America was officially at war, although it would be several months before it was prepared to go on the offensive against Germany and Japan, which had been building their military forces and equipment for a decade. The U.S. had only 335,000 men in the armed services in 1939 and 1.9 million in 1941, but that number grew to over 12 million at the height of the war in early 1945.

German submarines began patrols along the U.S. East Coast and in the Gulf of Mexico in early 1942 in an attempt to limit U.S. assistance to Great Britain and other European countries. The submarines sank more than 300 freighters and tankers loaded with arms, supplies, fuels, food and equipment over the next two years, including many within only a few miles of the U.S. coastline. More than 50 ships were sunk in the Gulf of Mexico, most of them oil-laden tankers departing from Texas and Louisiana, with hundreds of lives lost. With the aid of British sonar, the U.S. was finally able to drive the German submarines back across the Atlantic by late 1943.

Japan, meanwhile, was claiming island after island in the Pacific, setting up naval installations and airfields along the way as it reached toward Alaska and Australia. The Japanese occupied Attu and Kiska in Alaska's Aleutian Islands in 1942, and had even greater ambitions.

The Japanese even launched three attacks on the U.S. mainland in 1942. In the first attack, a Japanese submarine shelled the Ellwood Oil Field near Santa Barbara, CA, on Feb-

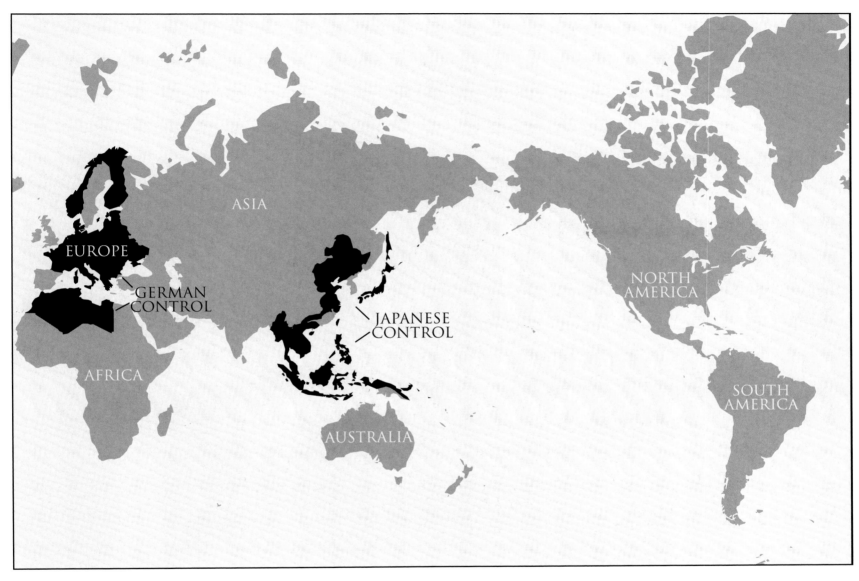

World map shows areas of German and Japanese control in January 1942.

ruary 23, 1942. The attack caused little damage but triggered an invasion scare along the West Coast. On the night of June 21, 1942, a Japanese submarine surfaced near the mouth of the Columbia River in Oregon and fired on Fort Stevens in the only attack on a U.S. mainland military installation. Again, there was little damage from the shelling. A Japanese seaplane launched from a submarine aircraft carrier dropped incendiary bombs near Brookings, OR, on September 9 and 29, 1942, in an attempt to start a forest fire, but again only minor dam-

age was reported.

America quickly rallied from its state of unpreparedness before Pearl Harbor. The Navy repaired as many of the ships at Pearl Harbor as possible and reorganized its Pacific fleet in an attempt to block further Japanese aggression. As manpower and equipment stockpiles grew, the U.S. finally began to fight back by the summer of 1942.

Soldiers marching along University Boulevard on the University campus was a common sight during the war years.

U.S. Navy forces first battled the Japanese navy to a standoff in the Battle of the Coral Sea in early May of 1942, blocking the Japanese attempt to occupy Port Moresby in New Guinea in the first military action in which aircraft carriers engaged each other. After breaking secret Japanese codes, U.S. Navy forces intercepted the Japanese Pacific fleet near Midway Island a month later and inflicted heavy losses on the enemy by sinking four aircraft carriers as it turned back the Japanese attempt to occupy the island.

U.S. land forces first attacked the Japanese at Guadalcanal in August of 1942 in the first major Allied assault, marking the transition from defensive to offensive operations.

The U.S. launched its first major offensive against German forces in North Africa during Operation Torch in November of 1942 as America joined the European fight in earnest.

More than 16 million American men and women joined the military services before the war finally ended in the summer of 1945. More than 291,000 servicemen and women were killed in action while 113,842 died of other causes and 800,000 more were wounded. Almost 125,000 spent time as prisoners of war and over 30,000 were listed as missing in action.

Worldwide, an estimated 50 million people died as a result of the war, many of them civilians in Russia, Germany and Japan. Almost six million of those were Jews exterminated by Nazi Germany in the Holocaust. Worldwide, more than 100 million people from 61 countries were mobilized for military service during the war.

The state of Alabama sent 321,000 men to war and more than 6,000 of those lost their lives, 4,600 in combat and 1,600 more in non-combat incidents.

Approximately 6,000 former University of Alabama students served during wartime. Of those, 343 men and one woman died in service. More than 300 of the former UA students who served during WWII were Alabama football players either before or after the war. At least 13 former players and a team manager lost their lives, eight of them in combat.

On the home front, there were shortages of automobiles, tires, gasoline, coffee, sugar, meat, shoes and other supplies during the war as all resources went toward arming, equipping and feeding the fighting men. Farmers were urged to grow more food; assembly line workers were urged to produce more planes and tanks, and people were urged to buy War Bonds to pay for it all.

Women manned production lines in truck, airplane and tank factories and shipyards. Colleges, including the University of Alabama, became training grounds for servicemen as Reserve Officers Training Corps (ROTC) programs were expanded and Army Specialized Training Programs (ASTP) established. Military units poured into Tuscaloosa by the trainload and marched from downtown to the college campus along what is now University Boulevard by the hundreds.

The University of Alabama had an enrollment of 4,921 students in 1941 but only 2,223 (856 males and 1,367 females)

U.S. troops stream ashore in the South Pacific.

by 1943 as the draft took most of the male students and many faculty members. Empty classrooms were used to train 12,880 servicemen, including many from foreign countries, in military, engineering and aerospace subjects from March 1943-December 1944. Thousands of those were pilots. Military barracks were built near the campus to house the army recruits who overflowed campus dorms and fraternity houses. Those barracks later housed married war veterans attending the University on the GI Bill as enrollment reached 9,105 in 1948.

The military draft, inducting men ages 18-38 at the rate of 12,000 per day nationwide by 1942, left too few players available for Alabama to field a varsity football team in 1943. The same was true for 60 other colleges. There were thousands of Army trainees on campus, but unlike their Navy counterparts at many other colleges, the soldiers were not allowed to participate in sports.

Wounded American servicemen returned to the states by the thousands during the war, overflowing existing military hospitals. Northington General Hospital, the second largest military hospital in the U.S. with 2,005 beds, was opened in Tuscaloosa in September 1943 to treat wounded servicemen from the area while bringing them closer to their families.

More than 450,000 German and Italian prisoners of war were sent to camps in the United States during the war, including 17,000 housed in the state of Alabama. The largest foreign POW camp in Alabama was in Aliceville, where over 3,000 German prisoners were housed.

The University of Alabama managed to field a football team again in 1944 with a roster made up mostly of freshmen and a few players who had been rejected by the military (4-F) because of physical limitations. Most of the 1944 players were 17 years old, not yet old enough for the military draft age of 18, prompting Coach Frank Thomas to call the team his "war babies."

It was a desperate and frightening time in America and in the world. Children scavenged for scrap metal and rubber to contribute to the war effort and saved their pennies for war bonds. Towns, including Tuscaloosa, held war bond drives to "buy" planes. War bond sales in the Tuscaloosa district helped purchase four heavy bombers, three medium bombers and 18 fighter planes during the war.

Wives and mothers came to dread a stranger's knock at the door as telegrams brought word of soldiers wounded, missing or killed in battle.

America went to war in 1942 and helped to finally bring World War II to an end more than three years later in the summer of 1945, although at a great cost. In addition to the more than 50 million lives lost, many Eden-like Pacific islands were bombed and burned to no more than stubble and sand while scores of European and Japanese cities were left in rubble by Allied bombing.

UA Enrollment Figures during WWII era

1940	5258
1941	4921
1942	4481*
1943	2223**
1944	2537
1945	3069#
1946	8626
1947	8729
1948	9105##
1949	8290
1950	6661

  * Included 1511 women and 2970 men.
 ** Included 1367 women and 856 men.
  # Included 1973 women and 1096 men.
Indicates peak of post-war veterans
    enrollment under GI Bill.

The RESPONSE

Athletes were in demand by all services

University of Alabama football players, as illustrated in the stories presented here, were at the forefront of World War II from the start, a fact that should come as no surprise. College athletes were among the most physically skilled, disciplined, trained and educated men in the country at the time and all the services wanted them.

The Marines, proudly claiming to be the toughest and bravest and proving it in Pacific assault landings against fanatical, fight-to-the-death Japanese defenders, chose athletes as their primary recruiting targets. Six Alabama football players responded by joining the Marines at halftime of the Tide's last home game in November 1942.

Football players, like the rest of the men in America, rushed to join the fight. At least 55 of the 61 players on the 1941 varsity roster and 58 of the 59 on one 1942 roster went into the service. There was similar response for most of the teams from the 1930s and 1940s. William T. "Bully" Van de Graaff, Alabama's first All-American (1915), is believed to have been the oldest former player to serve in the war. Many future Tide players went to war right out of high school and

Tide players Staples, Gambrell, Cashio, Killian, Gunnin and Reese (L-R) join the Marines during Alabama's last home game in 1942.

played college football after leaving the service.

Alabama football players, like all the men of military age in the early 1940s, grew up in the era of the Great Depression (1930s). They had endured the cold, the heat, the hunger and the pain of difficult times. They were hardened by the times and the elements even before they became football players, and they became good football players because of and in spite of those hard times.

Football taught the players teamwork, leadership, discipline, confidence, how to take orders and how to win. They were physically strong and fiercely competitive. Football helped make them not just good soldiers, but the best soldiers in the best fighting forces in the world.

University of Alabama football teams were consistently among the best in the nation from the 1920s on, and as one would expect, those same players excelled on the battlefield just as they had on the football field. Some reached the rank of general and admiral; some earned battlefield commissions for their leadership; some were wounded or became prisoners of war; some were killed in action; others died in training.

Many came home as decorated heroes. The highest known awards included Navy Cross presentations to Johnny Roberts and Hugh Barr Miller Jr. and the Distinguished Service Cross to Charlie Compton. Compton and Miller were also nominated for the Congressional Medal of Honor.

Some were Marines, storming the Pacific island beaches and jungles at Leyte, Bougainville, Iwo Jima and Okinawa. Some were Army infantrymen, fighting heroically in Sicily, the Battle of the Bulge and Bastogne. Many shared the glory with General George Patton as he daringly drove the Germans back toward Berlin in North Africa and France. Some

Former Crimson Tide players Paul "Bear" Bryant, Carney Laslie and Jimmy Walker (L-R) served in the Navy during World War II.

were paratroopers, jumping behind enemy lines in the predawn fog at Normandy on D-Day. Others drifted silently into the green farmlands of Holland aboard fragile wooden gliders during Operation Market Garden.

Some were pilots, braving enemy flak and fighter planes as they flew bombing missions over France and Germany. Some flew over the "Hump" in Burma, transporting fuel and supplies across the rugged Himalayan Mountains to the desperate Chinese Army in its war with Japan. Some, like Johnny Roberts, flew dive bombers off Navy aircraft carriers in the Pacific, attacking Japanese ships and planes in fierce air and sea battles. Others served on submarines and destroyers.

Two were doctors, serving in the front lines in the Pacific to help save the lives of Navy and Marine personnel wounded in such bloody battles as Iwo Jima, Midway and Okinawa.

Many former players who became coaches served as instructors, teaching discipline, physical fitness and toughness to raw recruits about to endure the supreme "gut check" that one famous coach often talked about.

The players and coaches served wherever they were called to serve, from Guadalcanal to Tokyo, from North Africa to Rome and from Normandy to Berlin, and they often took the lead in doing so. They helped win the war and came home heroes, but their stories didn't end there. They went on with their lives, and their lives are examples of remarkable success in almost every instance.

The brief personal stories of the former Alabama football players presented in this book are only a small representation

"Football, more than any other sport, prepares a young man for all the tough challenges of life."

—John Frank Bludworth

of the many others whose stories may now be lost to history. Information included here was collected from the veterans themselves in many instances and from family members in others during late 2009 and 2010 interviews.

The stories involve heart-breaking tragedy, daring heroism and improbable survival. A few even involve heartwarming romance, just like in the movies and just like in any war.

Many of the former players attributed their survival in wartime and their later success in life to their football training. There is no question that at some place and time these men learned to win. For most of them, it was on Denny Field at the University of Alabama.

To these men, and to the entire free world during World War II, winning was everything.

"They didn't like to talk about it much and didn't see their contributions as all that important or heroic, but we now know that they really did save the world."

— Joe Gammon

ARMY

"The roughest part of the war was seeing a dead GI."

— Don Salls

Opposite: Ships, planes, blimps, men and equipment are shown at Normandy Beach following the June 6, 1944, Allied invasion of France. U.S. and British forces attacked German forces in the largest invasion in military history on what is known as D-Day. (National Archives photograph)

Sumpter **BLACKMON**

'He never talked about his medals'

Sumpter Blackmon was among the first Americans to land on French soil in World War II when he was dropped behind enemy lines as a paratrooper well before dawn on D-Day, June 6, 1944. Blackmon served as an officer with the elite 501st Parachute Infantry Regiment attached to the 101st Airborne Division and jumped behind German lines twice during his 18 months of overseas duty during the war. He earned the Silver Star and Purple Heart in addition to other decorations as his regiment faced German forces in several major battles.

The 501st Parachute Infantry Regiment, first activated in November 1942, was the first airborne unit in the U.S. military. It was an all-volunteer unit and the first officers of the regiment were hand picked by its first commander, Colonel Howard R. Johnson, a rugged proponent of physical conditioning. While training in Georgia, the regiment once marched 105 miles in a move between camps.

Blackmon became a member of the 501st following graduation from the University of Alabama in March 1942. He received his Army commission in April of that year and trained with the unit in several locations before being deployed to England in January 1944. The 501st became a permanent attachment of the 101st Airborne Division at that time and began training for Operation Overlord, the secret allied plan for the massive air, naval, amphibious and airborne invasion of France.

Blackmon's regiment was dropped near the French town of Carentan shortly after midnight on June 6, five hours before the D-Day seaborne landing began, and although most men were dropped off target due to heavy fog and enemy antiaircraft fire, the 501st accomplished its missions of destroying bridges and taking control of key river locks due to the "initiative, stamina and daring of the individual parachutists," according to one historical account.

Blackmon landed in an open field alone in the darkness, according to his son, Dr. Sumpter Blackmon Jr. of Camden, Alabama, and soon located a fellow American by using his "cricket" (a tin toy that made a clicking sound). The two GIs joined three others as they

moved along a roadway, where Blackmon soon confronted his first German soldier. As Blackmon prepared to fire, the enemy soldier quickly surrendered and told the Americans that he was Polish and had been forced into the German army. The man then helped the Americans find their way to their targets.

Blackmon's unit remained in front-line action for more

Paratroopers jump into Holland during Operation Market Garden.

than a month with losses of 898 men killed, wounded, missing or captured. The 501st received a Presidential Unit Citation for its actions in Normandy. The unit returned to England in mid-July to receive replacements and prepare for Operation Market Garden, a massive airborne assault of

30,000 allied troops into German-held Holland scheduled for mid-September. The assault featured both the 82nd and 101st airborne divisions plus British airborne troops.

Again, Blackmon and the 501st dropped behind enemy lines, and it was during the Holland invasion that he earned the Silver Star for gallantry in battle on September 22, 1944. He also earned the Purple Heart during the same battle when he was wounded during an attack on the German-held town of Schijndel, Holland, after he was ordered to move his platoon to block an enemy attack force of 100 men supported by 20mm cannons and 88mm artillery.

Blackmon's Silver Star citation read: "Lieutenant Blackmon made contact with the enemy, disposed his men, and without regard for his personal safety remained in an exposed position directing his platoon's attack while under extremely intense shelling. He was on one occasion knocked off his feet by an 88mm shell fragment which struck his helmet and was later painfully wounded when a 20mm shell knocked his carbine from his hand. Lieutenant Blackmon refused to be treated or evacuated until he had finally stopped the enemy attack and accomplished his mission. His personal bravery and sound judgment inspired his men to continue to fight against overwhelming odds. His actions were in accordance with the highest standards of the military service."

The 501st spent 72 days in combat in Holland and lost Colonel Johnson to a fatal mortar attack in the process. Another 661 men were either killed or wounded before the unit received a much-needed rest.

Blackmon lettered at quarterback on the 1941 Crimson Tide team that defeated Texas A&M 29-21 in the Cotton Bowl on its way to a 9-2 record.

The unit was called back into action in mid-December when the Germans broke through U.S. lines in what became known as the Battle of the Bulge. The 501st was the lead combat team of the 101st in this battle and the first to fight at Bastogne, where it and the division held firmly to block the enemy advance and eventually earn the first Presidential Unit Citation ever awarded to a full division for service above and beyond the call of duty.

The 501st had 580 men killed, wounded or captured during the defense of Bastogne. The unit fought on into Germany and Bavaria before war's end. Following Germany's surrender in May 1945, the 501st returned to France to begin training for an anticipated invasion of Japan. The invasion never came, however. Japan surrendered in August 1945 following U.S. atomic bomb attacks on Hiroshima and Nagasaki. The surrender officially ended World War II and allowed Blackmon to soon return home to Columbus, Georgia.

"He never talked about his medals unless he was asked a question," Dr. Sumpter Blackmon Jr. said of his father. "He did talk often about the men in his company and what good soldiers they were. They were all fighting together for a common goal and all looking out for each other, much like the values instilled in him

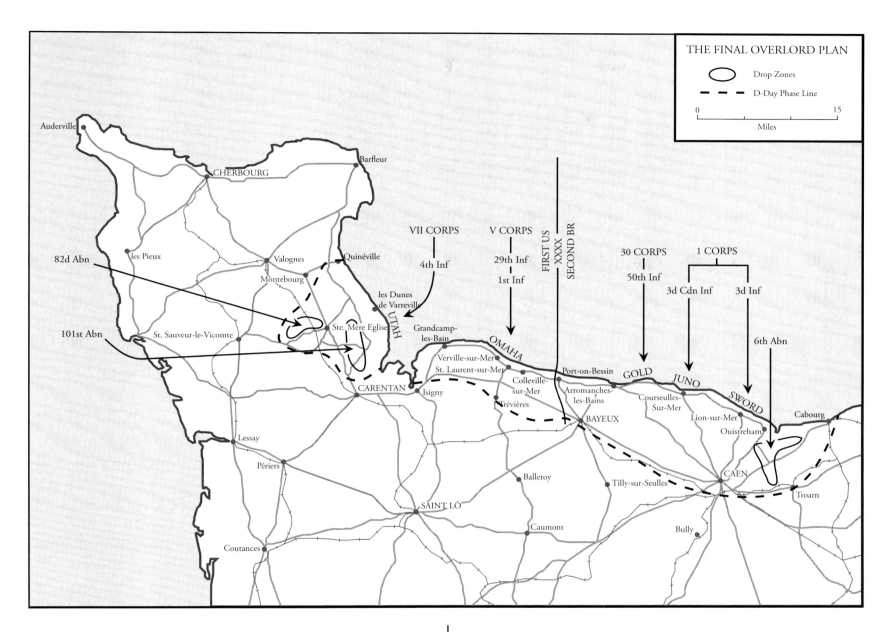

THE FINAL OVERLORD PLAN

◯ Drop Zones

- - - D-Day Phase Line

0   15

Miles

Auderville

Barfleur

CHERBOURG

VII CORPS

V CORPS

82d Abn

les Pieux

Valognes

Quinéville

4th Inf

29th Inf

1st Inf

30 CORPS

1 CORPS

Montebourg

les Dunes
de Varreville

FIRST US
XXXX
SECOND BR

50th Inf

3d Cdn Inf

3d Inf

101st Abn

St. Sauveur-le-Vicomte

Ste. Mère Eglise

Grandcamp-
les-Bain

UTAH

OMAHA

Port-on-Bessin

GOLD

JUNO

6th Abn

Verville-sur-Mer

St. Laurent-sur-Mer

Colleville-
sur-Mer

Arromanches-
les-Bains

Courseulles-
Sur-Mer

SWORD

Cabourg

CARENTAN

Isigny

Trévières

BAYEUX

Lion-sur-Mer

Ouistreham

Lessay

Balleroy

Tilly-sur-Seulles

CAEN

Troarn

Périers

SAINT LÔ

Caumont

Bully

Coutances

while playing on a winning football team," Dr. Blackmon added.

Blackmon was featured in at least two books dealing with World War II. He is quoted in *D-Day with the Screaming Eagles* and mentioned in *Look Out Below!* Movies have also been made of all the major battles in which Blackmon was involved.

Blackmon played football at Alabama 1939-41 and earned his degree in March 1942. He lettered at quarterback

Map shows details of D-Day invasion plan.

on the 1941 Crimson Tide team that defeated Texas A&M 29-21 in the Cotton Bowl on its way to a 9-2 record.

After the war, Blackmon returned to Georgia, where he coached high school football for 15 years then served as a principal for several years before retirement. He died in 1992. Dr. Sumpter Blackmon Jr. is a 1965 University of Alabama graduate and resides in Camden, Alabama.

John Frank BLUDWORTH

'They wrote a story in blood and courage'

John Frank Bludworth had been away from his high school coaching job less than a year and on the battlefield in Belgium only five days when he became engulfed in the infamous Battle of the Bulge, the largest and bloodiest battle of World War II. Bludworth was a private first class in the 422nd Regiment of the 106th Infantry Division, and his inexperienced division had just arrived in Europe from training in the U.S. when the Germans launched a massive surprise attack against thinly spread U.S. forces on December 16, 1944. By the time the Battle of the Bulge officially ended more than a month later, 19,000 Americans had been killed, 47,500 were wounded and 23,000 more were missing, according to official military records.

Bludworth was one of those missing. He was one of 6,697 members of his division captured by the Germans as they poured through American lines with wave after wave of troops, tanks and artillery, completely overwhelming and cutting off the 422nd and 423rd regiments from the rest of the division. The units surrendered after three bitter days of fighting when they ran out of food, ammunition and medical supplies.

The military newspaper "Stars and Stripes" praised the men of the 106th even in defeat, saying the troops "fought against superior forces with pulverizing artillery battering them from all sides; it was men against tanks, guts against steel. In one of the bloodiest battles of the war, the 106th showed the Germans and the world how American soldiers could fight—and die. The valiant men of the Lion Division wrote a story in blood and courage to rank with the Alamo, Chateau-Thierry, Pearl Harbor and Bataan. They never quit," the article said. Almost every man in the 106th was either killed or captured.

The Battle of the Bulge continued through January 25, 1945, before the Germans were finally pushed back. The powerful offensive proved to be the last for the Germans as Allied forces soon broke the Siegfried Line and drove through Germany to end the war in Europe in early May.

Bludworth, meanwhile, spent the final months of World War II as a prisoner of war at Stalag IV B near Dresden, Germany.

"After being marched about 200 miles, during which time it seemed that they made every town to show us off, we were finally placed in a barn," Bludworth later said of his ordeal. "We stayed there for five days waiting for box cars. Because of the cold and practically nothing to eat, 12 men died. We were at last placed on a train and sent to Stalag IV B." He added that the prisoners were forced to work long hours each day and given nothing to eat but a piece of bread and a bowl of soup. Bludworth was among the 6,500 members of the 106th Division to survive the internment. He was liberated by Russian troops at the end of the war and returned to the U.S.

to resume his coaching career.

Bludworth, speaking later about his war experience, said his football training helped him survive the difficult times. "Football, more than any other sport, prepares a young man for all the tough challenges of life," he said. "When I was a prisoner of war during World War II, I was locked up in a boxcar with 75 other prisoners for five days and nights. Several men died in the car during those five days without food or water. I feel I owe my life to the rigorous training I received while playing high school and college football," he said.

A native of Argyle, Florida, Bludworth was a graduate of Walton High School and attended the University of Alabama on a football scholarship. He was a reserve fullback 1934-36. The Crimson Tide went 24-2-2 during that period and won conference and national titles in 1934. Bludworth graduated from Alabama in 1937 and coached at Fayette, Bridgeport, Moulton, West Blocton, Scottsboro and Florala in Alabama and at DeFuniak Springs, Florida, before enlisting in the Army in January 1944.

Bludworth returned to Florala for one season (1945) after the war then returned to DeFuniak Springs as head coach at Walton High School in 1946. His 1947 team was unbeaten and won the Northwest Florida Championship for the first

Bludworth (left) was a fullback at Alabama and fought in the Battle of the Bulge.

time since 1931, when Bludworth was a member of the team. Bludworth also served as a principal and as superintendent of county schools before his retirement in 1973 after 35 years in education. He was elected mayor of DeFuniak Springs four times and served three terms for $1 per year. He died in 1981 on the same night he was elected to his fourth term as mayor.

Bludworth was married to the former Nina Culley of Birmingham and they had four sons and two daughters. John Frank (Jack) Bludworth Jr. played baseball at Auburn; David played football at Florida; Robert served two tours of duty in Vietnam, earning numerous decorations; Patrick attended Florida State; Nancy attended Montevallo, and Margaret attended the University of Alabama.

Left: American GIs captured by Germany in the Battle of the Bulge.

Below: Soldiers fought in deep snow and freezing temeratures during the winter of 1944–45.

Charley **BOSWELL**

'He didn't linger on what might have been'

Charley Boswell grew up dreaming of one day playing baseball for the New York Yankees, just like a million other youngsters of the 1930s playing sandlot or pasture ball on Saturday afternoons while idolizing Yankee greats Babe Ruth and Lou Gehrig.

Boswell might have made it to New York, too, had World War II not gotten in the way. He had signed a professional contract with the Atlanta Crackers in the summer of 1940 and was to report to Savannah for the 1941 season. He was drafted into the Army before reporting, however, and the turn of events drastically changed the course of Boswell's life, although he refused to let it keep him from athletic greatness.

Boswell was blinded in frontline fighting in Germany in 1944 but overcame the injury to become a successful businessman, the world's premier blind golfer and one of the nation's leading advocates for the handicapped.

He never got over his love of baseball, though, even with all his golf success, according to his wife Kathryn (Kitty) Boswell. "Oh, yes, he loved baseball," Mrs. Boswell said of her late husband. "He always talked a lot about the Yankees. He loved them, and he always listened to the games. But he didn't linger on what might have been. He never did look back and complain. He always got up and got going. He loved life and he always made people feel special," she said.

"He was very independent and was still working and golfing at 78," she added. Boswell died October 22, 1995, at age 78 following a fall at his home and is remembered as one of the state's best-known war veterans and one of the University of Alabama's most honored graduates and former athletes.

Boswell displayed a special determination to succeed early in life as he grew up in the Birmingham suburb of Ensley. Although rejected in his first tryout for the high school football team as a 105-pound 15-year-old, he was back the next fall and made the team. His first season was short-lived, however, when he suffered a broken hip in his first game. He spent two months in a cast then was back in action, playing basketball in the winter and track and baseball in the spring of 1935. He showed he was fully recovered by winning the 100-yard dash and placing second in the 220 in the state track meet.

Boswell finally hit his stride in football in the fall of 1935 as he led Ensley to the city championship while earning All-City, All-County, All-State and All-Southern honors at the important left halfback position in the Notre Dame Box formation. All the while, Boswell had continued to play baseball during the summers with an eye on the big leagues one day.

The University of Alabama recruited Boswell during his senior season (1935) and he enrolled in January, 1936, in time for spring practice. He showed promise as a freshman by punting for a 43-yard average and earned playing time the next three seasons despite various injuries. He threw a touchdown pass to future All-America end Holt Rast to secure a 7-0 win over Mississippi State in 1939. He was also a member of the Alabama track team.

Boswell left school in January, 1940, to begin workouts for summer baseball in the Birmingham semipro leagues as he had done throughout college. He did well enough that summer to get the professional contract he had always wanted, starting the next year. The threat of war was looming, however, with Germany and Japan invading country after country, and Congress passed a military draft law on September 14, 1940, requiring all men between the ages of 21-35 to register as the U. S. began building its forces.

Boswell got his call to the Army in early 1941 and was sent to officer candidate school at Fort Benning, Georgia, where he finished first in his class and was assigned to the 84th Infantry Division. He was eventually sent overseas in

September 1944, landing at Omaha Beach in October. The 84th fought its way across France to within a mile of Germany's formidable Siegfried Line, where on November 29 elements of the 335th Regiment attacked the enemy with the objective of taking the town of Lindern, Germany.

Boswell, a captain and company commander in the 335th, was injured the following day when he joined a tank crew in trying to deliver ammunition to men surrounded by the enemy in a forward position. The tank was hit by an antitank shell and caught fire. The men faced heavy enemy gunfire as they tried to escape the tank, and three of the four crewmen were killed. Boswell, the last man out after helping a wounded man, was met by a second antitank shell explosion as he crawled out of the tank.

"I was just rising to a crouch when the second round came in," Boswell later wrote of the incident. "If I'd had two seconds more I might have made it to a ditch alongside the road where I would have been protected from small arms fire."

That was around 4 p.m. on November 30. Boswell woke up a week later in a Belgium hospital with burns on his face and his eyes damaged beyond repair. He found out later that he had been left beside the demolished tank for several hours and found alive by a team recovering the dead after dark.

"Surprising as it may seem, I felt no pain when I was hit," Boswell wrote in recalling the explosion that cost him his eyesight. "Everything happened instantly. The concussion and shock of stopping those steel fragments blotted out my senses before it all registered," he wrote in his autobiography *Now I See,* in 1969.

After weeks and several surgeries in foreign hospitals, Boswell was sent to Valley Forge General Hospital near Philadelphia, where he and his wife Kitty (They were married April 5, 1942.) learned finally that he would never recover his eyesight.

Boswell threw a touchdown pass to future All-America end Holt Rast to secure a 7-0 win over Mississippi State in 1939.

"After a good cry for both of us, I doubt seriously if we talked about it for more than a few seconds at a time after that," Boswell wrote. "I think that was a little exaggerated," Kitty said. "But he handled it wonderfully," she said. "I couldn't have handled it as well without him."

Boswell had seen his share of disappointments and injuries, but this one had dashed all his dreams and left him with new and difficult hills to climb. "To be blundering around, groping, knocking into things and people embarrassed me to the point of bitter fury, but that was only part of it," Boswell wrote of his blindness. "I missed the sights I had always taken for granted—beautiful sunrises and

Charley Boswell (58) on the go for Bama.

sunsets, green leaves in the spring and the riots of color in the fall, faces of my loved ones, even the ugliness that makes the contrast with the beautiful so pronounced and exciting."

He underwent months of therapy at Valley Forge, learning to read Braille and to manage for himself as well as possible. He was introduced to several recreational activities, including bowling and horseback riding, but quickly rejected those. Finally, he was asked to try golf, and he grudgingly agreed to it, as he had the other activities. After he hit his first drive 200 yards, he was sold on the game he once called "the wildest waste of time man had ever devised," and it became his passion for the rest of his life.

Boswell played golf daily after that first outing, quickly regained his confidence and finally began to smile again, leading his doctors to transfer him to Northington General Hospital in Tuscaloosa by late 1945 for his last stop in the rehabilitation process. By Christmas, he was back home in Birmingham after more than a year of tragedy, surgeries and rehabilitation. Boswell received added happiness when his son Charles Boswell Jr. was born on December 30, 1945. Chuck joined a sister, Kay, who was born November 15, 1943, while Charley was in training in Louisiana. A second son, Stephen, was born in 1951.

Boswell's family and friends, including then current and former Alabama football players, coaches and fans, quickly rallied behind him, and the Crimson Tide's 1946 A-Day game was moved to Birmingham's Legion Field as a "Charley Boswell Day" benefit game to raise money for Boswell and his family. Tickets sold for $1 and the game was a sellout.

Bill Mogge lines up a Boswell drive.

With other donations, the game raised over $31,000, part of which went toward the Boswell family's first home.

Legion Field was the site of two of Boswell's worst disappointments. It was where he had suffered a broken hip in his first football game and it was where he was injured when playing against Georgia Tech in his last game for Alabama in 1939. On March 30, 1946, however, the loudest cheers in the stadium were for Boswell, and it was a day he never forgot.

"I heard some applause begin as I made my way to the sidelines to express my gratitude," Boswell wrote of the occasion, "and then the crowd broke into the loudest cheering I had ever heard in my life. It is just as well that I couldn't rely on notes, for tears were pouring down my face," he added. "To say that I am both proud and overjoyed would be a gross understatement," Boswell told the crowd. "The crowd let go once more. They were still cheering when I sat down by Coach Thomas on the Alabama bench for the second half," he wrote.

Boswell was honored at a dinner that night and given a set of golf clubs as 200 friends paid tribute to him again. Coupled with a job offer from Loveman's Department Store that same spring, Boswell's fortunes had changed dramatically following his return from the war.

Boswell used the new golf clubs regularly, playing with old friend Grant Thomas, but he was far from satisfied with just playing—he wanted to play well, and he wanted to compete, as he always had. He was invited to his first National Blind Golf Tournament in Los Angeles in December 1946, and Loveman's sponsored his trip. Although Boswell had been playing golf only 18 months, he finished second in the tournament. The next day Boswell and tournament champion Clint Russell were paired with entertainers Bob Hope and Bing Crosby in a round of golf that started a life-long friendship between Boswell and Hope.

The tournament provided Boswell with "just the kind of challenge I'd been seeking all my life," he said. Boswell defeated Russell, the nation's top blind golfer for 30 years, to win his first National Blind Golf championship a year later.

"I had needed that victory (1947) far more than anyone had known at the time," Boswell wrote. "The championship was actually the capstone achievement of another kind of competition I'd been engaged in for nearly three years—the fight to find a way of coping in life without vision." He skipped the next two tournaments, but competed again in 1950 and 1951, when he won both the national and international titles.

The 1953 tournament was held at Birmingham's Highland Park Course, and Boswell won by 10 strokes before a hometown crowd that exceeded all other tournament attendance records, and he continued to play throughout his life, winning a total of 17 national and 11 international championships. He won seven straight national titles 1955-61 and three more (1965, 1966 and 1970) after that. He won seven consecutive international titles 1955-61 and also won in 1965 and 1967. He once had a hole in one, and shot an 81 as his lowest score.

Success was not new to Boswell, of course. He had always displayed a competitive spirit and drive to excel,

Bob Hope (left) with Charley Boswell

starting with his *Liberty* magazine route at age 11, when he made up his mind to be the best salesman in the state and did it.

Boswell remembered that gift of salesmanship when he started a successful insurance business in 1954, even as he continued with golf and numerous other charitable activities. Along the way he received numerous honors, including "Hero of the Year" by the National Disabled Veterans in 1949; American Legion Comeback Award in 1951; Most Courageous Athlete Award by the Philadelphia Sports Writers Association in 1957; Ben Hogan Trophy as the golfer making the greatest comeback from physical disability in 1958; the 1959 Outstanding Athlete Award from the Sigma Chi Fraternity; the 1965 George Washington Medal as National Blind Father of the Year; the Football Hall of Fame Foundation Distinguished American Award in 1965; the 1966 Light House Humanitarian Award from the New York State Association for the Blind, and the 1961 Significant Sig Award from the Sigma Chi Fraternity.

He received the Sports Illustrated Silver Anniversary All-America Award in 1964 as one of 25 men honored for their accomplishments in the 25 years since playing their final football games. He also served as State Revenue Commissioner 1971-79; received the President's Distinguished Service Award in 1971; served on the Board of Directors for the Eye Foundation Hospital; served as the first chairman of the board of the Helen Keller Eye Research Foundation (1991); received the 1986 Women's Committee of 100 Citizen of the Year Award, and received the Tuss McLaughry Award from the American Football Coaches

Harry Edwards, Bob Hope, Boswell, Bo Russell and Paul "Bear" Bryant (L-R) at Boswell's Celebrity Golf Classic.

Association in 1994.

Boswell was inducted into the Alabama Sports Hall of Fame in 1972, the Alabama Academy of Honor in 1983 and the inaugural U. S. Blind Golf Association Hall of Fame in 2007. He received the University of Alabama National Alumni Association's Paul W. Bryant Alumni-Athlete Award in 1990 in recognition of his accomplishments and contributions to society after leaving the University. The Birmingham Veterans Administration Medical Center's Southeastern Blind Rehabilitation Center, which opened in 1982, was dedicated in his honor.

He also started and hosted the annual Charley Boswell Celebrity Golf Classic for many years, helping raise more than $1.7 million for the Eye Foundation while bringing to Birmingham celebrities such as Hope and Paul "Bear" Bryant in support of the event.

Boswell called Bryant "my model in terms of his devotion to the task at hand" in his autobiography, saying that Bryant "had been a tremendous influence on me when I was playing at Alabama." Bryant, later head coach at Alabama for 25 years and a close friend of Boswell's, was an Alabama assistant coach 1936-39.

Boswell was featured on the television show "This Is Your Life" in 1960. He was joined on the show by two members of his former Army unit; his family; Kenny Gleason, the former corporal who had introduced him to golf, and Hope, who called Boswell "America's greatest inspiration."

Boswell's brothers Jack and Billy followed behind him in football at Ensley, keeping a Boswell in the backfield there for nine years. Jack was also a member of the UA track team in the early 1940s and served as a lieutenant in the Army Air Forces during World War II.

Boswell lost his eyesight when a shell hit the tank in which he was riding.

Jack **BROWN**

'I stood on the crater of the atomic bomb blast'

Jack Brown saw dramatic evidence of the death and destruction of World War II more than 60 years ago and he has never forgotten the sight.

"I stood on the crater of the atomic bomb blast at Nagasaki," Brown said in recalling his World War II military experience at age 82. "It was a big one, and I wouldn't want to see another one. I didn't know anything about radiation at the time or I might not have done it."

Brown spent two years in Japan with the U. S. occupation forces. His unit's task was the destruction of military equipment, much of which was taken out to sea and dumped, he said. "Our unit basketball team won a weekend trip to Nagasaki," Brown said. "We went ice skating on a frozen lake in our combat boots and went to see the bomb crater."

Despite the outcome of the war and the destruction left by the August 9, 1945, bomb blast which killed an estimated 40,000 people while destroying half the city of Nagasaki, Brown said the Japanese people were not unfriendly toward the American occupation forces. "They were fine; we never had any trouble," the former Army sergeant said. "I never saw any bitterness or resentment."

The destruction of Nagasaki followed by three days the world's first atomic bomb blast at Hiroshima, which killed an estimated 100,000 people and destroyed most of that city. The two bombs, combined with Russia's declaration of war on Japan, brought about the surrender of Japan on August 15,

A mushroom cloud rises over Nagasaki, Japan on August 9, 1945.

1945, and officially ended World War II.

Brown joined the Army in 1946, just after graduating from Selma High School, where he had been a three-time All-State basketball player and an All-Southern end in football as a senior. "I played in one losing basketball game in three years," Brown said. "We won 88 straight games and state championships in 1944 and 1945." Brown was chosen the most valuable player in the state tournament in 1945.

After two years of military service, Brown returned home in time to enter the University of Alabama in the fall of 1948. He eventually earned four letters in football (1948-51) and two (1948-49) in basketball for the Crimson Tide.

Brown played halfback and defensive back for Tide coach Harold "Red" Drew's teams, starting out by averaging 39 yards a punt on 64 kicks as a freshman. He was captain of the 1951 football team and served as A Club president for two years. He was also a member of the national leadership honor society Omicron Delta Kappa (ODK) and brigade commander in ROTC, although a knee injury in football ended his hopes of a military career.

Instead, Brown returned to Selma as head football coach for five seasons, where he produced future Alabama football players Butch Henry, Elliott Moseley and James Estes. He joined Liberty National Life Insurance as an agent in 1959 and worked his way up to president of the company before retiring in 1993.

Brown was honored by the University of Alabama National Alumni Association in 2009 when he was presented the Paul W. Bryant Alumni-Athlete Award in recognition of his accomplishments and contributions to society after leaving the University.

Jack Brown played basketball and football at Alabama.

Byron CHAMBLISS

'A lot of us were sick or worn out from the war'

Byron Chambliss had dreams of being a bomber pilot in World War II like some of his high school friends, but a quirk of fate sent him to the Army instead.

Chambliss had wanted to be a pilot since seeing the famous flyer Charles Lindbergh once as a youngster. He grew up building model airplanes and hanging around the airports in Birmingham watching the planes take off and land.

"Lindbergh flew into Roberts Field in Ensley when I was just five or six years old and my daddy sat me on his shoulders so I could see him," Chambliss said. "My daddy always carried me to watch the planes and Lindbergh was always one of my heroes. I always dreamed of flying," he added.

Chambliss continued to hang around airports into his teen years until football and girls captured much of his interest, he said. "I used to take my date (future wife Ann)

there at night and watch the planes land and take off," he laughed.

"I tried to join the Army Air Forces when I got out of high school at Woodlawn in 1943, but I had a hernia and was turned down," Chambliss said. "They told me to have surgery and come back in six months. I talked my folks into paying $300 for surgery so I could get into the Air Forces, but I got drafted into the Army about three months after the surgery," Chambliss said.

Chambliss was inducted into the Army on November 12, 1943, and was discharged as a corporal in 1946 after serving in Germany and the Philippines. He spent time as a combat infantryman, a member of an antitank crew and as a physical fitness instructor. He served with the 86th Infantry Division in Germany and earned the American Campaign Medal, the European-Asian-Middle East Campaign Medal, the World War II Victory

"We had been sleeping on the ground, not eating well and being eaten up by mosquitoes. But I'm not complaining. I really had it easy if you can say anything about war is easy."

Medal, the Pacific Theater Medal and the Good Conduct Medal.

"I landed in France in April 1945," Chambliss said. "We moved on into Germany where we held about 500 German prisoners of war until the war ended in May. The prisoners were really very humble people," Chambliss said. When the war against Germany ended in early May, Chambliss was shipped to the Philippines in the South Pacific, where he served mainly as a physical fitness instructor until March 1946.

Chambliss was signed to a University of Alabama football scholarship shortly after his discharge from the Army in April of 1946. "Coach (Malcolm) Laney (Alabama assistant coach) came to our house the first night I got home," Chambliss said. "He had been my high school coach at Woodlawn, and he knew that I had always wanted to go to Alabama, so I signed that night," he added. Chambliss joined the Alabama football team in the summer along with many other returning war veterans.

"I had gotten sick in the Pacific with some kind of microscopic amoeba like a lot of others did," Chambliss said. "I lost a lot of weight and it took me years to get over it." He named Alabama teammate Kenny Reese as one other who had similar troubles. "A lot of us were sick and worn out from the war," he said. "We had been sleeping on the ground, not eating well and being eaten up by mosquitoes. But I'm not complaining," he added. "I really had it easy if you can say anything about war is easy."

Chambliss played football three years (1946-48) at Alabama and graduated with a teacher's certificate in the spring of 1949. He went to Livingston State College in the fall of 1949 and played an additional season of football, earning first-team all-conference and second-team All-America honors. Livingston State head coach George Darrow died of a heart attack following the school's first game in 1949 and former Alabama All-America center Vaughn Mancha was named head coach. Mancha and Chambliss had been teammates at Alabama 1946-47. After the 1949 football season, Chambliss coached at Livingston and Thompson high schools for seven years before beginning a successful career in insurance and real estate in Birmingham.

"The Lord blessed me," Chambliss said of his business and civic career, during which he was elected to the Million Dollar Roundtable and served as president of the Birmingham Sertoma Club. He was retired and living in Montgomery at age 85 in 2009. He went on an "Honor Flight" to visit the World War II Memorial in Washington, D.C., in 2008.

Chambliss grew up in Birmingham during the Great Depression and played his early football on the sandlots of Ensley, where his father, a Navy veteran of World War I, worked in the steel mills. "My uncle, Sam Scott, who was killed by a Japanese sniper on Guam during World War II, taught me to kick and throw a football," Chambliss said.

The Chambliss family later moved to Woodlawn where Byron earned All-State honors at end as a senior during the 1942 season. Woodlawn became famous for producing great teams and great players, including Alabama All-Americas Holt Rast and Harry Gilmer, under the coaching of Laney. Chambliss, a 6-3, 210-pounder as a Crimson Tide player, was later named to the Woodlawn all-time football team.

Chambliss and his wife Ann had four sons and one daughter. Sons Dave and Gordon played football at Kansas State while Sam played at Tennessee and Marion Military Institute. Son Dan was an outstanding intramural player at Alabama. Daughter Terry, now Mrs. Ron Beers, also attended Kansas State.

Herb CHAPMAN

'Daddy said he hid behind dead cows'

Herb Chapman's World War II souvenirs included an April 9, 1945, issue of *Life* magazine, its pages filled with dramatic photographs and stories from warfronts around the globe, including Iwo Jima, Belgium and Holland. Former University of Alabama football players could have been in any of the photographs; they were certainly in all the battles.

The photographs of Holland showed the sky filled with paratroopers; crumpled wooden gliders in trees and pastures, and soldiers crouching behind barns and houses as U.S troops took part in Operation Market Garden, the largest airborne battle in history, the second-largest invasion of the war and in the end a costly failure.

The invasion involved the dropping of 30,000 Allied paratroopers behind German lines in an attempt to capture bridges over the Maas, Waal and Rhine rivers along a 60-mile road heading from Holland to the German border. The allied force included the American 82nd and 101st airborne divisions, a British division and additional Polish paratroopers.

Although American forces accomplished their missions, the British were overpowered in their attempt to capture the bridge across the Rhine at Arnhem. British losses included 1,485 killed and 6,414 captured out of 10,600 troops. According to military estimates, the allies lost between 15,130-17,200 men killed, wounded and captured during the 10-day battle along a road that became known as "Hell's Highway."

The 1977 movie "A Bridge Too Far" told the story of the infamous battle for the bridge over the Rhine at Arnhem; the 1946 movie "Theirs Is The Glory" told the story of Operation Market Garden, and the HBO television miniseries "Band of Brothers" focused on the actions of the 506th Parachute Regiment of the 101st Airborne Division during the operation.

Chapman, a sergeant in the 82nd Airborne Division and former Crimson Tide football and baseball player, arrived in the middle of the war as a passenger in one of those crumpled gliders and spent 18 months in battles in Holland, Belgium and France during his three years of active service.

"Daddy said he hid behind dead cows," read a handwritten notation on a brittle yellow newspaper article about the Holland invasion, which took place on September 17, 1944, in the face of heavy German artillery, tank, machine gun and mortar fire.

"As soon as our boys got out into that open strip, they began catching it," the article quoted Capt. Ray Knuckles of Pontiac, Michigan, as saying. "They caught it every day, around the clock, for the whole time the attack lasted. Company F was magnificent. They stood there and took it and wouldn't yield an inch under the worst pasting you ever saw, and as a result the Germans had to call off their counterattack. But it was hell while it lasted, and their artillery was the worst we've ever seen. But we are the toughest fighting troops in the world and that sort of thing is what is expected of us," Knuckles added.

"He (Chapman) told about being in a foxhole with five other boys when a shell hit and all the others were killed," Mrs. Lula Chapman said of her late husband. "He said it was horrible. But I never would have met him if it hadn't been for the war because I was four years younger than he was," she added, finding a silver lining behind the dark memory of the war.

"I never understood how I got in the 82nd Airborne Division and how I was assigned to the glider group," Chapman said years later in an interview with the Paul W. Bryant Museum staff. He joined the Army in April 1943 after two years at the University of Alabama, hoping to become

Gliders delivered troops to the battlefront in Europe.

Chapman, a native of Elmore, Alabama, first joined the Alabama football team in the spring of 1941 after earning All-State honors in high school. He played center on the 1941 freshman and 1942 varsity teams, earning a trip to the January 1, 1943, Orange Bowl in which the Crimson Tide defeated Boston College 37-21. He also played baseball and batted .450 as a freshman and .347 as a sophomore in 1942 as Alabama won the Southeastern Conference championship for the sixth time in eight seasons.

Like most of Alabama's 1942 athletes, however, Chapman had his college life interrupted in the spring of 1943 when he was called into military service. He spent 35 months on active duty, including 18 months in the European theater, before he returned to play for the Tide again.

He returned to the states aboard the *Queen Elizabeth* with thousands of other servicemen, including actor Jimmy Stewart (an Army Air Forces pilot), and was discharged in March 1946. He rejoined the Alabama football team that fall and found it loaded with talent. "I had a harder time

a pilot. He was rejected for flight training because of color-blindness, however, and shipped off to paratrooper training. He joined the 82nd Airborne Division as a replacement in England soon after the unit had returned from the D-Day Normandy Invasion and immediately began training for the invasion of Holland as a member of the 325th Glider Group.

After fighting in Belgium, Chapman became a member of the 192nd General Hospital back in England, where he assisted with the rehabilitation of wounded soldiers and organized athletic events. As the war wound down, Chapman managed and played on a baseball team that won a championship in England and placed second in the European Theater. He won one of the championship games with a grand slam home run in the 10th inning.

"I think the associations that I had and being involved in sports at Alabama changed me completely."

getting playing time as a junior than I did as a sophomore," Chapman said. "The entire 1945 team returned and Vaughn Mancha (returning All-America center) was at my position. I didn't have much to look forward to."

Chapman did play, however, and earned a letter in 1947. He also earned letters in baseball in 1942, 46-47. He was the captain and leading hitter on the 1947 Tide baseball team that won the SEC championship and went to the school's first NCAA tournament while posting a 20-7 overall record. He also won the Jimmy Moore Memorial Trophy as the athlete with the highest grade-point average over four years as a senior in 1948.

Following graduation in May, 1948, Chapman went to Emma Sansom High School in Gadsden as an assistant coach for two seasons. He also played professional baseball for several years and gained national fame by hitting safely in 42 consecutive games in 1950. His mark is still tied for 11th place on the all-time minor league hitting streak list.

Chapman returned to his alma mater (Holtville) as head football coach for 12 years starting in 1950. His Holtville teams went 85-27-3, including three undefeated seasons and a 27-game unbeaten streak. He was head coach of the South squad in the 1956 High School Athletic Association All-Star game. He served as head coach at Prattville 1962-66 before leaving coaching at age 39. "I didn't have the spark anymore," he said. Chapman went into business and retired at age 65. He was named to Alabama's All-Century baseball team in 1993.

"I think the associations that I had and being involved in sports at Alabama changed me completely," Chapman said. "I very vividly can remember my personality changing. I used to be very timid, bashful and backward, and if I talked to you I wouldn't look at you.

"After being associated with the best for so long, you get

Chapman played center for Bama.

to where you don't back off from anybody and you figure that you're intelligent enough to carry on a conversation with anyone. In athletics you were taught to believe that. You were indoctrinated that way. If you were taught well that's the way you feel and that's your attitude toward life. It is mine," added Chapman, who died in 1998.

Mrs. Chapman is a former Alabama cheerleader (1946) and her granddaughter, Lacy Chapman, was a Tide cheerleader in 2002. The Chapmans had four sons, Joel, Jere, Jon and Jeff.

Ed *CLARK*

He helped liberate a Nazi concentration camp

Ed Clark joined the fight against Germany in World War II on Christmas Eve night, 1944, as a company commander with the famous 42nd Infantry Division, also known as the "Rainbow Division."

That first night of battle along the Rhine River near Strasbourg, France, was the first of 106 days of combat for the Rainbow Division before the war ended on May 8, 1945. The division suffered 5,949 casualties (killed and wounded) and took 59,128 prisoners of war in just over four months of action.

Battling the bitter ice and snow as well as the Germans, the 42nd broke through the Siegfried Line in March and advanced through Germany.

On April 29, 1945, the division, along with the 45th Infantry Division, liberated more than 30,000 prisoners at the infamous Nazi concentration camp at Dachau. It was only the second concentration camp to be liberated by allied forces and therefore was one of the first places where the Western world was exposed to the reality of Nazi brutality through photographs and newsreel accounts of the camp's conditions. Dachau housed large numbers of Christians and Jews and as many as 25,000 prisoners are believed to have died at the camp during the war.

Clark, commander of D Company in the 232nd Infantry Regiment, received the Silver Star for "conspicuous gallantry

in action" at Sessenheim, France, and the Bronze Star for actions near Wurzburg, Germany. The Rainbow Division also received a Distinguished Unit Citation.

Jimmy Gentry of Franklin, Tennessee, was a 19-year-old sergeant in E Company of the 232nd Infantry Regiment in

Top: Barbed wire held thousands of prisoners.
Right: Clark as a Tide football player.

1945, and painfully recalled the liberation of Dachau in March of 2010. He had fought in the Battle of the Bulge, but even that had not prepared him for what he saw at Dachau.

"We smelled, we saw, we touched, but we didn't know what we smelled, what we saw or what we touched at the time," Gentry said as tears welled in his eyes. "The smell was from the hundreds of bodies of the Jews who had been killed before we arrived and left in railroad cattle cars. I asked another soldier, 'Who are these people?' 'They are Jews,' he said. I knew soldiers died in war, but non-soldiers? Just people? Religious people? I couldn't take it all in. I didn't understand it. Not then, not now. I couldn't move. I knew what I had to do, but I was numb at the same time," he said.

"I was 19 years old and less than a year before had been in high school," Gentry continued. "It was all too much. I was a young boy, a simple foot soldier moving from one day to the next. I just wanted to get away from that place, away from smelling death.

"But the worst part was the eyes of the people still alive," Gentry added. "I saw a sea of faces behind the barbed-wire fences. They appeared to be dead, but they were alive. They were crying; they hugged us; they kissed our hands and boots.

"Some of the prisoners had typhus fever, and we had to burn our clothes, shave our heads, bathe and be sprayed with DDT to get rid of the fleas and germs," Gentry added. "I went nearly 40 years and didn't talk about it. I thought if I didn't talk about it, the memory would go away."

Gentry was tracked down by a Holocaust historian in the 1980s and interviewed about his experience at Dachau. That interview led to a meeting with a survivor of the camp a short time later.

"A man called and said he just wanted to come and see me and shake my hand," Gentry said. "When he came up to me he hugged me and started to cry. He was a Polish Jew and had been 13 years old in 1945," Gentry said. "He had been at Buchenwald and was moved to Dachau in one of the railroad cars. He survived by hiding under dead bodies when the Germans shot them when they heard that the Americans were coming," Gentry added.

Gentry, a high school coach in the Nashville area for 55 years after the war, returned to Dachau with his grandson in 2008 at the age of 83. "I saw the places where I had been in 1945 and I saw those faces I had seen in 1945 and I cried," he said.

Gentry, who earned two Bronze Star citations during the war, now speaks freely and frequently about the liberation of Dachau. "I think I'm supposed to pass it on," he said. "Why did the guy next to me get killed? Why did my brother get killed (in Italy) and not me? I feel like I owe God something. I think that's why I'm still here."

Clark's battalion moved from Dachau on to Munich, Germany, and was on a hill overlooking Salzburg, Austria, when the war ended on May 8.

An Alexandria, Alabama, native, Clark was a 155-pound halfback for the University of Alabama football team during the 1935-38 seasons and received a commission in the Army

Jimmy Gentry (inset) served with Clark in the liberation of the Nazi concentration camp at Dachau (above) on April 29, 1945.

through ROTC in 1939. He entered the service for duty in World War II in 1940.

Clark was recalled to duty during the Korean War (1951-52) and served as a battalion executive officer with the 45th Infantry Division. Clark held the rank of major while his division occupied defensive positions at Pork Chop Hill and Old Baldy.

He operated Clark and Son Dairy near Anniston following his military service and retired from the Army Reserve. He is survived by sons Edward II and Alan, both of whom served in the Army.

Scenes from the Nazi concentration camp
at Dachau, Germany

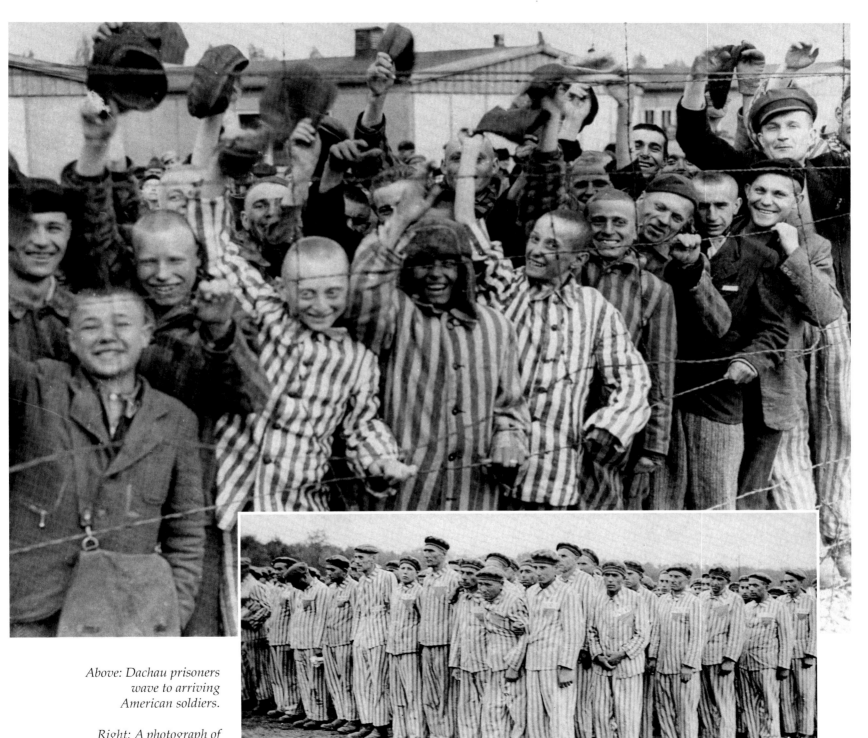

Above: Dachau prisoners wave to arriving American soldiers.

Right: A photograph of Jewish prisoners from German archives

Charlie COMPTON

'That one man who refused to withdraw'

Charlie Compton earned the nickname "Superman" during World War II and the nickname "Killer" on the football field, and there is no question that he deserved them both.

Compton was a unique man in many ways. He was a rugged and fearless 6-2, 205-pound football player at the University of Alabama 1941-42 and 1946-47. He was just as rugged and fearless as a soldier fighting in Europe, where he was nominated for the Congressional Medal of Honor, earned the Distinguished Service Cross and Bronze Star and was wounded twice.

He was deeply religious, disciplined and dedicated, never wavering from his teen years on in his goal to become a Southern Baptist foreign missionary, which he was for 22 years.

He was brilliant, and with a college degree that included several engineering courses, could build or do almost anything. He could read in several languages, yet could not write legibly enough to read his own handwriting.

He was courageous, daring and at times even reckless or funny.

Compton was the subject of a *Collier's* magazine article in 1947 entitled "The Gospel according to Charlie." Describing

Compton, the writer said "His eyes are deep-set and seem to hide in a cave protected by his bony, arched temples. Bald spots have receded on both sides of his head, leaving a tuft of hair in the middle front like a tonsure, but it is the eyes that fascinate and dominate the onlooker. They are serious except when Charlie lights them up with one of his jokes, and they could be taken as either spiritual or fanatical."

"I'm not fanatical," Charlie explained to the writer. "I'm just dog-near blind. Measles when I was a kid. The pupils are warped. Every time I blink I have to focus them again. I can't write, can't spell, can't read my own writing," Compton added.

Because of his handwriting, Compton's strangely scribbled letters home from the warfront from 1944-45 remain unread even today. Neither his mother during the war nor his children since have been able to break Compton's writing code. Compton's son, Dr. John Compton, believes his father's handwriting problems were caused by dyslexia.

Compton—officially Charles E. Compton Jr.—could speak and act, however, and he made lasting impressions wherever he went. His Alabama football teammates from 1942, when he helped the Tide to an 8-3 season and a 37-21 Orange Bowl win over Boston College, could probably have predicted his heroic actions in the war.

A native of Sylacauga, Alabama, Compton joined the Army in November 1942 and left for active duty in June of 1943. He was among the 57 players on the 1942 Alabama roster of 58 to serve in World War II. After training in the states, Compton was sent to France in October 1944 and saw his first action in northeast France in November. He saw seven months of combat during his 15 months of overseas duty.

Compton was a sergeant with the 398th Infantry Regiment of the 100th Infantry Division in Europe, and won several awards as the division's top marksman despite his eye problems. He served as communications chief in his company and carried a bulky radio in addition to the heavy 30-caliber Browning Automatic Rifle (B.A.R.) he preferred over his authorized carbine.

Compton was wounded in France on February 26, 1945, and in Germany on April 17, 1945, yet he chose not to wear his steel helmet throughout much of the war because he found it too heavy. He wore the lighter helmet liner instead.

Two major battles involving the 100th Division included the capture of the heavily fortified town of Bitche in the Low Vosges Mountains of northeast France in March of 1945 and the assault on the Neckar River and eventual seizure of Heilbronn, Germany, April 3-12, 1945.

Compton's 398th Infantry Regiment received a Presidential Unit Citation in each of the battles, and in the latter eliminated one of the last major centers of enemy resistance leading to the May 8 German surrender. In 185 days of uninterrupted combat, the 100th Division lost more than 4,600 men killed, wounded or missing in action while inflicting heavy losses on the enemy in addition to capturing 13,351 prisoners.

He was brilliant, and with a college degree that included several engineering courses, could build or do almost anything.

Charlie Compton at war in Germany.

Compton earned his recommendation for the Congressional Medal of Honor during the initial crossing of the Neckar River on April 6. A unit historical account of the battle includes details of Compton's heroics.

"About the same time that first boat pushed off an enemy machine gun cut the water in wide arcs and sent the battalion, less one man, scurrying over a mound some 30 yards to the rear. That one man who refused to withdraw was Charlie Compton," the account said. "For the following three hours while we were pinned behind the mound, Compton stayed on the river bank reorganizing the boats, calling encouragement and fire orders to the men on the opposite side and returning fire with his B.A.R." Compton also managed to carry the only boat not covered by enemy machine gun fire upstream for use in shuttling men across the river.

Compton continued his heroics after the river crossing, according to the historical account. "The company was then dispersed over a very large area, all on a bald ridge with absolutely no cover anywhere. Seemed as though the Jerries were waiting for us all to get on the ridge, for as soon as we did, we were pinned down by extremely accurate sniper fire from three directions. Before we could organize to do anything, one of the heaviest artillery barrages we ever had to sweat out came rolling in on top of us. Jerry was having a field day. It wasn't often that he got the drop as well as he had it then and he made the best of the situation.

"Again, here on Sniper Ridge, Charlie Compton went over the entire area, seemingly unaware of the danger. Compton directed mortar fire, Compton directed small arms fire, Compton used our 300 radio to contact battalion, and last but not least, Compton put himself to the maximum exposure when he went over the ridge unarmed and picked up men who where pinned down (more from fear than anything) and started them on their way back. For his actions that day, Compton was put in for the Congressional Medal of Honor.

"But even a distinction such as that could never express or replace the admiration we have for the man who under the worst possible circumstances went about helping all he could, doing more than any other ten men, and never wasting a thought of his own safety," the story said.

Compton received the Distinguished Service Cross, the nation's second highest award, for his courageous actions. He also received the Bronze Star; French Croix de Guerre with silver star; Purple Heart with bronze oak leaf cluster; European-African-Middle Eastern Service Medal; World War II Victory Medal; American Service Medal; Good Conduct Medal, and Combat Infantryman Badge, making him one of the most decorated Alabama football players in World War II.

Compton's Distinguished Service Cross citation cited him for "extraordinary heroism in action," saying that when his platoon came under enemy machine gun fire as it attempted to cross the river, "Sergeant Compton seized an automatic rifle and with one blast destroyed the enemy weapon and killed three members of the crew. He then

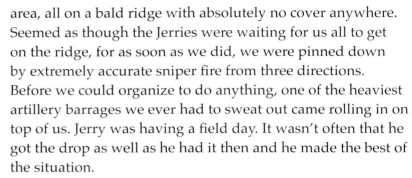

Compton baptizing a young convert in Brazil.

rescued four wounded men, carrying them boldly through fire-swept terrain, and rendered a hostile soldier unconscious with a single blow of his helmet when the enemy soldier, approaching from the rear, called upon him to surrender. The unparalleled gallantry displayed by Sergeant Compton contributed materially to the success of the operation and upon two occasions prevented infliction of severe casualties upon our troops."

Compton played on the 100th Division's football team against the 1st Armored Division team in Stuttgart, Germany, in late September of 1945 while serving with the occupation forces after the end of the war.

He returned to the University of Alabama following his discharge in January 1946 and lettered at tackle for the Crimson Tide in 1946 and 1947, earning the nickname "Killer" because of his rugged play. He earned third-team All-Southeastern Conference honors in 1947, placing him among the best six tackles in the conference.

A *Crimson-White* story on October 29, 1946, referred to Compton's play in a 21-7 win over Kentucky, saying "The rugged war hero literally tore the Kentucky line to shreds when Alabama had the ball and was the fifth man in the Wildcat backfield when Bear Bryant's team tried to move."

Birmingham sports writer Naylor Stone praised Compton's play following the Tide's 31-21 loss to LSU in 1946, saying he "gave his finest performance in the line. He was great, both on offense and defense."

A well documented illustration of Compton's toughness came during the 1946 Alabama-Georgia game in Athens, long before face masks became popular. Compton burst through the Georgia line on a third-down play in the second quarter and ran face-first into a quick-kick by Georgia's Charlie Trippi. The blow knocked

"Even a distinction such as that could never express or replace the admiration we have for the man who under the worst possible circumstances went about helping all he could, doing more than any other ten men, and never wasting a thought of his own safety."

Compton's helmet high into the air and the ball bounded 40 yards backward toward the Georgia goal, where Trippi recovered it himself on the five yard line.

Compton, meanwhile, trotted to the Alabama sideline, borrowed a pair of pliers from the trainer and pulled out the last of three teeth he lost on the play. He spit blood, walked over to Coach Frank Thomas and said, "Coach, I'm ready, get me back in there."

Compton received a serious cleat cut above the knee later in the game, came to the sidelines, taped the gash closed and nonchalantly asked to get back into the game again. Birmingham sports writer Zipp Newman called the game Compton's "finest performance."

"Oh, he was tough as nails," said fellow war veteran and teammate Norman "Monk" Mosley of Compton in 2009. "He was quite a football player and quite a guy—a good guy and a good football player. He didn't give you any problems, and he didn't take any."

"Compton played with reckless abandon," said former teammate Red Noonan. "He was all over the field and stayed after the ball carriers until he brought them down."

There are so many stories about Compton that one begins to wonder which ones are true. The truth is that they are all true, then some.

Harry Gilmer, the great Alabama All-America halfback

A U.S. soldier charges into battle in this National Archives photo.

"A minute later he stepped out with a rifle of some sort and BAM! Everybody ran—into the rooms, the showers, outside—and it got quiet all of a sudden. It scared the hell out of us; we were 18-19 years old and he's an ex-GI back from the war!"

(1944-47), played two seasons with Compton after Compton returned from his heroic duty in Europe and had his share of stories, of course. One involves the first-ever plane trip for the Crimson Tide.

"We were getting ready to fly to Boston to play Boston College in 1946, and we were going by plane for the first time," Gilmer said. "Charlie went to Coach Thomas on Wednesday and told him that he needed to get on the train and start for Boston so he could get there by game time. He said he wasn't going to fly.

"Coach Thomas talked to Charlie and promised to get him a parachute, just in case something happened," Gilmer continued. "Charlie gave it some thought and acted as if he would do it, then said, 'No—no, I'm not gonna do it. Just as sure as the world is round, if that airplane got into trouble you'd tell me, Compton, give Harry that parachute'."

Compton made the trip to Boston by plane after all, and later even earned a pilot's license and owned his own plane while serving as a missionary in Brazil.

Clem Gryska, an Alabama halfback 1945-48, recalled a more exciting episode involving Compton. "A lot of us were standing in the dorm hallway whooping and hollering after a night meal and Charlie was in the first room on the end of the hall," Gryska said. "He stuck his head out of his room and told us to keep it quiet, that he was studying. We joked back at him and kept cutting up. A minute later he stepped out with a rifle of some sort and BAM! Everybody ran—into the rooms, the showers, outside—and it got quiet all of a sudden. It scared the hell out of us; we were 18-19 years old and he's an ex-GI back from the war! There were bullet holes in the end of that hallway for years," Gryska said.

"I remember seeing the bullet marks in the wall," said Harry Lee, a four-year letterman for the Crimson Tide (1951-54) who played with Compton's brother Joe. "He read his Bible and cleaned his rifle every night. He was serious," Lee added.

In addition to playing football and keeping up with his studies, Compton was active in his religious endeavors. He led a Bible class at the Baptist Student Union, attended Calvary Baptist Church where he was a member and held church services for prisoners at the Tuscaloosa County Jail on Sunday afternoons. Most Sunday nights found Compton serving as a guest speaker at local churches.

Compton graduated in January 1948 and entered Southwestern Baptist Theological Seminary in Fort Worth, Texas, later that year along with his wife Betsy. They met in 1947 when Charlie spoke at Judson College, where Betsy was vice president of the student body. They were married June 19, 1948, at First Baptist Church in Betsy's home town of Kingsport, Tennessee.

After graduation from seminary school in 1950, Compton asked the Southern Baptist Foreign Mission Board to send him "where nobody else wants to go." The board responded by assigning Charlie and Betsy to the wilds of Brazil, in the geographical center of South America, with responsibility for helping minister to residents of a rural area twice the size of Texas.

Charlie and Betsy went to South America by boat in 1950. They went there empty handed, having to build their own adobe home and create whatever else they needed to survive in a virtual wilderness. They grew their own vegetables and Charlie hunted wild game for meat. The nearest doctor was a 12-hour drive away over bumpy dirt roads.

"Dad had some engineering training and we lived in a primitive area, so he would just build whatever we needed," Dr. John Compton, said. "He was creative yet practical. He did what needed to be done. It didn't have to be fancy."

Compton began his missionary travels in a 1929 Ford inherited from a retiring missionary, traveling from village to village and sleeping and eating meager meals of cornmeal mush in the vehicle for weeks at a time as he covered his

"When Dad came home from being on the road, he always went straight to Mom and gave her a big kiss and a hug that lifted her off her feet. Then he turned to us waiting children and we got our hugs. Mom was always first."

vast territory, according to Dr. Compton, pastor of First Baptist Church in Clinton, Mississippi. Compton later got a Volkswagen bus for use in his travels to the remote villages, according to Dr. Compton.

"Whatever village he showed up in and on whatever day it might have been, it was Sunday," said Dr. Compton. "He had a generator for loud speakers and he preached, showed films and counseled leaders. He did it again and again, village to village, for 22 years. There were no more than a dozen churches in his area when he arrived in 1950 and there were more than 200 when he died in 1972," Dr. Compton said.

"Mom and Dad were obviously madly in love," Dr. Compton said of his parents. "When Dad came home from being on the road, he always went straight to Mom and gave her a big kiss and a hug that lifted her off her feet. Then he turned to us waiting children and we got our hugs. Mom was always first."

Compton died at age 49, the victim of a head-on automobile accident as he rushed along a remote, dusty road 200 miles from home. His wife, daughter Virginia and sons William, John and Richard survived him and remained in Brazil as Betsy continued her missionary work for two years before returning to the states.

"He lived a Christian life," Dr. Compton said of his father. "All my courage and conviction come from Dad; any class I have comes from Mom. She was 'Miss Manners,' a true Southern Belle. My two brothers and I grew up afraid of nothing because we were Charlie Compton's sons and he was afraid of nothing," Dr. Compton added.

Compton maintained a strict physical fitness regimen throughout his life from his teen years until his death. He ran for miles and exercised daily, rain or shine, summer or winter,

and was still a trim 205 pounds when he died.

Calvary Baptist Church in Tuscaloosa continues to honor Charlie Compton's memory by presenting the Charlie Compton Award to the University of Alabama football player who has demonstrated the most outstanding Christian leadership each year. The award is presented at the Squad Sunday Service each fall, and was first given in 1964.

Among the players who have received the award through the years are Mike Ford, John Croyle, Steadman Shealy, Keith Pugh, Major Ogilvie, Jay Barker and Shaun Alexander. Dr. John Compton was speaker at the Calvary Squad Sunday service in 2007.

Ernest Wilson, a fellow missionary of Compton's in Brazil, wrote a book (*The Good News according to Charlie*) about Compton, detailing his life from childhood until his death. "The example of a strong, masculine personality who denied himself is helpful to those of us who are preoccupied with luxurious creature comforts," Wilson wrote. "My hope is that his example will inspire young people, especially men, to follow the Lord in sacrificial service."

Charlie's brother Joe lettered at fullback for the Crimson Tide 1949-51. He gained 88 yards and scored a touchdown on 31 carries in 1951. Joe worked at the Tuscaloosa tire factory during summers and rode a bike to and from work while living on campus. He took a great deal of ribbing from older brother Charlie for riding the bike, however. Charlie had worked at the tire plant a few summers also, but had walked or jogged back and forth, according to John Compton.

Joe Compton became a high school football coach and had an overall record of 177-49-4 in 25 seasons, including state championships in Alabama, Georgia and North Carolina. He also served as an Army officer during the Korean War, spending a year at Inchon. Joe was retired and living in Fitzgerald, Georgia, in 2009.

A third Compton brother, Byrd, served in the Merchant Marines during World War II and in the Army during the Korean War. He received a Purple Heart for wounds received in Korea.

Cary **COX**

'The fighting was bitter and it was bloody'

Cary Cox kept several souvenirs from his World War II experiences in North Africa, Sicily and Europe, but one stood out as the framed centerpiece over his home's fireplace.

Surrounded by drawings of battle scenes was a water-stained, screen-printed silk map Cox had carried folded inside his belt from the time he hit the beach in Normandy in June 1944 until the end of the war in May 1945. It was a map detailing escape routes from Germany back through France in the event he was captured. Fortunately, he never needed it.

The map was similar to those smuggled to prisoners of war in the board game Monopoly. The Monopoly games, secretly produced by the British and distributed to POWs by charity groups along with coats, food and personal items such as soap, also often included real money hidden among the game's play money. Silk maps were used because they could be folded tightly for concealment and would not make noise when opened.

Cox spent almost three years in front-line action, leading troops into battle on numerous fronts as an infantry officer while earning Silver Star and Bronze Star decorations for bravery.

The former University of Alabama All-America center also earned several battlefield promotions as he advanced from lieutenant to lieutenant colonel during his overseas duty, an indication of his leadership and courage.

Cox displayed the same leadership as a member of the Crimson Tide football team during the 1937-39 seasons. He moved into the starting lineup at center and linebacker midway through his sophomore season (1937) and kept the role through his senior season, when he was named to the Liberty Magazine Players All-America team.

Alabama went undefeated (9-0) in 1937 before losing to California 13-0 in the Rose Bowl then went 7-1-1 in 1938 and 5-3-1 in 1939. Cox was elected team captain for the 1939 season. A Bainbridge, Georgia, native, Cox joined the Tide as a freshman in 1935 and was redshirted in 1936.

Cox was also outstanding in the classroom at Alabama. He was elected to the honorary organizations of Jasons, Omicron Delta Kappa and Scabbard and Blade and was a member of Phi Delta Theta fraternity. He graduated with a degree in business in June 1939 and was commissioned a second lieutenant in the Army Reserve even before he completed his football eligibility.

Cox was ordered to active duty on December 1, 1940, and sent to Fort Benning, Georgia, for training with the Ninth Infantry Division. He played his last football game as a member of the Army All-Star team in October 1942 against Yale University in New York City. A few days later, Cox and other members of the Ninth Infantry Division shipped out to North Africa.

He became one of the first American troops to engage the Germans in World War II when his regiment spearheaded the November 1942 invasion of French Morocco in Operation Torch. The unit later received a Presidential Unit Citation for repelling a massive German attack on Easter Sunday, April 18, 1943. Cox was promoted to captain during cleanup operations in North Africa while his unit fought along the Algeria-Tunisia border.

Cox's unit landed at Palermo, Sicily, on August 5, 1943, and infiltrated enemy lines to lead the offensive in the capture of Messina on August 17. He received the Bronze Star for bravery and a battlefield promotion to major for his leadership during the Sicilian campaign. His unit then moved to Winchester, England, in November, 1943, to prepare for the June 6, 1944, Normandy Invasion.

Cox waded onto Utah Beach a few days after D-Day as a newly promoted lieutenant colonel commanding the

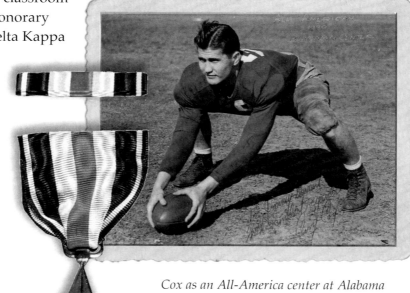

Cox as an All-America center at Alabama

first battalion of the 60th Infantry Regiment. The unit immediately joined the battle in relief of units decimated during the D-Day invasion. The 60th Infantry Regiment later became a part of Operation Cobra, a plan to breach the German lines near St. Lo, France, to allow General George S. Patton Jr. and his Third Army to break through and exploit the German defenses on its drive toward the Brest Peninsula.

Operation Cobra evolved into one of the war's worst friendly fire disasters as U.S. forces were pounded by hundreds of U.S. bombers on two consecutive days when wind blew signal smoke over American lines.

The first errant bombing occurred on July 24, 1944, and killed and injured nearly 200 men. A planned infantry attack on German lines for later that day was called off and another bombing run was scheduled for the next day. Division artillery fired its red smoke shells again on July 25 and again the wind blew the smoke over American lines. Again, allied bombers bombed the American lines, killing 64, wounding 374 and leaving 60 missing in action, according to historical records.

Cox escaped the bombings unhurt, but the driver of a jeep in which he was riding was killed. "He (Cox) said it was awful," Cox's wife Elizabeth, 92, said of the friendly fire incident. One American killed in the second day of bombing was Lt. Gen. Leslie McNair, who had moved forward as an observer after the first disaster. There was no ground-to-air communications at the time, so there was no way ground troops could contact the planes to stop the bombings.

Even after the two tragic events, the planned attack was

carried out on the second day as the American troops moved forward to break the enemy line and allow Patton's Third Army to advance.

Cox received the Silver Star for gallantry in action on August 9, 1944, while commanding a task force assigned the

Lt. Gen. George S. Patton (left) talks with one of his officers in Sicily.

mission of stopping a large-scale enemy counteroffensive near Mortain, France. The Germans had launched a surprise attack on U.S. forces with three armored divisions, including

"By his outstanding leadership and coolness under fire, the mission was successfully accomplished. Colonel Cox remained with the most advanced elements of his troops throughout the fight and was continually exposed to heavy enemy fire."

more than 100 Panzer tanks, on August 7 in an attempt to divide American forces and reclaim recently lost territory. The battle involved six days of fierce, close-range fighting and cost the division an estimated 2,000 lives. The Americans stood their ground against overwhelming German numbers and firepower, however, and with the aid of air and artillery support stopped the German offensive with what one historian called "plain, old-fashioned guts."

Cox was at the forefront of the fight, and his Silver Star citation read: "By his outstanding leadership and coolness under fire, the mission was successfully accomplished. Colonel Cox remained with the most advanced elements of his troops throughout the fight and was continually exposed to heavy enemy fire. The leadership and personal bravery of Colonel Cox on this occasion inspired his troops to their maximum efforts and are in keeping with the highest traditions of the Armed Forces."

Associated Press war correspondent Don Whitehead mentioned Cox and his troops in an October story from the front lines, saying "A First Army infantry unit under the command of Lt. Col. William C. Cox engaged in hand-to-hand fighting with the Germans. The fighting was bitter and it was bloody. The first German surge drove the American infantry from the heights and gave the Germans control of seven of the pillboxes which they had lost, but on the side of the ridge, Colonel Cox and his men held fast."

Cox fought through France, Belgium and Holland and then on into Germany as his 60th Infantry Regiment advanced alongside Patton's Third Army units. He saw action in the Hurtgen Forest and the Battle of the Bulge, where his unit won another Presidential Unit Citation. His regiment was

Holt Rast (left) and Cary Cox during training at Fort Benning, GA.

the first to cross the Rhine River at Remagen and was on occupation duty in Germany when Japan surrendered to end World War II.

In addition to the Silver and Bronze stars, Cox was awarded the American Defense Service Medal, Combat Infantryman Badge, European-African-Middle Eastern Theater Service Medal and Bronze Arrowhead for the North African Invasion. He was discharged in September 1945 after serving three years overseas without receiving a battle wound.

Mrs. Cox said her husband ran into former Alabama teammate Charley Boswell briefly in November of 1944, shortly before Boswell was blinded in battle on November 30. He also crossed paths with Holt Rast, another former

Alabama teammate who was also a member of the Ninth Infantry Division. Rast had also played for the Army All-Star team against Yale in October 1942.

Cox operated an automobile dealership in Alexander City for 25 years before his retirement in 1984. He was active in numerous civic organizations and served as president of the Rotary Club, Kiwanis Club and Chamber of Commerce. He served as a member of the city school board for five years and as chairman for one year.

Cox was inducted into the Alabama Sports Hall of Fame in 1988. He died in 1991 and is survived by his wife Elizabeth, son Cary and daughter Elizabeth (Buffie) Cox Marks.

Cary Cox (with ball) and 1937 Tide teammates line up against Hollywood movie stars, including Humphrey Bogart and Ronald Reagan.

The World War II escape map that Cary Cox kept on his wall for decades.

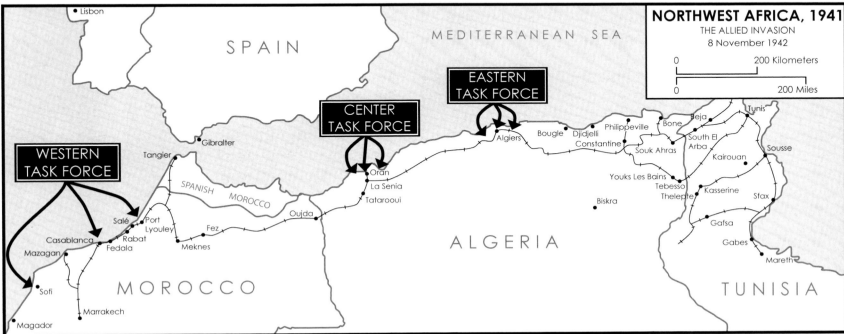

Top: American troops go ashore in North Africa. Above: Map shows areas of attack against German forces.

Russ CRAFT

'It certainly wasn't the best of duty'

Russ Craft helped the University of Alabama to a 9–2 football record in 1941 as the school's outstanding athlete for 1940-41.

Craft starred on both the football and baseball teams as a junior to win the honor then earned second-team All-Southeastern Conference honors as a senior halfback in 1942.

Craft was a three-year (1940-42) letterman on the football team and helped the Tide to an overall 24-7 record during his career on the varsity. He was also a regular on the baseball team and led the team in hitting by averaging over .400 and leading the team to SEC titles in 1940, 1941 and 1942.

The fastest player on the Alabama team, Craft scored two touchdowns to help the Tide defeat Texas A&M 29-21 in the January 1, 1942, Cotton Bowl to claim one of its 13 national championships. A year later, Craft rushed eight times for 80 yards in a 37-21 Tide win over Boston College in the Orange Bowl to cap an 8-3 season. Although hampered by injuries, Craft had 68 carries for 394 yards and caught seven passes for 109 yards and scored seven touchdowns as a senior in 1942.

Craft was commissioned as a second lieutenant in the Army through ROTC in early 1943 and served three years on active duty during and after World War II. He was stationed at Fort Benning, Georgia, where he played football with the Fort Benning Doughboys and conducted physical fitness training before serving overseas in graves registration (accounting for dead and missing soldiers).

"It certainly wasn't the best duty, but it could have been worse," Craft's widow Frances said of Craft's military service. Craft served in Germany 1945-46, earning the European-Africa-Middle Eastern Campaign Medal, the American Campaign Medal and the Victory Medal.

He was discharged as a captain in June 1946 and soon joined the Philadelphia Eagles of the NFL, who had drafted him out of Alabama in 1943.

Craft played on offense, defense and special teams with the Eagles 1946-53 and set several team and NFL records, including four interceptions in one game; a 103-yard kickoff return, and three blocked extra points in one exhibition game. He was selected for the

Craft (18, with ball) also played baseball (left) for Alabama.

first three Pro Bowl games; led the Eagles in fumble recoveries with 15 and pass interceptions with 22 (451 yards returned and two TDs); served as team captain 1952 and 1953, and was named the team's most valuable player in 1952. In 1950, Craft returned 10 kickoffs for 327 yards. He played on two NFL championship teams with the Eagles and also played two years with Pittsburgh.

One of Craft's defensive plays was selected among the NFL's "Top 100 Touchdowns." The play took place in the 1948 NFL championship game when Craft, a defensive back, snatched the football from the arms of Elroy "Crazy Legs" Hirsch and ran 81 yards for a score. Craft was named to at least one all-time all-pro team.

Following his retirement from professional football, Craft returned to his native West Virginia where he operated a business and served two terms as sheriff of Brooke County, where he had earned letters in four sports at Wellsburg High School. Craft died January 12, 2009.

Joe DOMNANOVICH

'When Joe tackled you, you stayed tackled'

University of Alabama head football coach Frank Thomas (1931-1946) once called Joe Domnanovich "the best center to play at Alabama on any team I have coached here." Tide assistant Pete Cawthon (1942), a former head coach at Texas Tech, echoed the praise, calling Domnanovich "the best center I have seen in 22 years of coaching."

That was high praise for a 6-1, 195-pound center, even in the 1940-42 seasons when players were smaller and when Domnanovich was a starter for the Crimson Tide. At least one teammate, halfback Russ Craft, felt the same way, according to Joe's widow Elizabeth Domnanovich.

"Russ always said, 'When Joe tackled you, you stayed tackled'," Mrs. Domnanovich said, recalling in 2009 how close the two were as teammates, opponents in Army and professional football and lifetime friends.

Domnanovich played center on offense and linebacker on defense as a 60-minute player in almost every game during his last two seasons at Alabama, earning All-America and All-Southeastern Conference honors. He

Following his military discharge, Domnanovich played professional football for six years with the Boston Yanks, New York Bulldogs and New York Yanks.

also served as team captain in 1942 as he helped the Tide to an 8-3 record, including a 37-21 Orange Bowl win over Boston College. He returned two interceptions for touchdowns as a senior and called defensive signals.

A native of South Bend, Indiana, Domnanovich was commissioned a second lieutenant in the Army in 1943 and spent three years in the service. He served as an instructor with the Army Specialized Training Program (ASTP) at Alabama for a few months after his commission, then played football while training at Fort McClellan, Alabama, before going overseas to help set up athletic and entertainment events in England and Europe as a special services officer in Third Army, then commanded by Lt. Gen. George S. Patton Jr.

Following his military discharge, Domnanovich played professional football for six years with the Boston Yanks, New York Bulldogs and New York Yanks. "He played

Col. William T. Carpenter swears Tide football players Jimmy Nelson, George Hecht and Joe Domnanovich (L-R) into ROTC.

against Russ (Craft) in the Army (Craft played with the Fort Benning Doughboys.) and in pro football for six years," Mrs. Domnanovich recalled, "but they were always close friends. They were teammates; we were in each others' weddings; they went into service at the same time and came home two days apart; we vacationed together, and they even died two days apart in January 2009," she said.

Following his professional football career, Domnanovich served as a supervisor at U. S. Steel in Birmingham for 30 years before his retirement. He was inducted into the Alabama Sports Hall of Fame in 1984 and was a second-team selection on Alabama's All-Century team.

Clockwise from top: All but one member of this 1942 football team served in World War II; Joe Domnanovich prepares for war; Alabama Coach Frank Thomas and team captain Joe Domnanovich accept Orange Bowl Trophy

Frank KENDALL

Coach takes time out for military service

Frank Kendall was well on his way to legendary status as a high school coach and educator when the United States entered World War II in December of 1941.

Kendall had served as an officer in the Warrior Guards and State Home Guards (now National Guard) for several years and had also taught military classes at Tuscaloosa High School in addition to coaching several sports when he was called to active duty with the Army as a first lieutenant in May 1943. He reached the rank of captain while serving with the Coast Artillery near New York City until the war's end in 1945. The Army's Coast Artillery units provided wartime antiaircraft protection at coastal ports in the U.S. and nearby territories.

Kendall played football at the University of Alabama 1928-30 and was a reserve end on the 1930 national championship team that went 10-0, beat Washington State 24-0 in the Rose Bowl and outscored opponents 271-13 for the season.

Kendall completed his University of Alabama studies in the spring of 1932 and began an outstanding 26-year coaching career that fall. He coached high school sports at Brookwood (1932), Pell City (1933-34), Tuscaloosa County (1935-39) and Tuscaloosa (1940-58, except for time off for military duty), and he coached from two to four sports many of those years.

His football teams went 112-53-15 with five unbeaten

Kendall coached numerous outstanding college players, including Cecil "Hootie" Ingram and Jack Smalley, both All-Southeastern Conference players at Alabama.

seasons and win streaks of 28 and 19. His track teams won two state championships and finished second twice. In basketball, his teams won one state title and finished second once. He also coached a state championship golf team and led his baseball teams to the state playoffs several times. His best year was 1954, when his teams were unbeaten in football, won state titles in basketball and track and lost only one baseball game.

A North Carolina native who moved to Tuscaloosa in 1924, Kendall played end on Tuscaloosa High's powerful football teams of the 1920s. As a high school coach, he produced scores of college athletes during his career and was instrumental in starting the Alabama High School Athletic Association All-Star games when he served as president of that organization in 1947.

Kendall coached numerous outstanding college players, including Cecil "Hootie" Ingram and Jack Smalley, both All-Southeastern Conference players at Alabama; Clell Hobson and George Albright (Alabama), and Billy Henderson (Alabama and The Citadel).

"He was a brilliant coach," Ingram said of Kendall. "He knew how to get the most out of people." Kendall served as principal of Tuscaloosa Junior High School for several years after his retirement from coaching. He also remained in the National Guard for several years following World War II.

Kendall, known widely as "Swede," was elected to the Alabama Sports Hall of Fame in 1980. Kendall's sons Frank Jr. and Tommy both played varsity tennis for the University of Alabama. Tommy received an Army commission through ROTC at the University and earned a Bronze Star as a first lieutenant in Vietnam.

Kendall found his way to the University in unique fashion. His father died when he was a teenager in Laurinburg, NC, forcing him to drop out of high school to work as a clerk in a drugstore to help his family. After several years, his sister Kathryn, who was married to then-Alabama assistant football coach Hank Crisp, persuaded Kendall to come to Tuscaloosa to live with the Crisps and finish school at Tuscaloosa High.

Kendall played end on the THS football team except on passing downs, when he moved to quarterback. His play helped the Black Bears win a mythical national championship in 1926 with an unbeaten season capped by a win over Senn High of Chicago. He was 23 years old at the time. He went on to play at Alabama along with Tuscaloosa High teammate John Henry "Flash" Suther, and they were both members of the Crimson Tide's 1930 national championship team.

Kendall was married to Sara Hart Coleman, the sister of long-time University athletic business manager Jeff Coleman, for whom Coleman Coliseum is named. Kendall, Coleman and Crisp have all been elected to the Alabama Sports Hall of Fame.

The Kendall family has established the Swede and Sara Hart Kendall Endowed Athletic Scholarship at the University in their honor.

Frank Kendall (third from right, second row) was a member of Alabama's 1930 national championship team.

Jack McKEWEN

'I don't think I'd be here today if not for those bombs'

Jack McKewen was an Army officer on his honeymoon in August 1945, daring not to think of what lay ahead of him as war with Japan still raged in the Pacific.

"I was on leave just before shipping out to the Pacific and Ruth and I were on our honeymoon when the bombs were dropped to end the war," McKewen, 90, said in November 2009. "We're still together 64 years later, but I don't think I'd be here today if not for those bombs."

The U.S. was training its military forces worldwide for an anticipated land invasion of Japan in the summer of 1945 when the first of two atomic bombs was dropped on Hiroshima, Japan, on August 6, 1945, with an estimated death toll of more than 100,000 people. The second bomb hit Nagasaki on August 9, taking up to 40,000 more lives. Japan surrendered on August 15, officially ending the conflict with the U.S. that began with the December 7, 1941, Japanese bombing of the U.S. Pacific Fleet at Pearl Harbor, Hawaii.

McKewen graduated from the University of Alabama in 1942 and soon became a first lieutenant in the Army's 124th Infantry Regiment at Fort Benning, Georgia. At that time, ROTC graduates had to complete officer candidate's school after graduation to receive their commissions. He had played football for the Crimson Tide 1939-42 and lettered his last two years at tackle, which helped him land a spot on the regiment's football squad in 1943.

"We played anyone we could, even a prison team," McKewen said. "We played other division teams and bases, including Fort Jackson and Jacksonville Naval Station." McKewen played well enough to be named first team on the Associated Press Southeastern All-Service team.

"There were a lot of ex-college and professional players on those teams," McKewen said. One of those players was Bob Waterfield, a former UCLA star who was married to actress Jane Russell. "I danced with her at the Fort Benning Officer's Club once; she was a nice lady," McKewen said of Russell.

McKewen spent 18 months (1944-45) in Panama, guarding the Panama Canal and patrolling the nearby jungles. He returned to Fort Benning for additional training in anticipation of the invasion of Japan in the summer of 1945 but was discharged soon after the war ended in August. He was called back to active duty for the Korean War in 1950 and spent two years with the 31st Division at Fort Jackson, South Carolina. "I was very lucky; I never got shot at," McKewen said of his wartime experiences.

McKewen enjoyed his military experiences enough that he joined the Alabama National Guard for an additional 14 years and eventually retired as a full colonel.

McKewen spent 50 years in the life insurance business in Birmingham with Fidelity Mutual Life. In 1978 he was elected president of the Million Dollar Round Table, an insurance organization of 19,000 members worldwide. He helped establish the Jack L. McKewen Endowed Scholarship Fund for the University of Alabama Culverhouse College of Commerce and Business Administration through gifts donated by Fidelity Mutual in his honor in addition to a substantial gift to the scholarship made by McKewen and his wife.

McKewen was a recipient of the University of Alabama National Alumni Association's Paul W. Bryant Alumni-Athlete Award in 2001 in recognition of his professional accomplishments and contributions to society after leaving the University. His son Jack McKewen Jr. played football at Alabama during the 1960s, overcoming a serious shoulder injury as a junior to earn a letter at tackle in 1968. Jack Jr. earned engineering and business degrees (MBA) from Alabama and later joined his father in the insurance business.

"I always wanted to play football at Alabama," McKewen said. He was recruited by several colleges despite being slowed by a knee injury as a senior at Woodlawn High School. He played on back-to-back state championship teams at Woodlawn alongside Holt Rast and Sam Sharpe, both of whom also played at Alabama. McKewen was a member of

McKewen was a recipient of the University of Alabama National Alumni Association's Paul W. Bryant Alumni-Athlete Award in 2001 in recognition of his professional accomplishments and contributions to society after leaving the University.

Jack McKewen as an Alabama tackle.

the 1941 Alabama football team that went 9-2 and defeated Texas A&M 29-21 in the Cotton Bowl.

McKewen also played in the Orange Bowl on January 1, 1943, helping the Tide defeat Boston College 37-21. McKewen and Tide end Sam Sharpe had already entered OCS training prior to the Orange Bowl, but were allowed time off to play in the game.

McKewen died April 11, 2010.

Walter **MERRILL**

'The most dependable man on the team'

Walter Merrill was a football player, and a good one. He played the game most of his life, and always as a star.

Ironically, an injury received while playing service football during World War II likely contributed to his untimely death at age 35.

Merrill was a big man for his day at 6-3, 223 pounds, and he earned All-State honors at Andalusia High School before signing a scholarship with the University of Alabama in the spring of 1936.

Tales persist that Merrill brought along his own helmet and shoes when he joined the Crimson Tide team because his sizes were hard to find. He wore a size eight helmet and size 13EEE shoes.

He became the only sophomore starter for the Crimson Tide in 1937, playing both offense and defense, and earned third-team All-Southeastern Conference honors in 1938 and 1939. He was one of only two Alabama players chosen by Tide head coach Frank Thomas on his 1938 All-South team. He was also named to the writers' first-team All-Southeastern team and was elected alternate captain in 1939.

Alabama went 21-5-2 during Merrill's varsity years, winning the SEC championship in 1937 and finishing the regular season at 9-0. The Tide lost to California 13-0 in the Rose Bowl. Alabama went 7-1-1 in 1938 and 5-3-1 in 1939.

Merrill was chosen the Tide's most valuable player by the Birmingham Alumni Association in 1939. He was a second-team selection on Alabama's All-Time Eleven chosen by the media in 1943.

Thomas once called Merrill "the best offensive tackle I ever coached," and former Alabama head coach Paul "Bear" Bryant, who was an Alabama assistant when Merrill played for the Tide, once said "Walt was one of our great players, a great person and a warm friend of mine." Birmingham sports writer Zipp Newman described Merrill as "rugged and powerful, quick and agile, smart and aggressive, the most dependable man on the team and probably the best tackle in America today."

ALABAMA CRIMSON TIDE vs **KEESLER FLIERS**
Flier Field
Saturday, September 29

Souvenir program from 1945

Merrill played in the East-West Shrine All-Star game and the College All-Star game against the Green Bay Packers after the 1939 season and was chosen 34th overall in the National Football League draft of 1940 by the Brooklyn Dodgers. He started 22 of 28 games with the Dodgers before joining the Army Air Forces on January 12, 1943.

Blindness in one eye limited Merrill's service options. He was sent to Non-Commissioned Officers' school and attained the rank of sergeant. Then, like many former college and professional athletes, he was assigned to duty as a physical fitness instructor and athletic coach. Merrill ended up playing football for the Keesler Air Force Base Commandos (1943) and the Randolph Field Ramblers (1944). His teammates at Randolph included former Alabama players Hal Newman and Joel (Macky) McCoy and the Ramblers won the service championship in 1944 with a perfect record.

A serious kidney injury received in a 1944 game and subsequent major surgery ended Merrill's playing career. He later coached at Keesler along with former Alabama end Albert Elmore Sr. and was on the sideline when Keesler played Alabama in the first game of the 1945 season. Alabama won the game 21-0 and went on to a 10-0 season, including a 34-14 Rose Bowl win over Southern California.

Randolph Ramblers Merrill, McCoy and Newman (L-R) all played at Alabama.

Former Alabama head coach Paul "Bear" Bryant, who was an Alabama assistant when Merrill played for the Tide, once said "Walt was one of our great players, a great person and a warm friend of mine."

Merrill was discharged at the end of the war and returned to his home town of Andalusia to join his father's construction company. He continued to have medical problems related to his service injury and surgery, however, and died on March 12, 1953, at age 35. "It was as though Hercules had died," a younger cousin said of Merrill's death.

Merrill's grandson, Seth Moates, was a walk-on linebacker at Alabama 1985-86.

Floyd 'KO' MILLER

He earned his nickname as a Golden Gloves boxer

Floyd Dean Miller earned the nickname "KO" as a boxer during high school and it stuck with him throughout his life, including his four years as a rugged football player at the University of Alabama.

Miller, a husky 6-2, 220-pounder, won a Golden Gloves boxing tournament in Birmingham to pick up his nickname, according to his wife Virginia. "Everyone called him 'KO' for knockout from that time on," Mrs. Miller said.

Miller was named the state's outstanding football player at Blount County High School as a senior tackle in 1942-43 and signed a scholarship to Alabama in the spring. His college football career was delayed for three years, however, when he was drafted into the Army in May 1943 for service during World War II.

The Oneonta native served in the 4th Field Artillery Regiment and with a rehabilitation company in the Pacific. Miller also served as an instructor in various classes, including marksmanship, mortar and machine gun tactics and first aid before being discharged in February 1946 as a sergeant.

Miller enrolled at Alabama in 1946 and played football for four years, lettering in 1948 and 1949 at tackle. "He was a tough player," said former teammate Clem Gryska of Miller in 2009. Alabama went 27-14-2 during Miller's playing seasons, including a 27-7 loss to Texas in the January 1, 1948,

Miller also served as an instructor in various classes, including marksmanship, mortar and machine gun tactics and first aid before being discharged in February 1946 as a sergeant.

Sugar Bowl.

Miller earned B.S. (1949) and M.A. (1950) degrees from Alabama and went into coaching in the fall of 1950 as an assistant at Emma Sansom High School in Gadsden. He became head coach a year later and held the job for five years. He left coaching in 1956 to develop the Trades and Industrial Education Program at Oneonta High School, where he remained as coordinator until his retirement in 1980. He died in 1991.

Miller was an active member of the A Club throughout his life and helped organize the Blount County University of Alabama Alumni Chapter, in which he served as president. He also served as vice president of the University of Alabama District Alumni Association. Miller was founder of the Oneonta/Blount County Pee Wee Football Association and the Oneonta Recreation Board for Youth Sports. He was also a member of the Alabama Council on Physical Fitness and a member and officer in several state and local professional education associations. Miller was inducted into the Blount County Sports Hall of Fame and the Emma Sansom Hall of Fame.

Miller was survived by his wife Virginia, whom he married in 1946, and children Noah Dean Miller and Carolyn Miller Kirby.

Noah Dean played football at Alabama 1970-73, earning a letter at linebacker under Coach Paul "Bear" Bryant in 1973. Noah Dean's sons Marc (1998-2001) and Matt (2000-2003) also played football at Alabama, giving the family three generations of Crimson Tide players. Noah Dean is now a dentist in Gadsden.

Carolyn served as a "Bear Girl" 1973-77 and was director of athletic hostesses during the coaching tenures of Ray Perkins and Bill Curry. She is now a professor at the University of Montevallo.

The Military in World War II

The Air Force was a part of the Department of the Army from its beginning until September 18, 1947, when it became a separate branch of the military service. From June 20-1941-September 17, 1947, it was known as the U.S. Army Air Forces. From July 2, 1926-June 20, 1941, it was known as the U.S. Army Air Corps. From May 24, 1918, until July 2, 1926, it was known as the U.S. Army Air Services.

The Army Air Corps had only 26,500 men and 2,200 aircraft in 1939. At its peak during World War II, the Army Air Forces had approximately 2.4 million men and women and 80,000 aircraft.

The U.S. Army had an authorized active strength of 227,000 men in 1939 with another 235,000 authorized for the National Guard. By December 31, 1941, the Army strength had grown to 1.6 million men, with 867,462 of those ground forces. At its peak on March 31, 1945, the Army included 8,157,386 men and women with 2,753,517 of those ground troops.

The U.S. Navy had an active strength of 337,349 men on December 7, 1941. On July 31, 1945, the Navy had 3,405,525 men and women on active duty. The Navy had 225 surface warships on December 7, 1941, with a total of 790 ships. On December 31, 1944, the Navy had 827 surface warships and 6,084 total ships.

Holt **RAST**

'He took a bullet in the chest; he was lucky to survive'

Holt Rast had plenty of stories to tell about his heroic actions in nearly three years of combat during World War II, but few people ever heard them.

An All-America end at Alabama in 1941, Rast had to pass up an offer from George Halas to play professional football with the Chicago Bears and report to the Army shortly after graduation in 1942. He went on to become one of the most decorated former Tide football players in World War II.

Rast served in North Africa, Sicily, France and Germany and was wounded twice as his division saw 304 days of combat during the war. He earned the Silver Star, Bronze Star; Purple Heart with Oak Leaf Cluster; eight battle stars for French Morocco, Tunisia, Sicily, Normandy, Northern France, Ardennes, Rhineland and Central Europe campaigns; Victory Medal; Distinguished Unit Badge and European-African-Middle Eastern Medal.

Rast received the Silver Star, the nation's third-highest decoration for combat valor, for gallantry in action in February 1945, near Zerkall, Germany. His citation read: "Displaying his aggressive initiative and devotion to duty,

Rast served in North Africa, Sicily, France and Germany and was wounded twice as his division saw 304 days of combat during the war.

Captain Rast repeatedly exposed himself to direct enemy observation and fire to personally reconnoiter the Roer River for sites for an assault crossing. While moving forward with another officer, the other man was seriously wounded after having accidently detonated a mine. Realizing that the wounded man needed immediate medical attention, Captain Rast carried the man through the mine field to a position from which he could be quickly evacuated to the rear for medical treatment."

Recounting his heroic actions years later, Rast said it wasn't courage that made him carry a wounded man through a minefield. "I wasn't brave; I was terrified," he said. "I went after him because I knew that if I let him die because I was too scared to get him out I would never be able to close my eyes and sleep again."

Rast received the Bronze Star on October 1, 1944, for "meritorious service during military operations in the North

"When a grandchild asked about his war wounds in the 1990s, Dad said, 'A sniper was waiting for us in a tree as we were moving along. I was shot in the buttocks, just like Forrest Gump'," Bob Rast laughed. "Dad said when he went down his entire squad turned around and cut down on the sniper with everything they had and killed him. He always said he felt a little sorry for the sniper," Bob laughed. (Ironically, the "Forrest Gump" character in the book and movie by the same name was a mythical member of the 9th Infantry Division in Vietnam.)

The war stories Bob Rast tells today were hard to come by when he and his seven siblings were growing up. "He wouldn't talk about the war at all when we were young," Bob said. "It was a chapter in his life he kept closed for a long time. He said all he ever wanted to do was get it over with and come back home alive."

Rast graduated from Alabama with a degree in engineering and an ROTC commission in the spring of 1942 and within months became one of the first U.S. troops to engage in offensive ground combat operations during the war when he landed at Safi, French Morocco, North Africa, on November 8, 1942, as part of Operation Torch. His division later fought in Tunisia (March 1943) and in Sicily (August 1943) as part of the 7th Army under the command of General George S. Patton Jr.

The 9th Division moved to England in November 1943 for training for the Normandy invasion and hit Utah Beach on June 10, 1944, (D-Day plus 4). The division fought its way through France, Belgium and Germany during the remainder

African Theater of operations November 8, 1942-August 17, 1943" while serving as a company commander with the 15th Combat Engineer Battalion. "His skill and untiring efforts in the supervision of road construction were largely responsible for the success of the operations during this period," the citation read.

Rast received his most serious wound on July 25, 1944, near St. Lo, France, when he was cut down during an assault on a German machine gun position. "Mother said he was missing for about a month," said Rast's son Bob, "but she finally got a letter from a nurse who told her that he was alive in a hospital. He had taken a bullet in his chest and was lucky to survive." Rast even received a commendation for his assistance in the rehabilitation of other patients in the 250th Station Hospital while recovering from his wounds (August 16-November 11, 1944).

Rast returned to the front lines in November and was wounded again on February 6, 1945, as U.S. forces drove toward the Roer and Rhine rivers on their way to relieve the 82nd Airborne Division in the Hurtgen Forest.

of the war, participating in the Normandy, Northern France, Ardennes, Rhineland and Central Europe campaigns. The division had 22,292 battle casualties during the war, according to military records, with 4,581 killed, 16,961 wounded, 750 missing and 868 captured.

When the war finally ended in May, 1945, Rast and the rest of the 9th Infantry Division returned to England, where Rast was able to make a brief telephone call home to his wife Anne to say he was coming home. "It was the first time she had heard his voice in three years," said Bob Rast. "Dad said they had only three minutes to talk and she cried the entire time."

Rast was discharged from the Army as a major in 1946 and became a founding partner in a Birmingham construction company known today as Rast Construction Company. He served as president until the mid-1980s then as CEO until his death. Bob Rast now serves as president.

Holt's brother Tom served as an Army captain in the Pacific during the war after being the captain of the boxing team and a member of the track team at Alabama. He returned from World War II to enter the real estate and insurance business (Johnson, Rast & Hayes), and both brothers became business and civic leaders in Birmingham and in the state of Alabama, earning numerous honors and awards through the years.

Holt Rast was elected to the Alabama Sports Hall of Fame in 1977 and the Alabama Academy of Honor in 1989. He was chosen Distinguished Engineering Fellow by the University

"The more you do, the more you can do was his philosophy," said Bob Rast of his father. "He was a true believer in the adage 'To whom much is given, much is expected,' and he lived it."

of Alabama College of Engineering in 1988 and received the Admiral Thomas J. Hamilton Award and the Pioneer All-American Award from the All-American Football Foundation in 1996. He was selected to receive the SEC Living Legends Award in 1998, but died a month before the ceremony and was honored posthumously. He also served in the Alabama House of Representatives 1957-66, as president of the Alabama Utility Contractors Association, president of the Birmingham Monday Morning Quarterback Club and as a member of the Jefferson County Planning and Zoning Board.

Holt and Tom Rast shared the University of Alabama National Alumni Association's Paul W. Bryant Alumni-Athlete Award in 1993 in recognition of their accomplishments and contributions to society after graduating from the university.

"Going to the University of Alabama made a tremendous difference in my life," Holt Rast said at the time. "There is no way to say what my life would have been like had I not had the opportunity to go to Alabama."

"My dad and Uncle Tom loved the University of

Rast overseas (top) and with wife Anne.

Alabama," Bob Rast said. "They attributed everything they had to the University." Tom Rast served on the University of Alabama System Board of Trustees in addition to numerous other civic and professional organizations.

Holt Rast earned a scholarship to Alabama in 1937 as an All-State end from Woodlawn High School, where he earned three letters in football, basketball and track and served as captain of the football team, president of his senior class and president of the student body.

He almost left Tuscaloosa after only a few weeks as a freshman, according to Bob Rast. "He said he felt out of place at Alabama in his worn out, hand-me-down shoes, even in the Depression era," Bob said. "He made up his mind to leave and started walking. He was only a mile or two down the road when Coach (Frank) Thomas caught up with him. He bought Dad some shoes that maybe cost three or four dollars. Coach Thomas said 'A pair of shoes shouldn't keep a person from getting a college education'," Bob added. Similar stories have been told by numerous Crimson Tide players from the Depression days as Coach Thomas and assistant coach Hank Crisp helped players stay in school during hard times.

The shoes paid off for Rast, who went on to earn All-Southeastern Conference honors as a junior and senior and was selected to every 1941 All-America team, including the "Kate Smith All-America, All-Collegiate Team." He also earned his degree in engineering, served as president of the A Club, took part in ROTC and earned his pilot's license while at the University.

Thomas once called the 6-0, 180-pound Rast "the best

Top left: Rast takes a break from war to play with a puppy. Above, Rast seated in front passenger seat.

all-around end in the South, a demon on defense, excellent pass receiver and one of the best downfield blockers on the squad." Rast, although playing end, called the offensive signals in 1941.

"The more you do, the more you can do was his philosophy," said Bob Rast of his father. "He was a true believer in the adage 'To whom much is given, much is expected,' and he lived it. He worked hard for all his material success, but he believed he had been blessed with wonderful

Above: American troops cross the Seigfried Line.
Right: Rast was a recipient of the Silver Star.

opportunities, good family and friends. He was a giver. He thought you had to pay back. He was generous with his time and resources.

"He pushed himself exceedingly hard, but he never pushed others as hard as he did himself. He was tolerant and patient with people. He never got onto people for mistakes, but he would really get on them for doing nothing. Although he was the president of a good-sized company, he never hesitated to pick up a shovel and work. He admired good works and good workers," Bob added.

"They (Holt and Tom Rast) came up during the Depression. They had a hard early life, but they were achievers—true Americans, symbols of what this country is. They lived it in words and deeds," Bob said.

Holt Rast's oldest son, Holt Rast III, served in Vietnam as a master sergeant under the command of Colonel George S. Patton IV, the son of the famed World War II general under whom his father had served.

Rast (center) with
GIs in Europe

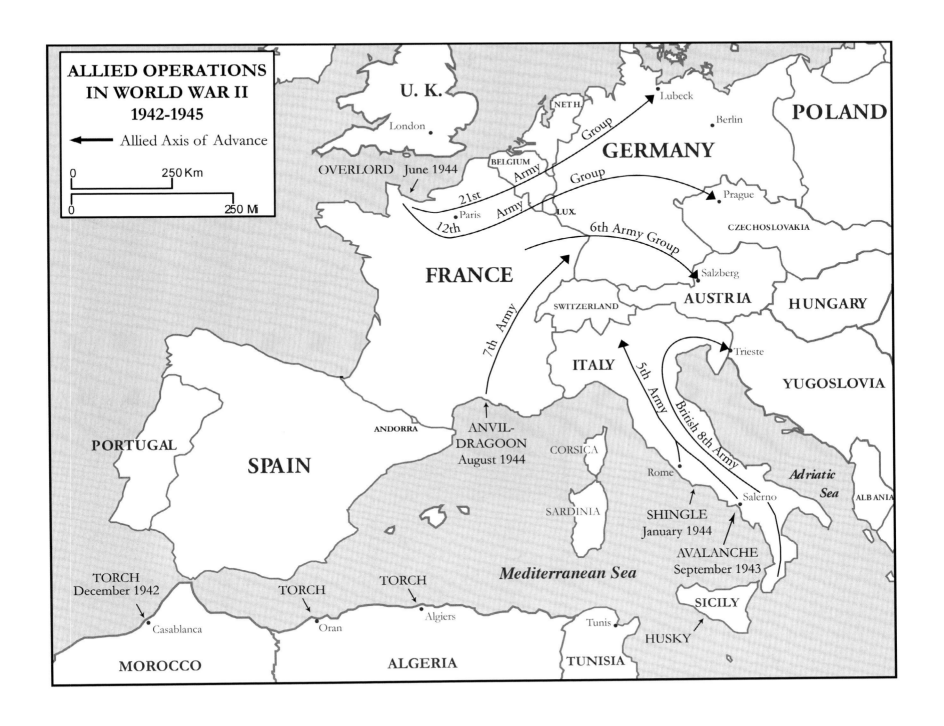

ALLIED OPERATIONS
IN WORLD WAR II
1942-1945

← Allied Axis of Advance

0 _____ 250 Km

0 _____ 250 Mi

U. K.

London

NETH.

OVERLORD June 1944

BELGIUM

21st Army Group

Group

Army

12th

Paris

LUX.

Lubeck

Berlin

POLAND

GERMANY

Prague

CZECHOSLOVAKIA

6th Army Group

FRANCE

7th Army

SWITZERLAND

Salzberg

AUSTRIA

HUNGARY

PORTUGAL

SPAIN

ANDORRA

ANVIL-
DRAGOON
August 1944

CORSICA

ITALY

5th Army

British 8th Army

Trieste

YUGOSLOVIA

Adriatic
Sea

ALBANIA

SARDINIA

Rome

SHINGLE
January 1944

Salerno

AVALANCHE
September 1943

Mediterranean Sea

TORCH
December 1942

Casablanca

TORCH

Oran

TORCH

Algiers

Tunis

SICILY

HUSKY

MOROCCO

ALGERIA

TUNISIA

Don **SALLS**

'I developed a foxhole religion like everyone else'

Don Salls said in 2009 that he had been blessed with an angel on each shoulder during his 90 years of life, and he offered plenty of evidence to back up his claim.

Salls was a hard-driving fullback and linebacker for the University of Alabama football team from 1940-42 before serving in the Army in France during World War II, and he returned to become one of the state's top small college coaches and leading educators.

Salls was wounded in France after two months of combat with the 79th Infantry Division. He joined the fighting near St. Lo in the summer of 1944 as a replacement officer and earned the Bronze Star with oak leaf cluster, Purple Heart, American Campaign Medal, European Campaign Medal, World War II Victory Medal and Combat Infantryman Badge during his time in the service.

"I've been blessed at every turn," Salls said of his long and productive life. "I certainly didn't expect to live this long."

Salls rode a bus from White Plains, New York, to Alabama in the summer of 1938 to accept a Crimson Tide football scholarship that included room, board, tuition and $10 a month, and other than his time in service, he has made the state his home since.

"My high school coach was a former roommate of Coach Red Drew (former UA assistant and head football coach), so I was offered a scholarship to Alabama," Salls said. It didn't hurt that Salls was his high school team's leading scorer, captain and most valuable player as a senior, of course. "My father asked them to put the scholarship offer in writing and they did, so I came here," Salls said. "When I rode the bus from New York to Alabama, it seemed like another football player headed for the University of Alabama got on at every stop along the way," Salls said with a laugh. "And I'll bet we had a hundred freshman out there my first year."

Salls almost didn't stay in Tuscaloosa, however. "I hated the heat and the tough practices, and the smell of wild onions on the practice field and the stench of the paper mill made me sick," he said. "I wanted to leave. That first year we were just tackling dummies for the varsity, and I only weighed 169 pounds." Salls stuck it out, however, when he discovered that transferring would cause him to sit out of football for a year.

Salls played on the freshman team in 1938 then was redshirted in 1939 before he finally got to play as a sophomore in 1940. The first time he went into a game he returned an interception 76 yards for a touchdown against Kentucky and his playing time increased steadily after that.

He lettered at fullback-linebacker in 1941 and 1942 and drew frequent media praise for both his offensive (eight touchdowns) and defensive play. He scored the only touchdown in a 9-2 win over Tennessee in 1941 as the Tide posted a 9-2 record that included a 29-21 win over Texas A&M in the Cotton Bowl. He was the team's second-leading rusher in 1942 with 291 yards on 78 carries and recovered a fumble and gained 31 yards rushing in the January 1, 1943, Orange Bowl win over Boston College. Salls drew media praise in the 37-21 win for his "great defensive work" and was called "a human pile driver" on offense.

"We played 60 minutes most of the time," Salls said. "Coach Thomas didn't like to play a lot of people. He was a bug about that. If you didn't start, you didn't play. He didn't letter a lot of people." Salls said Thomas only corrected him once during his career at Alabama. "I cut the wrong way once and he said, 'Salls, that may be the way they do it in New York, but you're in Tuscaloosa now.' I was glad to know that he knew my name and where I was from," Salls added.

Salls returned home to White Plains, New York, during the summers while attending college and worked at two and often three jobs. "I pushed a lawnmower at the cemetery in the day time, ushered at the movie theater at night and pumped gas on weekends," the silver-haired Salls said. "I was making good money and was able to take my date to the Astor Hotel in New York City in my daddy's Reo (car)," Salls boasted. "We went to the Astor Rooftop where the big bands played under the stars," he added with a broad smile.

Salls might well have been drafted into the Army prior to his senior season had he not been able to enroll in the advanced Army ROTC program, he said. "That was a changing moment in my entire life," Salls said. "That allowed me to complete my education and become an officer in the Army rather than going in as a private."

Salls and practically the entire 1942 Alabama football went into the military in early 1943, leaving Coach Frank Thomas with too few players to field a team in 1943. "They (the government) were drafting everyone and others were joining up to defend the country," Salls said. Salls received

Salls and practically the entire 1942 Alabama football went into the military in early 1943, leaving Coach Frank Thomas with too few players to field a team in 1943.

his training at Fort Benning, Georgia, starting in March 1943, and was shipped overseas for duty in France in the summer of 1944. Salls had married Margaret Ruger in 1943. They were together for 45 years before her death.

"I reported to a combat unit as a replacement officer and lasted about two months," Salls said of his time in France. "I was wounded near Lamath, France, on September 19, 1944. I was lying in a field trying to avoid German fire and was hit in the hand. There was no pain, but my hand and my rifle had been shattered. I didn't even know I was hit until I looked at my hand," he said. Although his hand was permanently disfigured to some extent, Salls said he considered the wound that took him out of combat a blessing. "It was what you call a million dollar wound," he said.

"After 60 days of combat I was about to go psycho," Salls said. "We had overhead fire, mortar, machine gun, artillery, planes—and a lot of it was our own. My nerves were on edge. We were fighting hedgerow to hedgerow and it was slow, difficult fighting. We were pinned down a lot," Salls

Salls returned to the University of Alabama in the fall of 1945 to pursue a master's degree and a year later was named head football coach at Jacksonville State University.

added. "Once, on the other side of Paris, my platoon was in a church and we heard artillery—our own—working toward us. I wanted to get out of there. Our captain was on the radio trying to stop it, and finally it stopped just short of us," he added.

"The roughest part of the war was seeing a dead GI," Salls said. "You knew a mother, a father, a son or wife had lost someone dear to them. I developed a foxhole religion like everyone else in the war. I was a Catholic with regular attendance, but you develop a deeper relationship with the Lord when you have bullets flying over your head," he added. Salls did have one pleasant experience in France, however, when his platoon took part in the liberation of a town near Paris. "We were the first Americans they had seen. The people poured out of their homes and hugged us and cheered us. That was the proudest moment of the war for me," he said.

Salls was sent back to England for surgery on his hand, and doctors there soon discovered that he also had five fractured vertebrae and seven fractured transverse processes. That explained why his back had hurt so badly during his march across France, he said. "We had walked a lot—from St. Lo to Paris—and my back had ached a lot," he said. "I had to throw away a lot of my gear because of it." Salls saw limited duty from that time on, serving as a rehabilitation officer in England until the end of the war in May 1945. He was finally discharged as a captain in July 1945. He said the back problems have remained with him since.

Salls returned to the University of Alabama in the fall of 1945 to pursue a master's degree and a year later was named head football coach at Jacksonville State University. "They

Don Salls on duty in Europe

made me head coach and head of the physical education department and I had never coached a day in my life," Salls said. His pay was $3,000 for the first year, and he said that he would not have taken the job had he visited the campus first. "We really had no facilities and had to play our games on the local high school field," he said.

Salls said his inexperience in coaching was evident during his first season as the Gamecocks won only one game. "I got smart after that lesson," Salls said. "I hired a defensive coach—Ray Wedgeworth, a high school coach who had played some professional football—and he taught me more football than I had learned in five years of college. He was a defensive genius. We went undefeated in 1947 and had one of the best defenses in the country." One of the 1947 wins was 7-0 over Florida State in Tallahassee. Salls spent 19 seasons (1946-64) as head coach at Jacksonville, posting a 95-57-11 overall record. His teams won seven conference championships and played in four bowl games. His only unbeaten season came in 1947, but the Gamecocks went 10-1 in 1955 and 8-1 in 1948. The 95 wins by Salls was still the most by any coach in JSU history in 2010.

Salls spent his first few summers at Jacksonville back in his home state of New York working toward his doctorate degree, which he earned in 1955 to boost his rank at JSU to full professor. After he left coaching at the end of the 1964 season, Salls remained at JSU for another 18 years as a professor. A campus dorm there is named Salls Hall in his honor.

In 1962, Salls developed a program of isometric exercises that he labeled "XSXIM, which stands for Ten Static Exercises In One Minute. The program was based on the theory that it takes only six seconds of isometric exercise to develop a muscle to its full potential. Salls sold thousands of copies of the exercise booklet. He said the booklet helped him send his four children to college in addition to helping others through the exercises. Salls has also authored a book entitled *Live and Love to be 100* which offers hints for a long, happy and healthy life.

Salls was presented the University of Alabama National

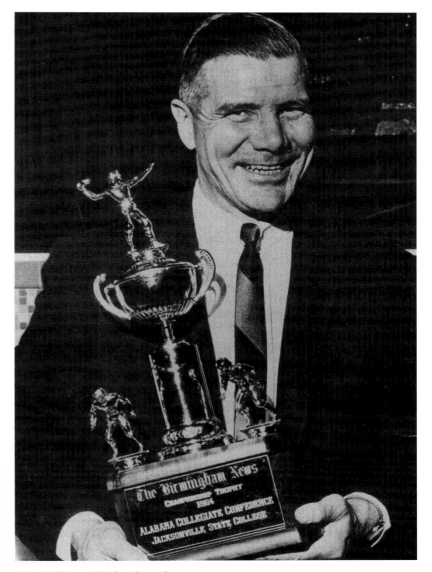

Don Salls as JSU head coach.

Alumni Association's Paul W. Bryant Alumni-Athlete Award in 2003 for his professional accomplishments and contributions to society after leaving the University. He has also been inducted into the Alabama Sports Hall of Fame, the Jacksonville State University Hall of Fame, the Westchester County, NY, Hall of Fame and the All-American Foundation Hall of Fame.

Salls and his wife of 22 years, Diane, live in Tuscaloosa. He has four children, Donald II, Patricia, Donna and Sherrie.

Cullen **SUGG**

'We tried to fill the air with lead'

Cullen Sugg said he was in "some pretty hot spots" as an officer in General George Patton's Third Army as it attacked German defenses in France, Belgium, Germany and Austria during World War II.

The 1940 University of Alabama graduate commanded a battery in the 24th Antiaircraft Artillery Group throughout the European campaign. His mission was to protect American troops and tanks from German airstrikes. "We tried to fill the air with lead," Sugg said at age 93.

Although Sugg was a captain under Patton's command, he said he never came face to face with the famous general. "I never had any close contact with him and I'm glad I didn't," Sugg said of Patton. "Everybody was scared of him. We knew of his fame and we were proud to be a part of his outfit. We would have given our lives for him," he added. Although Patton was often outspoken and controversial, he was known for daring successes in numerous battles during the war.

Sugg played football at Alabama 1936-39 and took advanced ROTC to earn an Army Reserve commission following graduation in 1940. "I wasn't thinking about going in the Army at the time," Sugg said. "I

Opposite: Sugg directs artillery fire against Germans

did it to get the extra money. I sure didn't learn enough in ROTC to fight a war. I found that out when I got over there against the Germans."

Sugg was called to active duty in early 1942 and sailed from Boston to England in February of 1944. "We had to zigzag to avoid German submarines and I got seasick," Sugg said. "Then I had submarine watch and was sick *and* scared," he recalled with a laugh. "We docked in England beside the Queen Mary," Sugg said. "That was the biggest thing I'd ever seen."

Soon after arriving in England, Sugg's unit began training for the anticipated D-Day invasion. "We set up our artillery along the white cliffs at Dover and tried to shoot down the German buzz bombs that were coming over at the time," he said.

Sugg went ashore at Normandy on D-Day plus six. "We saw a lot of dead animals and wrecked equipment along the way, but the dead soldiers had already been picked up," he said. "As we moved through France to St. Lo, I saw a dead paratrooper still hanging in a tree. It was awful. I knew then that we were in the thick of it. I was in some pretty hot spots and exposed to a lot of war, but luckily I was never hit," he said. Sugg mentioned Metz, the Siegfried Line, Battle of the Bulge, Ardennes, Bastogne, the Moselle and Rhine rivers and several other memorable battlefronts

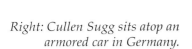

Right: Cullen Sugg sits atop an armored car in Germany.

Below: U.S. artillery pounds German lines in Europe.

throughout Europe in which he saw action.

"It was wet and cold and we took any shelter we could find," Sugg said. "We took over a bank building in Metz and got in a big old iron safe trying to dodge German planes strafing us once," he said. "There was mud and snow and our tanks and trucks kept slipping off the road. It was terrible; a lot of lives were lost. I don't want to go back," Sugg said.

Sugg was in the Bavarian Alps when Germany surrendered on May 8, 1945, but he had little time to celebrate with the war against Japan still raging in the Pacific. "I was in command of some troops training for the invasion of Japan when the A-bomb was dropped (in Japan to soon end the war)," Sugg said. "I was sure glad; I knew there would be a lot of losses there."

Above: Sugg (right) with fellow GI. Right: Sugg in Germany

According to military records, Third Army forces killed 144,500 enemy troops, wounded 386,200 more and captured 765,483 prisoners during their year-long European campaign. American losses included 16,596 killed, 96,241 wounded and 26,809 missing in action. Third Army Artillery units, including Sugg's, fired 5,870,843 rounds of ammunition as they "tried to fill the air with lead" in defense of Third Army troops.

Sugg was discharged in December 1945 and returned home to his wife Dorene, whom he had married in 1943, and to the Russellville, Alabama, area of north Alabama where he grew up. "We fixed up an old farm house in Town Creek and raised our family (two boys) there," Sugg said. "We farmed

and went to a lot of ball games."

Sugg grew up six miles out of Russellville and attended Russellville High School, where he played football under Charles "Buster" Kindig, a University of Alabama graduate. "I sort of starred as a senior and someone from Auburn came up to try to recruit me," Sugg said. "Coach Kindig called Coach Hank Crisp at Alabama and told him that Auburn was after me and Coach Crisp said, 'Put him on the bus and send him down here.' That's how I ended up at Alabama," he added.

"They gave me a job trimming hedges when I got there," Sugg added. "I was a country boy and didn't know my way around much, but I met a fullback from Pensacola (Dallas Wicke) who had more experience in city ways and he helped me along some. And Bear Bryant (assistant coach 1936-39) seemed like he was always pushing 'ol Sugg along."

Sugg came to college against all odds, he said. His father died when he was two and his mother raised his family and ran the farm alone during the trying times of the Great Depression. "She had to sacrifice to help me get to college, and she trained me well," he said. Sugg and his wife were still a lively couple after 66 years of marriage in 2009, and Sugg continued to plant a tomato garden each year.

Bully *VAN de* GRAAFF

1915 Tide All-American served during WWII

William T. "Bully" Van de Graaff has been remembered for almost a century now as the University of Alabama's first All-America football player.

He earned the honor as a senior tackle, punter, placekicker, linebacker and fullback in 1915 and was the third Van de Graaff brother to star for the Crimson Tide over seven seasons (1909-1915). He also earned All-Southern Conference honors at tackle in 1914 and at fullback in 1915.

The Van de Graaff brothers were the offensive stars of the era and Bully was the star of the stars. The brothers scored many of Alabama's points during their playing days as football grew from a club sport to a more competitive level. Bully Van de Graaff helped Alabama defeat Southern Conference power Sewanee for the first time in 11 meetings by scoring 17 points in a 23-10 victory in 1915.

All three Van de Graaff brothers were on the Alabama team in 1912 when Bully was a 16-year-old freshman, Hargrove a junior end and Adrian a senior halfback. Adrian

and Hargrove each scored a touchdown in 1911 when Alabama beat Birmingham Southern 47-5, and they repeated the feat two more times during their careers. Hargrove and Bully each scored a touchdown in 1913 as the Tide defeated Birmingham Southern 81-0.

Although records are incomplete, press clippings show that Bully kicked nine field goals and scored a total of 50 points in only three games in 1915 on his way to earning All-America recognition.

Bully also had the honor of throwing Alabama's first forward pass in a game against Georgia Tech, and it went for a 60-yard touchdown, according to the press report. His punts were said to travel 50-60 yards and his tackling on defense was called brutal.

Bully kicked 45 extra points and 15 field goals during his career and amassed a scoring total of 162 points in four seasons—impressive numbers even by today's standards. The 1915 Corolla called Bully the "best punter in Dixie, a wonder

Bully (left) and C. Hargrove Van de Graaff

at place-kicking, the most powerful man at carrying the ball seen on the field and an impregnable backing to the line."

Following graduation from Alabama in 1916, Bully went to the U.S. Military Academy at West Point and earned a commission in the Army. He returned to the University of Alabama in 1922 as an ROTC instructor. While at Alabama he served as assistant football coach under Xen Scott and Wallace Wade (1922-25). He led the Tide freshmen to three straight unbeaten seasons and helped develop the Crimson Tide linemen who played in Alabama's first two Rose Bowls following the 1925 and 1926 seasons.

Bully served as athletic director, head football coach and professor of physical education at Colorado College from 1926-42, when World War II prompted his return to military duty. He served as a major in Special Services with the Eighth Army. As a physical fitness instructor, Bully coached various service football teams, including an Army team that played in a New Year's Day bowl game in Yokohama, Japan, on

January 1, 1947. He remained on active military duty until his retirement in 1954. As a 1916 graduate, Bully is thought to be the oldest former Alabama football player to serve in the military during World War II. He was inducted into the Alabama Sports Hall of Fame in 1970 and lived his final years in Colorado.

Adrian, who played football 1909-1912, earned a law degree from the University and practiced law in Tuscaloosa until his death in 1938. He also served in the Army during World War I.

Hargrove, a 1914 Alabama graduate who played football 1910-1913, became a highly decorated hero in World War I as a member of the 15th Field Artillery Regiment in France. He was awarded the Distinguished Service Cross, second only to the Congressional Medal of Honor, for "extraordinary heroism" in action near Villemontoire, France, on July 21, 1918. "On duty with the infantry as liaison officer, Lt. Van de Graaff displayed marked courage in passing through an

Bully Van de Graaff (second from left) takes aim on ball carrier

Adrian Van de Graaff

enemy artillery barrage several times, in carrying information to his battalion commander and administering aid to wounded men under heavy shell fire," his citation read.

Hargrove also received three Silver Star citations "for gallantry in action against an enemy of the United States" and two French Croix de Guerre awards during his WWI service. The Tuscaloosa airport was named Van de Graaff Field in his honor. Hargrove was later a coal mine operator in Tuscaloosa County.

A fourth Van de Graaff brother, Robert, played football at Tuscaloosa High School and was a reserve on the 1918 Alabama football team before giving up the sport due to an injury. He earned a degree in mechanical engineering from the University in 1922 and went on to become a world-famous physicist. He attended Oxford University as a Rhodes Scholar, earning his doctor of philosophy degree there in 1928 while participating in several sports. Robert spent three years as a national research fellow at Princeton University before joining the Massachusetts Institute of Technology as a research associate in 1931. He designed and developed what became known as the Van de Graaff high voltage electrostatic generator, which proved critical to the development of the atomic bombs which helped bring an end to World War II.

Bully Van de Graaff (right) as a member of the UA ROTC staff.

The Van de Graaff brothers were descendants of some of the area's oldest and most aristocratic families. Their maternal grandfather, Andrew Coleman Hargrove, was a colonel in the Confederate Army, a dean of the University of Alabama law school and presiding officer of the Alabama state senate. Their maternal great-grandfather, Robert Jemison Jr., was a Confederate Senator who argued against seceding from the union in January 1861. He was also the builder of the well-known Jemison Home, one of the area's antebellum landmarks, on Greensboro Avenue in Tuscaloosa.

The Van de Graaff boys apparently came by much of their athletic and scholarly prowess through their father, Adrian S. Van de Graaff, a native of Gainesville in Sumter County, Alabama. The elder Van de Graaff attended Yale University and played on the school's first 11-man football team in 1880, according to local historical records. He returned to Tuscaloosa, earned a law degree from the University and later served as a University of Alabama law professor (1890-97 and 1910-1911) in addition to practicing law. He served as judge of the 6th Judicial Circuit from November 1915-December 1916 and was elected to the state house of representatives in 1918.

Lloyd **WISE**

'He attributed all his success to football'

Lloyd Wise received a box of melted chocolate candy from back home while serving in the Pacific during World War II, and that candy eventually led him to the love of his life after the war ended in the summer of 1945.

Wise was drafted into the Army in 1942 following his junior year at the University of Alabama, where he had been a reserve tackle on the football team. He completed officer candidate's school in Australia and was commissioned a second lieutenant in 1943.

Wise then served as a combat engineer in the Pacific with the 532nd Engineer Boat & Shore Regiment of the 2nd Engineer Special Brigade. His regiment participated in the assault landing at Leyte in October 1944 and Wise's company was chosen to clear the beach for General Douglas MacArthur's famous "return" to the Philippines.

McArthur, then the Supreme Commander of Allied Forces in the Southwest Pacific, had been ordered to leave the Philippines in February 1942 in the face of advancing Japanese forces. He vowed to return, however, and he waded ashore at Leyte on October 20, 1944, as American forces pushed the Japanese back across the Pacific. Less than one year later, on September 2, 1945, MacArthur was aboard the *USS Missouri* in Tokyo Bay accepting the Japanese surrender that ended the war.

Wise returned home to Blytheville, Arkansas, following

his discharge from the Army in late November 1945, and accompanied his family on a Christmas trip to St. Louis soon afterward. The box of candy Wise had received during the middle of the war had come from St. Louis, and he decided to look up the young lady who sent it. Wise met Julia Mae Fears that December in St. Louis, and they went on only three dates before he asked her to marry him. They announced their engagement on February 23, 1946, and were married June 6.

Julia Mae Fears had sent the candy to Wise as part of a city-wide program in St. Louis. She got his address from a coworker at the DePaul Nursing School who knew Wise's mother and the box of candy was their only contact until after the war.

Lloyd and Julia Wise, circa 1946

"He attributed all his success to football and to the University of Alabama. He was proud of the University and what it did for him, and he taught us to love the University of Alabama."

Wise passed up his final year of football when he returned to Tuscaloosa in the fall of 1946 to earn a degree in business. Following graduation, he returned to Blytheville and went into the insurance business with former Alabama teammate Russell Mosley. He reenlisted in the Army during the Korean War and saw duty overseas again as he became a career Army officer. He also saw duty in Vietnam before retiring as a lieutenant colonel. He earned the Bronze Star with oak leaf cluster and other decorations for his service. He retired in St. Louis and died in 1998.

"He often told us that the opportunity he had at the University of Alabama and the values he developed as a football player shaped his life," Wise's daughter Julia said of her father. "He always said that if Pop Mosley hadn't helped him get to Alabama his life would have been different. He attributed all his success to football and to the University of Alabama. He was proud of the University and what it did for him, and he taught us to love the University of Alabama," she added.

Wise was a 6-6, 229-pound junior tackle on the 1941 Alabama football team. He had played football at Blytheville High School under Joe Dildy, a former University of Alabama center, and was encouraged to attend Alabama by Sylvester "Pop" Mosley, whose sons Herschel (Herky), Russell, Norman (Monk) and Tommy all played for the Crimson Tide.

Wise's father, Lloyd V. Wise, served in the Army in France during World War I and carried a gold locket given to him by his wife throughout the war. The locket is a family heirloom with a medal inside that was once blessed by the Pope. Lloyd Wise carried the same locket during his duty in World War II, and it is still worn or carried by family members on such special occasions as weddings and graduations, according to Julia Wise.

George _ZIVICH_

'In those days I would fight at the drop of a hat'

George Zivich was once featured in an Associated Press story from the front lines of World War II when he jumped into a fox hole with a war correspondent after being slightly wounded by a Japanese sniper.

Zivich was in the jungles of Burma at the time, fighting alongside Chinese troops to clear the Burma Road so fuel, ammunition and supplies could reach the struggling Chinese army in its war against the invading Japanese.

At the same time, U.S. transport planes were flying supplies over the treacherous Himalayan Mountains ("The Hump") from India to Kunming, China, in an attempt to aid the Chinese, whose land supply lines had been cut when Japan conquered Burma in 1942.

Zivich, an Army ranger captain from East Chicago, Indiana, who had played football at the University of Alabama before the war, served as an advisor to the Chinese army and supervised supply air drops and controlled tactical air support as part of his duties in the China-Burma-India Theater from April 1944-September 1945.

He also served as a company commander with the 475th Infantry Regiment during the Mars Task Force operation. The force included 3,000 men and hundreds of pack mules and their task included defeating Japanese forces blocking the Burma Road while also facing such obstacles as steaming jungles, raging monsoons and narrow, treacherous trails

Zivich at UA, circa 1938

through icy, 8,000-foot mountain passes. The MARS soldiers included the survivors of the heroic all-volunteer Merrill's Marauders and was the first to make combat use of night sighting devices then known as "snooperscopes" or "sniperscopes."

Zivich earned several decorations for his World War II service, including Purple Heart, Bronze Star, Army Commendation Medal, Combat Infantryman Badge, Asiatic-Pacific Campaign Medal, European Campaign Medal, World War II Victory Medal and National Defense Service Medal. He also received the Breast Order of Yun Hui with ribbon from the Republic of China.

A 5-11, 200-pound halfback at Alabama, Zivich played

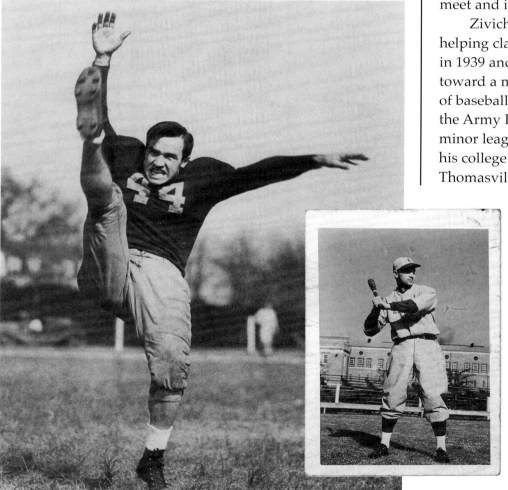

"They said stay put; they would get in touch with me when my name came up." Zivich recalled. "They said they were going by alphabetical order, and I said 'By the time you get to me the damn war will be over'."

for the Crimson Tide 1936-38, lettering his last two seasons. He was on the Tide's 1937 team that went 9-1, won the Southeastern Conference championship and lost to California 13-0 in the January 1, 1938, Rose Bowl. Zivich recalled in later years that he had met actors Humphrey Bogart and (future president) Ronald Reagan while on the Rose Bowl trip. "They were two of the nicest people that I ever had the privilege to meet and interact with," Zivich said of the movie stars.

Zivich also played on the Tide baseball team 1939-40, helping claim an SEC title in 1940. He earned his B.S. degree in 1939 and remained in school an additional year working toward a master's degree while playing his final season of baseball. He was commissioned a second lieutenant in the Army Reserve through ROTC in 1939. Zivich played minor league baseball for two seasons (1940-41) following his college career, batting .233 with two teams, including Thomasville, Georgia, where he met his future wife Mary.

After the Japanese bombing of U.S. ships at Pearl Harbor, Hawaii, on December 7, 1941, Zivich contacted Army officials to inquire about active duty, only to be put off. "They said stay put; they would get in touch with me when my name came up." Zivich recalled. "They said they were going by alphabetical order, and I said 'By the time you get to me the damn war will be over'." He was called to duty three weeks later. He went back to Thomasville during his first leave to marry Mary in March 1942. He was shipped overseas in December 1943 and returned in October 1945.

Zivich coached high school football at Rockmart, Georgia, and Gadsden, Alabama,

Zivich played football and baseball for the Tide

following World War II and completed work on his master's degree at the University of Alabama in 1949. He was called back to military duty during the Korean War and remained in the Army until August 1967, when he retired as a full colonel. He served in numerous positions, including that of commanding officer, U.S. Army Alaska Headquarters Command. He also received the Korean Service Medal, Armed Forces Reserve Medal, the United Nations Service Medal and the Army Commendation Medal with oak leaf cluster.

Zivich had wanted to attend Notre Dame as a youngster growing up in nearby Chicago, even though his older brother had earned All-Big Ten honors at Indiana University. Zivich broke his collarbone as a senior in high school, however, and Notre Dame, Michigan and Indiana all withdrew their scholarship offers, leaving only Alabama on the list, according to comments by Zivich

in 2002. "Alabama recruiters said they still wanted me to play for them and to get well," Zivich said. He enrolled at Alabama as a freshman in the fall of 1936.

"I was the Yankee, the outsider from the north," Zivich said of his freshman season at Alabama. "I did not talk or act the same as those country boys. I had to prove to them that I was not going to be pushed around. In those days I would fight at the drop of a hat, and sometimes the hat didn't even have to be dropped," he said, noting that he had grown up on the tough streets of Chicago.

Zivich died November 13, 2003, in Atlanta, Georgia, and is buried at Arlington National Cemetery near Washington, D.C. He is survived by a daughter, Ann Zivich Bishop of Atlanta, and other relatives.

Travel through the jungles of Burma was difficult for U.S. troops.

General Douglas MacArthur returns to the Phillipines in October 1944.

American troops faced rugged terrain and harsh weather during World War II.

ARMY AIR FORCES

"I wouldn't take anything for the experience of fighting for our country and helping stop Hitler."

— Emmett Dendy

Opposite: A U.S. plane is shown on a bombing run over German targets in Europe during World War II. (National Archives photograph)

Tom **BORDERS**

'I'm just a guy that likes his life...'

Tom Borders became one of the first American heroes of World War II when the plane he was piloting shot down the first German fighter plane over occupied France on August 17, 1942.

The former University of Alabama football player was the pilot of a B-17 bomber he had christened "Birmingham Blitzkrieg" in the first daylight bombing raid flown by Eighth Air Force planes against a European target. Major Paul Tibbetts, who later flew the B-29 bomber called the "Enola Gay" to drop the world's first atomic bomb on Hiroshima, Japan, on August 5, 1945, was among the other 11 pilots who flew on that first high-altitude attack on German targets near Rouen, France.

The "Birmingham Blitzkrieg" had an all-Alabama crew, and belly gunner Sgt. Kent West of West Blocton fired the shots that downed the enemy fighter plane, thus becoming the first American to shoot down a German plane in the war.

Borders, a Birmingham native, was later awarded the Air Medal with two oak leaf clusters for extreme bravery in action as his bomber accounted for heavy damage to enemy installations and several Nazi planes during numerous missions over enemy-held territory.

The above portrait of Tom Borders appeared in Life Magazine _in 1942._

"We are all proud of our success over here," Borders wrote in a letter to a close friend back home in September 1942. "The English think we are the last word in precision bombing. Funny, they told us it couldn't be done, that our proposed manner and tactics were contrary to all rules of modern warfare. Well, we wrote a new rule book!"

Borders was an early hero of World War II as a B-17 bomber pilot in Europe.

"I can't go into detail about it all but it really makes me feel good to actually put in my four bits worth, so to speak, a feeling of doing something toward or against a force that wants to destroy our manner and way of life.

"Sounds like I've been given a pep talk, but I'm just a guy that likes his life and is damn willing to do something when it is threatened. There are a lot of us that feel that way and that's why we've got the top team! I'm just a little angry now because we lost a good guy," Borders added.

Borders became the subject of a color portrait in *Life* magazine as part of a tribute to the men of the Army Air Forces Bomber Command in England. The portrait appeared in the February 15, 1943, issue, shortly after Borders, then a first lieutenant, had been killed on December 26, 1942, during a bombing raid over Tunisia. The portrait is reportedly now on display at the Pentagon.

The shocking details of Borders' death were revealed by a fellow pilot soon after the hero's final raid.

"I turned for a look at Tom Borders, flying number two

Left: Borders' first plane became a "Judas Goat."

in the 'Birmingham Blitzkrieg,' to see his bombs go," said Lt. H. M. Locker, another pilot on the December 26 raid, in an *Air Force* magazine article shortly after the incident.

"I've always had a mania for watching those beautiful golden eggs come sliding out. This time, I wished I had curbed my curiosity, for just as my eyes found him there was a blinding flash and the loudest explosion I've ever heard. I saw the tail of Tom's ship fly backward then down toward the ground five miles below. It was the only visible piece of the 10-man crew and airplane. A direct flak hit in his bomb bay had set off three tons of TNT. When the flash and smoke cleared, there just wasn't anything left. I remember saying 'Poor boys, God bless them'," Locker said in the article.

Only 12 planes of the 97th Bomb Group flew to Rouen in northern France on that first daylight bombing run on August 17, 1942, and all the

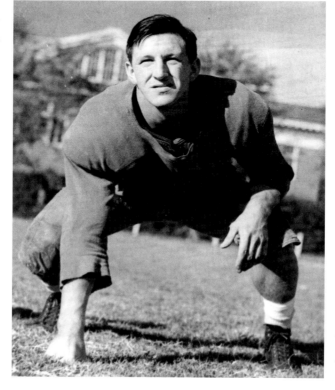

planes and the 111 men aboard returned safely. Before the war ended, however, 31 of those men would die in action, including those aboard the Birmingham Blitzkrieg.

John Hanson, an Army Air Forces officer who had played football with Borders at Alabama, wrote to a friend upon hearing of Borders' death, saying "With boys we have known getting popped off all around it seems more like they've just had a change of station—moved to a better outfit, and by golly, that's what happened in their case if we believe as we should in our God. When I think of Tom and all the others I just think of them as being where I last heard from them, somewhere that I can't quite find time to getting around to look them up, yet still doing their jobs the best they can."

Borders was one of the biggest players on the Alabama football team during his playing days (1937-40) as a 6-3, 240-pound tackle. The Tide posted an overall 21-5-2 record during those years, including a Southeastern Conference championship and 9-0 regular-season mark in 1937 before losing to California 13-0 in the January 1, 1938 Rose Bowl.

Borders graduated in 1941 with a degree in business and enlisted in the Army Air Forces a month later. He received his wings and commission at Randolph Field in January 1942.

Borders flew at least two planes bearing the "Birmingham Blitzkrieg" name. The first was later used as a formation assembly plane, or "Judas goat," after it became damaged from war duty. The formation assembly planes, brightly painted for easy recognition, circled in a designated area until bombing groups reached altitude and formed on the lead plane for their bombing missions over Europe. Attaining altitude and getting into

Borders (with goggles) with flight crew.

near Bizerte (North Africa), but never could seem to get together," Bob Borders said on his return to Birmingham. "Then one day I got some time off and hitched a ride over to Tom's base. A private from Alabama—I think he is dead now—was driving the jeep. He asked me where I was going, and when I told him he got the queerest look on his face and asked me hadn't I heard. Then he told me that Tommy had gotten it that day. That was the first I knew of it," he added.

The younger brother of Tom Borders, Lt. J. H. Borders, also served in the Army Air Forces in Africa.

A B-24 Liberator built in Birmingham and paid for with War Bonds bought by the Jefferson County Savings and Loan Association was christened the "Tom Borders Birmingham Blitzkrieg" in his honor shortly after his death.

proper formation for a bombing run could take two hours or more on each mission. "Judas goat" is a term given to an animal trained to mingle with others and lead them to a specific destination, such as a truck or pen. In stockyards, a Judas goat will lead other animals to slaughter while its own life is spared. The term is used in reference to the Biblical character Judas Iscariot.

Bob Borders, a nephew of Tom Borders though only a few years younger, was also a bomber pilot during World War II. He named his plane "Birmingham Blitz IV" and flew 47 missions over enemy territory. Bob Borders, who also attended the University of Alabama, earned the Air Medal with eight oak leaf clusters and a rare silver cluster and was recommended for the Silver Star.

"We (Tom and Bob) were stationed 30 miles apart once

The University of Alabama Air Force ROTC chapter of the Arnold Air Society is also named the Thomas H. Borders Squadron in honor of Borders.

The 1949 motion picture "Twelve O'Clock High" starring Gregory Peck featured pilots such as Borders who flew daylight bombing missions over enemy territory during the early stages of the war in Europe. The movie was introduced by the following caption:

"This motion picture is humbly dedicated to those Americans, both living and dead, whose gallant efforts made possible daylight precision bombing. They were the only Americans fighting in Europe in the fall of 1942. They stood alone against the enemy and against doubts from home and abroad. This is their story."

Emmett **DENDY**

'I was 19 years old; I didn't know what fear was'

Emmett Dendy was so anxious to join the action in World War II that he skipped his high school graduation exercises in Luverne, Alabama, and headed off to training with the Army Air Forces in May of 1944, leaving his diploma for his mother to pick up.

"I wanted to be a pilot, but they needed gunners more, so I became a gunner," Dendy recalled. "After training, I was shipped to England aboard the *Queen Elizabeth* along with about 10,000 other GIs in December of 1944."

Dendy was assigned to the Eighth Air Force's 467th Bomb Group and made his first bombing run as turret gunner in a B-24 bomber on Wednesday, February 24, 1945. Dendy kept a log book detailing that mission and the 21 others in which he participated before the war ended. His log book showed that his B-24 crew hit targets throughout Germany, Czechoslovakia and Austria, where he noted that they flew "over the heart of the Alps and got a good view of the beautiful, snow-covered tops."

Dendy's log book, which he still had in 2010, reported

only minor damage from German anti-aircraft fire, and his plane arrived back in England with an engine on fire only once.

He said he had little apprehension about his flights over enemy territory. "I was 19 years old, flying over Germany and having a big time; I didn't know what fear was," Dendy said. "Our bombers had cut off their fuel supplies, so they couldn't get their planes off the ground late in the war. Flak was all we had to worry about, and we were hit only a few times and only had one man in our crew injured," he added.

Many other airmen were not so lucky, however. The Eighth Air Force had 26,000 men killed in action and another 28,000 shot down and taken prisoner from 1942-1945.

After Germany surrendered on May 8, 1945, Dendy's crew returned to Nebraska for training in B-29 bombers, preparing for an anticipated invasion of Japan. Japan surrendered in August, however, after U. S. atomic bombs destroyed the cities of Hiroshima and Nagasaki, and Dendy was discharged later that year in time to enroll at the University of Alabama under the GI Bill in January 1946.

"I had played three years of high school football at High-

Dendy (second from left, kneeling) with B-24 Bomber crew.

Dendy did play in the March 1946 A-Day game in Legion Field, and that remains a special memory for him. "It was Charley Boswell Day and the stadium was full," Dendy said. "I was about a third-string right halfback on the team with Vaughn Mancha as our captain and I got to play in two quarters."

Dendy earned his degree in 1949, married Joy Pearson and joined her father at Pearson Lumber Company in Tuscaloosa in 1950. At age 84, Dendy was still a working partner in the business with his son Walt in January 2010. Dendy has been an active business and civic leader in the area throughout his business career. He has been honored as Chamber of Commerce Member of the Year, served on the Tuscaloosa County Park and Recreation Board and been honored by that organization, and been named "Mr. Pi Kappa Phi" as the national member of the year (1979).

land Home and Luverne, so I went out for football at Alabama in the spring," Dendy said. "There must have been 150 scholarship players out there with all of that 1945 Rose Bowl team, all the freshmen and all the players returning from the service."

Dendy stuck with the team through spring and summer and into fall practice before being offered a job in the intramural department that included living quarters in Foster Auditorium, an offer he simply couldn't refuse. "I weighed about 155 pounds and was not much more than a tackling dummy," Dendy said of his football days. "Coach Thomas kept telling me to stick with it and I could play in about three years, but I didn't want to be a tackling dummy for three years."

"I've had a wonderful life since coming home from the war," Dendy said. "But I wouldn't take anything for the experience of fighting for our country and helping stop Hitler."

George **GAMMON**

'He named his plane Alabama Gal for me'

George Gammon flew a B-17 bomber he called the "Alabama Gal" in bombing raids over Germany during World War II. The "Alabama Gal" didn't survive the war, but Gammon did, even after 33 missions over flak-filled enemy skies.

"He named his plane for me," said Mrs. Frances Gammon in October 2009. Mrs. Gammon is the former Frances Conway of Fort Deposit, Alabama, and she and George were married during Thanksgiving weekend 1942 while seniors at the University.

Gammon was a handsome, All-America-type big man on campus at the time. He was a senior half-back on the Alabama football team; member of the track team; president of the A Club; member of Omicron Delta Kappa, Officer's Club and Pi Kappa Phi, and listed in Who's Who in American Colleges and Universities. Frances was a catch as well. She was a member of Mortar Board, Triangle, Kappa Delta Pi, Chi Delta Phi, vice president of WSGA and also listed in Who's Who.

Gammon earned letters in 1941 and 1942 at halfback for the Crimson Tide, helping the team to a 9-2 record and a Cotton Bowl win over Texas A&M in 1941 and an 8-3 record and an Orange Bowl win over Boston College in 1942. He was also a captain in the advanced ROTC program, which meant he went directly into the Army after graduation in early

Gammon (front left) with flight crew in Italy.

March of 1943.

A Cullman native, Gammon transferred to the Army Air Forces and was trained to fly the new four-engine B-17 bomber before being assigned to the 483rd Bombardment Group with the 15th Air Force. The 483rd left Hunter Field, Georgia, in March 1944 on a 49-hour, six-stop flight to Foggia, Italy. Lieutenant Gammon painted "Alabama Gal" on the nose of his plane before leaving Georgia and called it his, although crews flew whatever planes were serviceable during their bombing runs.

From their base in Italy, pilots of the 483rd flew a total of 215 missions in 14 months of combat duty before Germany surrendered in May 1945. Their targets included the heavily defended areas of Ploesti, Berlin, Munich, Vienna, Budapest and Bucharest, where they attacked refineries, factories, railway systems and supply dumps.

Of the original 646 pilots and crewmembers sent to Italy in 1944, 39 percent were either killed or missing in action.

From their base in Italy, pilots of the 483rd flew a total of 215 missions in 14 months of combat duty before Germany surrendered in May 1945.

Including replacements over the 14 months, a total of 214 men were killed, 315 became prisoners of war and 231 others evaded capture and returned to duty. The 483rd lost 81 planes during its bombing runs, including Gammon's "Alabama Gal."

Gammon returned home uninjured after the war and flew with the "Home Bound Air Lines" ferrying troops around the country until discharged at Wright Field in Dayton, Ohio, on January 22, 1947. He received the European Theater Ribbon with five battle stars, the Air Medal with two oak leaf clusters and the American Theater Medal.

Gammon and his wife moved to Vicksburg, Mississippi, in 1955, where he operated a Western Auto store for 28 years before going into real estate. He died in 1999.

Bomber crew checks gear before long and dangerous raid

Roy *JOHNSON*

'Mighty Mite' did his share on the field and in the war

At first glance, most people wrote Roy Johnson off as being too small for college football at only 5-2, 137 pounds, but he proved them wrong as a triple-threat halfback for the University of Alabama.

Johnson was considered too small for military duty in World War II at first glance, too, but he also proved those judges wrong by eventually flying 35 missions over Southeast Asia as a bombardier in the Army Air Forces.

Johnson, labeled the "Mighty Mite" by the media, is likely the smallest man ever to play football for the University of Alabama, and he became a crowd favorite during the 1941-42 seasons because of his size, speed and determination. Fans chanted "We want Roy! We want Roy!" at very game, according to media reports, and head coach Frank Thomas responded by sending Johnson onto the field for at least one series in many games.

Thomas called Johnson "pound for pound the best player on the field," and Johnson proved Thomas' point regularly with exciting runs, punt returns and even pass completions despite his size. The former Phillips High School star from Birmingham returned a punt 18 yards and completed passes for 19 and 20 yards against Howard College in 1941, drawing roars from the crowd. He completed 13 of 21 passes for 170 yards in a "B-team" game against Mississippi State in 1942 in his best overall performance. He also played second base on the 1942 Crimson Tide Southeastern Conference championship baseball team.

Although rejected by ROTC and turned down for pilot training soon after the start of World War II because of his size, Johnson persisted in his attempts to join the fight and was finally accepted by the Army Air Forces in February 1943. He reported to Miami Beach, FL, for training and became a B-24 bombardier with the 5th Air Force.

Stationed in India, Johnson eventually flew 35 missions over Burma and Thailand with the 9th Bomb Squadron, 7th Bomb Group, helping defeat Japanese forces in the area.

"We flew 16-hour missions into Burma, going after Japanese troops and the bridges over the rivers," said Henry Nixon, a pilot in Johnson's squadron and Birmingham native who also attended Alabama before the war. "The Japanese were using British prisoners of war as slave labor to build railroads and bridges and we were trying to destroy them," Nixon said.

"Roy was the only decent bombardier in the squadron," Nixon added. "He was going to hit that target if it killed us. He'd insist on another run if we missed on the first one, and there was a lot of flak. There must have been 20 antiaircraft guns protecting each target. Roy was always the lead bombardier and the only one I ever trusted."

Nixon recalled one particular bombing run for which Johnson was selected as somewhat historic. "We sent a single plane armed with a 1,000-pound bomb to attack a railroad bridge over a river but the British had already destroyed it," Nixon said, noting that it was the same bridge depicted in the fictionalized movie "Bridge on the River Kwai." The bridge was one of several railway bridges built over the Mae Klong River in Thailand in 1943 by British prisoners of war used as slave laborers. The river was renamed the Khwae Yai River in the 1960s.

Nixon also recalled seeing Johnson play football for the Crimson Tide while a student at the University before the war. "The crowd would chant 'We want Roy! We want Roy!' and Coach Thomas would send him in for a few plays. He (Johnson) was an exciting player and a great athlete," Nixon said.

"Dad had great hand-eye coordination," said Johnson's son Roy III. "He was always proud of that. And he was good at math, too. He said he missed his targets on his first few bombing missions, but once he started hitting them he never

missed again. For years he kept pictures of the targets they had bombed." A first lieutenant, Johnson earned the Distinguished Flying Cross and the Air Medal while in service.

Johnson remained determined to become a pilot, according to Nixon, even after completing his 35 combat missions. "Some pretty famous general in India pulled some strings to get him into flight school and he was on his way there when the war ended," Nixon said.

Johnson was actually home on leave with his wife Margaret prior to going to flight training when he heard the news of the war's end, according to Roy III. "He and my mother were fishing on the Coosa River when they heard horns blowing and people cheering and found out that the war was over," said Roy III. "He was discharged soon after that and returned to the University to finish his degree and attend law school."

Johnson also returned to the baseball diamond at Alabama and played on the 1946-47 teams, helping the Crimson Tide to another SEC title and its first NCAA tournament appearance in 1947. He led the team in runs scored in 1946 with 30.

Roy III said his father rarely went to movies but did go to see "Patton" and "The Bridge on the River Kwai."

Johnson was named a first-team halfback on the 50-year All-City team in Birmingham in 1974. He practiced law in Birmingham for 58 years and one of his hobbies was researching and speaking on the trial of Jesus Christ.

Johnson died in 2006 of lung cancer, an illness he blamed on a smoking habit picked up from the free cigarettes given to GIs during World War II, according to Roy III. "He never smoked before he went into the service, but he later smoked three packs a day. He cursed them (the cigarettes) but he never was able to quit them," Roy III said.

Johnson's brother Robert also attended the University and served as a ball turret gunner aboard a B-24 bomber in World War II.

Above and left: American planes in action during World War II

The P-51 fighter plane (above left) was one of America's primary air weapons during the war. A B-29 bomber (above right) is shown in flight during World War II. Colonel Paul Tibbetts (left) waves from the cockpit of the B-29 bomber "Enola Gay" after returning from a flight to drop the world's first atomic bomb on Hiroshima, Japan, on August 6, 1945. Crew members from the B-17 bomber Memphis Belle (below) celebrate after their final mission during World War II.

America's air weapons during World War II included the B-17 bomber (top right) and the P-38 (left) and P-47 (below) fighter planes.

BROTHERS *at war*

"We applied for flight training. We went to Maxwell Field in Montgomery for our first training then we were separated."

— *Ray Hutson*

Opposite: Triumphant U.S. troops display a German flag captured in battle in Europe during World War II. (National Archives photograph)

Ray and Robert HUTSON

'One day a soldier came to our house...'

Twin brothers Ray and Robert Hutson were leading storybook lives as athletes at the University of Alabama on the eve of World War II in 1940.

They were stars on the freshman football and basketball teams and limitless athletic success surely lay ahead for the younger brothers of Don Hutson, a former Alabama All-America end and Rose Bowl star in 1934.

The handsome identical twins arrived at the University of Alabama in the fall of 1940 with even greater credentials than their older brother, who was setting receiving records in professional football with the Green Bay Packers as his brothers began their careers with the Crimson Tide.

Ray had earned All-State and All-Southern honors at right halfback for two years at Pine Bluff High School in Arkansas and Robert had been All-State and All-Southern at left halfback as a senior. They had led Pine Bluff to the state championship as seniors and scored 24 of their team's 25 points against Baton Rouge, Louisiana, in what was billed as

Robert (left) and Ray Hutson as Tide freshmen in 1940.

the 1939 national high school championship game. Robert had also scored both touchdowns in a 12-0 win over Blytheville High for the state championship. They also played basketball and baseball, with Ray serving as team captain in basketball.

The twins were 5-9 and about 160 pounds, and between them could do it all. Ray was acclaimed as an outstanding runner, receiver, punter and kicker while Robert was an outstanding passer and runner.

As freshmen at Alabama, the Hutson twins accounted for 19 points in their first game, a 25-6 win over Howard College, and they drew frequent media attention throughout the fall and in the spring of 1941 with their passing, catching, running and kicking. "They gave a good account of themselves," Alabama head coach Frank Thomas said of the twins after the spring A-Day game. "They are both able runners and punt and pass well."

The twins were said to have much of Don's speed (He ran a 9.8 100-yard dash on the UA track team.) and elusiveness, and their ambition was to play in a Rose Bowl game as Don

Hutson brothers trained as pilots.

drafted that fall, so they joined the Army Air Forces instead of reporting back to Alabama for fall practice. No one could imagine at the time that their athletic careers were over.

"We applied for flight training," Ray said. "We went to Maxwell Field in Montgomery for our first training then we were separated." It was the first time in their lives that the twins had been apart. They were together once more while training at Augusta, Georgia, in mid-1942.

After training in various locations, Robert was shipped to the South Pacific, where he was assigned to the Fifth Air Force's 317th Troop Carrier Group. He was flight officer on a C-47 transport with the 46th Troop Carrier Squadron, moving men and supplies to the front lines in New Guinea and returning casualties to the rear near Australia.

"While I was stationed in Wilmington, Delaware, my mother called to tell me that Robert had been reported missing in action," Ray said. "She didn't have any other information on how or where it happened. Several months later a soldier came to our house to confirm that he had been killed," he added. One report said Robert was among 26 servicemen who died when their plane was either shot down or crashed on takeoff from a battle zone. Ray spent time at home with his family following the news of Robert's death then returned to Delaware, where he was ferrying planes all over the world.

had done, although they had only seen him play one game while he was earning All-America honors at Alabama.

"We had heard nothing but Alabama football since we were kids, so there was no question where we would go. Bear Bryant came to Pine Bluff and signed both of us," Ray Hutson said in 2009. A photograph of the twins in their Alabama football uniforms in 1940 showed them with happy smiles as they seemed destined to follow in Don's footsteps to athletic stardom.

War raged in Europe, Southeast Asia and across the Pacific at the time, however, as Germany and Japan expanded their empires by conquering country after country. Congress passed the Selective Training and Service Act on September 16, 1940, requiring all men ages 21-35 to register for the draft, and the Hutson twins turned 21 that year. They learned during the summer of 1941 that they would likely be

Robert was reported missing on August 27, 1943. His parents wrote to his commanding officer seeking details of his loss and received a response from Major James J. Evans Jr. dated October 13, 1943, saying that he had witnessed the

Robert was reported missing on August 27, 1943. His parents wrote to his commanding officer seeking details of his loss and received a response from Major James J. Evans Jr. dated October 13, 1943, saying that he had witnessed the crash in which Robert was killed.

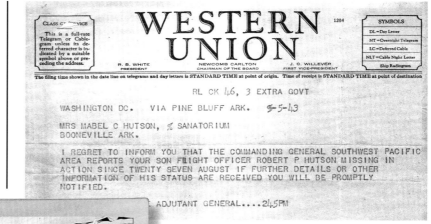

crash in which Robert was killed.

"I was flying directly behind Robert and saw his plane go down," Evans wrote. "A search party was sent out immediately, but upon reaching the wreckage found all the occupants had been instantly killed. The bodies were given a Christian burial by the chaplain in the party. Only your loss of Robert as a son can be greater than our loss of him as a splendid officer and a good friend," Evans added.

Ray was first trained to fly B-24 bombers then was assigned to the 22nd Ferrying Group as a copilot flying the new C-46 Commando transport planes from the U.S. to India before soon being ordered to India to fly over the "Hump" himself.

"I had to tell my mother about this and it was very hard," Ray said of the assignment, which was one of the most dangerous of the war. The mission was to fly transports heavily loaded with fuel, ammunition and supplies over the treacherous Himalayan Mountains from airfields in India to Kunming, China, to support China in its war with Japan. The Japanese had cut off China's supply lines by sea and land.

American transport planes took off from airfields in India's eastern jungles and flew 525 miles one way at 16,000-20,000 feet over the jagged mountains in the face of violent blizzards, 125-mile per-hour crosswinds, dense fog

Robert Hutson

and bitter cold, making each flight a challenge. Add to that the threat of possibly having to ditch in the jungles of Japanese-held Burma, where tribes of headhunters still roamed, and one easily recognizes the dangers of flying over the "Hump."

In addition to offloading the drums of fuel from the transports, any excess fuel from the transport planes was drained in China, leaving the pilots with just enough fuel to return to the bases in India, and many didn't make it back due to stiff headwinds. Official military losses from April 1942-November 1945 show that 590 aircraft were lost and 1,314 crewmembers killed while flying over the Himalayans. In addition, 1,171 crewmen bailed out and survived and 345 more were missing in action as flyers averaged only 30 missions without trouble.

Ray Hutson beat the odds, however. He flew a grueling 77 missions over the "Hump," averaging close to 10 hours per round trip in the air. All the flying was done at night to avoid enemy planes. During his last few months overseas, Hutson served as operations officer and check pilot for new pilots

Ray Hutson

before they were allowed to fly over the hump alone. He later ferried troops in the U.S. from the end of the war until being discharged in January 1946.

"I was lucky," Hutson said modestly of his return from his dangerous war-time service unharmed. For his heroic service, Hutson received the Distinguished Flying Cross with two oak leaf clusters and the Air Medal with two oak leaf clusters. Ray's 22nd Ferrying Group also received a Presidential Unit Citation. Robert received the Purple Heart.

Hutson chose not to return to Alabama to continue his athletic career after the war. "I enjoyed both football and basketball at Alabama, but it just seemed too much to go back after nearly five years," Ray said. Instead, Hutson went to Wisconsin to work with his brother Don in the automobile business for a few years before opening his own Chevrolet dealership in La Crosse in 1953. He, and later his son Mike, operated the business for more than 50 years until his retirement. Hutson, 89, was living in Naples, Florida, in 2010.

Hal and Harwell **JONES**

'Just no wonder people go crazy'

Hal Jones wrote to his mother often during World War II, knowing that she worried for his safety as he fought with General George S. Patton's Third Army in Germany.

Jones wrote to his mother on April 9, 1945, just a month before the war in Europe ended, saying , "Mama, I thought a lot about you last night and this morning…I wanted to write today to let you know I'm still safe and sound. Things are still looking up and we are all praying for a speedy victory…Take care of the one I love and regards to all. Hal."

The young lieutenant from Tuscaloosa sent a short note on April 16, assuring his mother again that he was well. "Hello, Mom, just this note to let ya know I'm fine," he began. "Have been seeing a good bit of territory lately. Almost like being on a sight-seeing tour…Just wanted to let ya know I'm O.K. Love to all. Hal."

Jones, a heavy weapons platoon leader in the 41st Infantry Regiment, was killed by a German sniper three days later, just 19 days before Germany surrendered on May 8, 1945.

Ed Swain, a member of his platoon, wrote of Jones' death

in a letter home on April 23, saying "Since we left Bayreuth several days ago we have had it more rugged that I ever thought human beings could stand. Each day we would say 'How much longer can we stand this?' The worst of all was the sudden death of our platoon leader. It was almost impossible to believe even after seeing," Swain wrote. "He was really one swell guy (was killed by a sniper). He was a prince, that guy. The weapons platoon I'm sure will never forget him nor forgive the — — Germans."

Jones had just turned 22 years old. His regiment arrived in France in February, 1945, as part of the 71st Infantry Division and had taken the towns of Coburg and Bayreuth in the week prior to his death as U.S. forces pushed toward Berlin.

"On the day he was killed, we were coming over a rise and in front of us was some firing from the Germans," wrote Ken Hermann in a letter to Jones' family in 1998. Hermann was a member of the same company (G) as Jones, and was responding to inquiries about his death. "We were held up

Above: Hal Jones

for some time for the company CO and the platoon leaders to plan our next move. I remember it was a bright, sunny day. I could see the officers in this huddle and all of a sudden shots rang out and I saw somebody fall. He was shot by a sniper. At the same time all hell broke loose. We got whoever was responsible for his death. After 53 years, that day will stay with me."

Another member of G Company, Sam Vutetakis, wrote of the incident in a letter home also, recalling that Jones was a "quiet and good-natured young man, well liked and respected…and I found it ironic that such a gentle human being was in charge of the murderous machine guns, mortars,

etc., of the company.

"I vividly remember the position of his body. It was as though he was taking a break, sitting on the ground, leaning back on his knapsack. Gently, I took his carbine rifle. It was one of the saddest events of my life," wrote Vutetakis of the incident.

Jones is buried in the Lorraine American National Cemetery in St. Avold, France, the final resting place for 10,489 of the Americans who lost their lives in Europe. He was awarded the Purple Heart. A book on the history of G

Below:: Hal Jones, number 59, with his 1941 Alabama teammates.

A GI writes home from the warfront.

"Mama, believe me as soon as I can I'm getting out of this army and am going to hurry back to Tuscaloosa to spend the rest of my days pestering you. Promise you won't worry. I'm fine and having a big time."

February 11, 1945, Jones said "Mama, believe me as soon as I can I'm getting out of this army and am going to hurry back to Tuscaloosa to spend the rest of my days pestering you. Promise you won't worry. I'm fine and having a big time." A week later he sent another letter ending it with "Mama, be sweet and take care of yourself and don't worry about me. I'm living the life of Riley. The officers really have a gravy train."

On March 25, in a long letter Jones wrote "Mama, don't worry for there is nothing to this stuff. I'm really living the life of a king now…I predict this war will be over by the last of May…I can see the end of anybody getting hurt that stays on the ball, which I am."

His next letter said "I'm along the front now and although there is quite a bit of fighting going on I am in a quiet and safe place. I am out in the woods and mountains and have a foxhole in the side of a hill for home. It is nice here except for the planes and artillery."

On April 7, just 12 days before he was killed, Jones wrote: "Mama, now you take care of yourself and quit that foolish worrying. No need of worrying for nothing. If anybody should worry it should be me and I'm perfectly content."

Jones, whose full name was Crawford Haralson Jones, spent three years at the University of Alabama prior to joining the Army. He was a member of the football team and was listed as a reserve quarterback on the 1942 roster. He entered the Army in June 1943 and earned his commission through Officers Training School at Fort Benning, Georgia.

He had been an outstanding athlete at Tuscaloosa High School, where he played football, basketball and tennis. He was the seventh of eight children by Henry Heard Jones and Alline Cleveland Jones. Henry Heard Jones was a letterman on the 1901 Alabama football team and also played baseball

Company from its formation at Fort Benning through the end of the war was dedicated to Jones.

Hal's mother, who had discouraged his impulse to join the Army at the onset of the war, expressed her continuing anguish over his death in a letter to her children 14 years later, writing, "…Just no wonder people go crazy."

Jones apparently wrote to his mother each week throughout his time in the Army and even remembered to send Valentine and Easter cards. One letter, written while he was aboard a ship headed for France, said "Well, Mama, I hope you will take this in fine spirit for it will help me lots by knowing you are O.K. and are not worrying yourself sick. I didn't want to give you this news till the last minute for I saw no need of it. When you get this I'll be on the other side of the big pond from you and safe and sound."

In another letter, written from a small French village on

at Alabama. He earned his degree in 1905 and was a long-time area educator.

Harwell Jones, an older brother of Hal Jones, was on the Alabama football and track teams in the late 1920s. He earned a letter in track in 1928 and was a member of the A Club. He served in the Army Air Forces in the states and later in occupied Japan during World War II. Harwell Jones remained in the service for 34 years, reaching the rank of lieutenant colonel while serving in the U.S., Japan and Korea with the Strategic Air Command. Harwell Jones received the American Campaign Medal, the Army of Occupation Medal, the Asiatic-Pacific Campaign Medal, the World War II Victory Medal, the National Defense Service Medal and the Armed Forces Reserve Medal.

The Jones family has a long history with the University of Alabama. All eight of the Jones children attended the University, as did the five siblings of Henry Heard Jones. In

Harwell Jones

The Jones family has a long history with the University of Alabama. All eight of the Jones children attended the University, as did the five siblings of Henry Heard Jones.

addition, seven grandchildren and five great-grandchildren of Henry Heard Jones attended Alabama.

Halcyann Badham, a daughter of Harwell Jones, served as UA band sponsor in 1966. Robert Jackson Eubank, a grandson of Harwell Jones, was a walk-on member of the Alabama football team in 1996 and later served as a staff sergeant with the Army in Iraq and Afghanistan.

Hal Jones' siblings included brothers Harwell and Fritz Robert Jones and sisters Mary Helen Jones Hughes, Mildred Zoe Jones Siler, Marjorie Alline Jones Hinton, Eleanor Nell Jones and Jesse Jean Jones McBrayer.

Joe and Benny KILGROW

'It's the day I've been waiting for so long'

Joe Kilgrow was known as much for his modesty as he was for being an All-America halfback on a University of Alabama Rose Bowl football team.

More than anything, however, Kilgrow was known as a quiet leader who gave his all in every endeavor, including athletics, overseas action with the Army in World War II and in everyday life.

Kilgrow earned All-State and All-Southern honors three years (1931-1933) at halfback for Sidney Lanier High School in Montgomery and joined the Alabama football squad as a freshman in the fall of 1934. Because of his versatility, Kilgrow earned a starting spot as a sophomore in 1935 and played in every game from that time on.

Kilgrow punted, passed, kicked extra points, played safety on defense and was known as a speedy and elusive runner. He threw his first touchdown pass as a sophomore, connecting with team captain Jimmy Walker on a 33-yard toss. Kilgrow ran for three touchdowns and passed for two as a sophomore.

As a junior in 1936, Kilgrow became a 60-minute player as he rushed for five touchdowns and passed for four more. One of his touchdowns came when he faked a punt and ran 83 yards to score in a 7-0 win over Mississippi State. Alabama was 8-0-1 in 1936 as Kilgrow earned second-team All-Southeastern Conference honors.

Kilgrow accounted for ten touchdowns while leading

Joe (left) and Benny Kilgrow at UA football practice.

Alabama to a 9-0 record and the SEC championship during the regular season as a senior in 1937. He threw touchdown passes to give Alabama the winning points in its last two games. Although Alabama fell to California 13-0 in the Rose Bowl for its only loss of the 1937 season, Kilgrow drew media praise for his typical outstanding play during another 60-minute performance.

Kilgrow led the Tide to a 17-1-1 record his last two seasons and a 23-3-2 mark during his varsity career. As a senior he rushed for more than 400 yards and five touchdowns and completed 20 of 57 passes for 302 yards and five touchdowns. He also kicked 12 extra points to lead the team in scoring with 42 points.

He earned All-SEC and All-America honors and finished fifth in the Heisman Trophy balloting to cap his outstanding career for the Crimson Tide. He was also selected third overall in the 1938 NFL draft.

Even then, Kilgrow wasn't finished at Alabama. He returned in 1938 and 1939 to play baseball while serving as an assistant coach with the football team. He earned All-SEC honors at third base in 1939.

Kilgrow joined Mercer College in 1940 as backfield coach and played professional baseball during the summer with the Troy Trojans of the Alabama State League, hitting .295 and fielding .978 in 35 games as he pursued his dream of playing major league baseball.

World War II stepped in to spoil his plans, however, as Kilgrow's Alabama National Guard unit (104th Antiaircraft Battalion) was called to active duty in February 1941. Kilgrow was a platoon sergeant serving in New Guinea by early 1942 as U.S. forces began the battle to turn back advancing Japanese forces.

Kilgrow received a battlefield commission for "outstanding leadership displayed under fire" after his platoon shot down four Japanese planes during an attack in August 1942, and he advanced to the rank of captain before returning home

Joe Kilgrow in New Guinea and as a Crimson Tide halfback.

after 38 months of fighting in the Pacific theater. His unit earned three battle stars and a presidential unit citation.

In a post-war interview, Kilgrow called New Guinea a wild country when his unit arrived, and he brought home photographs of natives in grass skirts living in primitive

Joe Kilgrow as UA coach.

conditions to prove it.

"The country was wild, but that was nothing to compare with the Japanese when we first got there," Kilgrow said. "It was two months after Pearl Harbor and the Japanese were in full command; we were at their mercy," he added, noting that the Japanese regularly shelled American troops from their ships.

In a letter home, Kilgrow once described the Pacific battles as "damn rough and the jungles thick and dangerous," but added that American ships, planes and infantry were taking a toll on the Japanese. "I have seen plenty of dead ones," he wrote.

Kilgrow also spoke of seeing Bob Hope and Bing Crosby at USO shows and listening to football games and Jack Benny on the radio even in the remote Pacific islands.

Kilgrow was discharged after Japan surrendered in August 1945, and his first act was to write his wife-to-be, Susan Miller of Greensboro, Alabama, to let her know that he was on his way home. "Will be well on the way home by the time you receive this letter. I expect to leave within the next few days," he wrote. "Well, honey, it's the day I've been waiting for so long. It won't be long now. Will wire you when I reach the states. All my love, Joe."

He returned to the University of Alabama following military duty and served as an assistant coach for the football and baseball teams 1945-57. He was superintendent of the University of Alabama golf course when he died on July 21, 1967, at age 52.

While Joe Kilgrow was fighting in the Pacific theater, his younger brother Benny, also a former Alabama football player (1938-40), was serving in Europe as a bombardier on a B-17 Flying Fortress with the 8th Air Force.

Benny's plane was shot down near the coast of France

Joe Kilgrow (left) with Johnny Roberts, circa 1938.

"I regret to inform you that your son, Second Lieutenant Benedict A. Kilgrow Jr., is missing in action…" the telegram began in words that became all too familiar during the war years.

on July 4, 1943, following a bombing raid on German installations near LeMans, France. Kilgrow's family received a telegram from the War Department in mid-July informing them that he was missing in action after eight bombers were shot down by German fighters during the bombing raid.

"I regret to inform you that your son, Second Lieutenant Benedict A. Kilgrow Jr., is missing in action…" the telegram began in words that became all too familiar during the war years. A later letter from Colonel Eddie Tracy of the 8th Air Force offered sympathy and hope as he said there was a "50-50 chance" that Kilgrow was safe somewhere as a prisoner of war.

Because parachutes had been seen drifting toward the coastal waters of France as Benny's plane went down, the Kilgrow family held out hope that he was among the survivors of the crash. Good news finally came on September 2 when Kilgrow's family received a second telegram saying

U.S. troops man an artillery post in the Pacific Theater.

Allied POWs in Germany surround a U.S. jeep as they are liberated.

that the International Red Cross had confirmed that Benny was in fact a prisoner of war.

Even better news soon followed when a letter from Kilgrow himself dated July 28, 1943, arrived in Montgomery two months after the crash. The letter said:

"Dear Daddy,

"I am here now almost a month. Guess by now you have heard I went down on the 4th of July. Landed in water off the south coast of France. Entire crew all right, thank God! We are in a pretty good camp, getting plenty to eat. The Red Cross sends us a lot of canned food and the Germans give us a few vegetables. We have a small garden just outside of barracks and from that we get a few fresh vegetables, but all in all, we are eating pretty good.

"We play softball, volleyball and touch football occasionally. I met a bunch of my classmates here that I was surprised to see. We have started a school and go to classes every day except Sunday. Study math, chemistry, languages, physics, etc. It isn't too bad here and I'll be glad to get home again. Take care of yourself and let me hear from you. All my love. Benny."

Above: Joe Kilgrow as UA baseball star.

Right: Joe Kilgrow, Ronald Reagan, Jim Tipton (L-R) at 1938 Rose Bowl.

Kilgrow enlisted in the Army Air Forces on December 12, 1941, just five days after the Japanese bombed U.S. ships and installations at Pearl Harbor, Hawaii. He received training as a bombardier in Albuquerque, New Mexico, where he appeared in scenes from the motion picture "Bombardier," which was being filmed there at the time. He was serving with the 381st Bombardment Group out of England when his plane was shot down.

Kilgrow was liberated when Germany surrendered in early May 1945. He returned to Montgomery and died at an early age.

A former All-State and All-Southern fullback at Sidney Lanier High School in Montgomery, Benny had followed in Joe's footsteps by winning the Paramount Trophy as the school's outstanding athlete in 1936 and 1937. Like his older brother, Benny was known as an outstanding runner, passer, punter and defensive player.

Kilgrow came to the University of Alabama on a football scholarship in 1938 and was a redshirt back in 1939. He was listed as a 178-pound sophomore fullback on the 1940 roster.

The **MOSLEY** Brothers

'The Good Lord was looking after us'

Sylvester "Pop" Mosley sent four sons away from home in Blytheville, Arkansas, to play football for the University of Alabama, and three of them went on to fight in World War II.

Herschel, Russell, Norman and Tommy Mosley were all outstanding athletes in high school, earning All-State and All-Southern honors as triple-threat left halfbacks in the then-popular Notre Dame Box formation, and all four earned scholarships to Alabama.

Herschel, best known as Herky and the oldest of the Mosley boys, lettered for the Crimson Tide 1937-38-39 and was the team's leading rusher in 1938 with 465 yards on only 78 carries, an average of six yards per carry. Herky also led the Tide in passing in 1938 with 334 yards and three touchdowns on 28 completions and in 1939 with 174 yards and three touchdowns on 15 completions.

Alabama was 21-5-2 during Herky's playing days and won the Southeastern Conference championship in 1937 with a 9-0 regular-season record before losing to California 13-0 in the Rose Bowl.

"When you speak of left half you speak of Herky Mosley, the Blast from Blytheville," a 1938 newspaper article boasted. "Everyone says that he's a better passer than Dixie Howell. He kicks superbly and in the open he's as shifty as a gambler's eyes."

Left: Norman "Monk" Mosley
Above: Russell Mosley

And the Mosley boys were all cast in the same mold.

Russell lettered for the Tide 1941-42, and Norman, known as "Monk" to his teammates, lettered 1942, 1946 and 1947. Russ led Alabama in passing in 1942 by completing 24 of 48 passes for 352 yards and two touchdowns. All three players were skilled at running, passing and punting, and all three saw starting time for Coach Frank Thomas' talented Alabama teams of the day. All three also played halfback on defense in the era of one-platoon football.

Russell helped lead Alabama to a 9-2 record in

1941, including a 29-21 win over Texas A&M in the Cotton Bowl. The Tide went 8-3 in 1942 with Russ, Monk and Johnny August sharing left halfback duties, and capped the season with a 37-21 win over Boston College in the Orange Bowl. Monk helped the Tide to an 8-3 mark in 1947, including a 27-7 loss to Texas in the Sugar Bowl, as the Mosley boys together played in the four major bowls of their day.

Monk's playing career was interrupted by service during the war and he had the misfortune of returning to an Alabama team in 1946 that featured returning All-America left halfback Harry Gilmer, who had led the Crimson Tide to a 10-0 record and a 34-14 Rose Bowl win over Southern Cal in 1945.

Monk played enough to letter his last two seasons and was perhaps the Tide's best punter, but his playing time was greatly limited by the presence of Gilmer. The same was true

Below: Herschel "Herky" Mosley (50) carries the ball for the Tide.

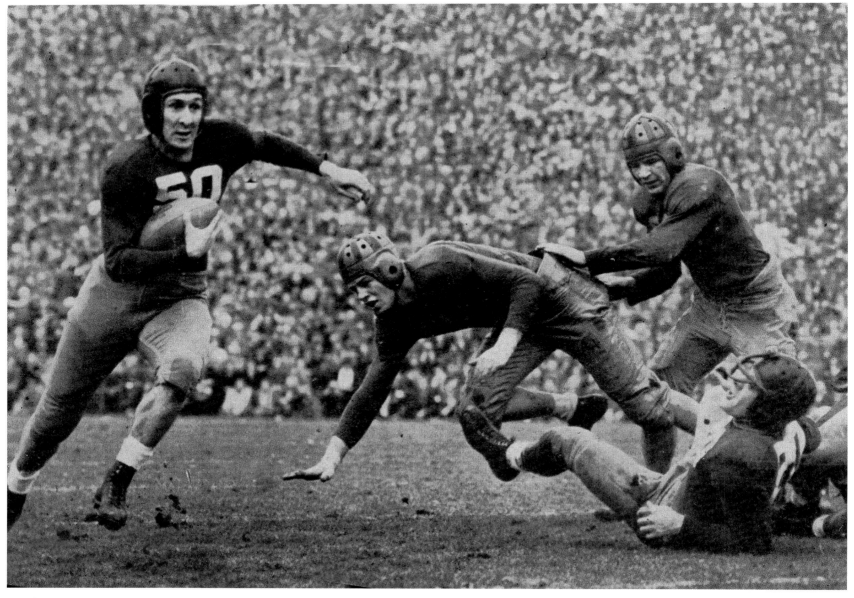

Herkey Mosley and his crew prepare for a bombing run.

for returning war veterans at several positions at Alabama and at every other college in the U. S.

The three older Mosley brothers each took a turn at professional football after leaving Alabama. Herky played one season (1940) with the Long Island Indians before being sidelined by a knee injury. Russ played two seasons for Green Bay (1945 and 1946) and Monk played one season (1948) with the Pittsburgh Steelers.

Monk's playing career was interrupted by service during the war and he had the misfortune of returning to an Alabama team in 1946 that featured returning All-America left halfback Harry Gilmer, who had led the Crimson Tide to a 10-0 record and a 34-14 Rose Bowl win over Southern Cal in 1945.

Tommy, the youngest brother by several years, played two seasons (1954-55) at Alabama under Coach J. B. Whitworth but did not letter. Whitworth was also a native of Blytheville and was a member of Alabama's 1930 national championship team.

The Mosley boys came by their football talent through their father, who had been a star athlete in high school in Missouri, and the coaching of head coach Joe Dildy and assistant Carney Laslie at Blytheville High School. Both coaches were former Alabama players. Laslie lettered at tackle 1930-32 and was later a long-time assistant coach under Paul "Bear" Bryant at Alabama while Dildy, a native of Nashville, Arkansas, lettered at center 1933-34.

Monk led Blytheville to the 1940 Arkansas state championship as team captain while earning All-State and

All-Southern honors, just as his older brothers had done.

Pop Mosley knew his football, too. He coached the Blytheville Junior High team to a state championship as interim coach during World War II while the regular coach was away in military service.

Herky and Russ joined the Army Air Forces in 1943 and became bomber pilots for the 8th Air Force in Europe. Both flew B-17 Flying Fortresses in raids on German targets and beat the odds by completing all their missions without being shot down by enemy fire.

"The first day Dad rotated off after about eight missions, his plane and crew

Right: Herky Mosley, wife Peggy and daughter Margaret

were shot down with another pilot aboard," Joe Mosley said in relating one of Herky's wartime experiences. "They spent the rest of the war in a prison camp. He (Herky) saw the bombardier in Boston 40 years later, and although my dad was a hard-nosed guy, he teared up."

Herky served in the 324th Squadron of the 91st Bomb Group, which included the famed "Memphis Belle" bomber. The 91st suffered the greatest number of losses of any heavy bomb group in World War II, with 37 percent of its crews killed, missing or taken prisoners of war during 340 missions from 1942-45. Of the 35 original flight crews in the 91st, 47 percent were lost in combat. The 91st earned two Distinguished Unit Citations for its deep bombing raids into heavily defended German territory.

Herky earned the Distinguished Flying Cross, Air Medal with three oak leaf clusters and the European-African-Middle East Theater ribbon with two bronze stars while flying his required overseas missions. He then served as a flight instructor on B-29 bombers in the states until the end of the war. He coached for a few years then was a salesman for Wilson Sporting Goods until his sudden death at age 89 while attending an NCAA Coaches Convention.

"That generation, whatever the challenge, just went and did it and went on. They didn't talk about it a lot," said Joe Mosley. "They came home and went about their lives."

Russ enlisted in the Army Air Forces in early 1943, soon after completing the 1942 football season at Alabama. He became a pilot with the 381st Bomb Group stationed at Ridgewell Airdrome in England. He flew 230 combat hours on 26 missions over enemy territory, many of them in a plane christened the "Stage Door Canteen" in honor of the opening

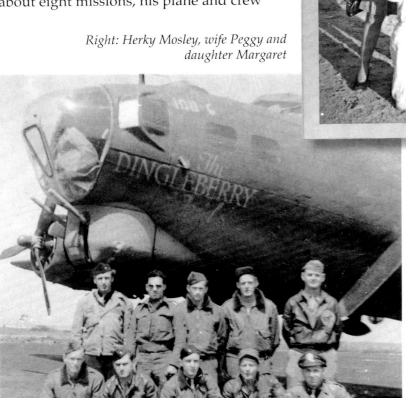

Russ Mosley (left rear) with crew.

Russ Mosley as pilot of the "Stage Door Canteen."

of the Stage Door Canteen in London. Stage Door Canteens, where film and Broadway stars hosted and entertained soldiers departing for the war, were already open in several U.S. cities, including Los Angeles, San Francisco, Boston and New York.

Among those present for the christening of the Stage Door Canteen plane at Ridgewell were British Prime Minister Winston Churchill's daughter Mary, actor Laurence Olivier and actress Vivien Leigh, who played Scarlett O'Hara in the movie "Gone With The Wind."

Russ earned the Air Medal with three oak leaf clusters and the European-African-Middle Eastern Theater Medal with three bronze stars for the Rhineland, Ardennes and Central Europe campaigns. His 26 bombing missions included raids on German factories and refineries in addition to air support for the Battle of the Bulge.

Russ flew back to the states after the war in a B-17 bomber called "Dingleberry Kid," bringing 15 former

Monk Mosley was involved in Pacific fighting.

"We hadn't been over there any time at all when five or six of us were standing around and a sniper shot one guy in our group in the jaw," Monk said. "It makes you wonder why the sniper shot him instead of me.

"The Japanese were good fighters," Monk added. "You had to kill them; they wouldn't give up. We didn't fight every day," Monk added of his wartime experience. "We had patrols and set up defenses for airfields. It wasn't so much the bullets. What bothered most of us were the mortars. They could drop that thing in your hip pocket," he said.

"We were training, getting ready to invade Japan, when the bomb ended it all, thank goodness," Monk added, referring to the atomic bombs dropped on Hiroshima and Nagasaki, Japan, in early August 1945, leading to Japan's surrender on August 14.

Monk spent 24 months overseas and reached the rank of master sergeant. "All three of us (brothers) returned home," Monk said proudly. "The Good Lord was looking after us."

Both Russ and Monk became high school coaches after earning their degrees from Alabama in the late 1940s. Russ coached at Huntsville, Alabama, in 1948 then returned to Blytheville as head coach for 11 years, winning state championships there in 1949 and 1954, before moving to

prisoners of war from Buchenwald as passengers.

Monk chose the Army in 1943 instead of following his brothers into the Army Air Forces. "I didn't want to fly," Monk said. "On the ground I could run; there's no place to go on a plane," he joked.

Monk went through basic training in California, where he said his football training and conditioning came in handy, then was shipped to the Pacific, where he joined the 182nd Infantry Regiment of the Americal Division. He saw his first action at Bougainville then fought in the Northern Solomon Islands, the Battle of Leyte and on Cebu. He served in occupied Japan from September 1945 until being discharged in 1946.

"We had patrols and set up defenses for airfields. It wasn't so much the bullets. What bothered most of us were the mortars. They could drop that thing in your hip pocket."

An American plane drops bombs over Europe.

nearby Gosnell High as head coach for 11 years. Tommy Mosley was a member of the 1954 Blytheville state championship team. Another former player for Russ Mosley was Fred Akers, who played college football at the University of Arkansas and later served as head coach at Wyoming, Texas and Purdue.

Monk spent five years as an assistant coach at Talladega High School under former Alabama player Ralph Gandy then served as head coach there for eight seasons. Several of Monk's Talladega players came to Alabama on football scholarships, including Buddy Wesley, Tommy Tolleson and All-America tackle Dan Kearley. Monk moved to Woodlawn as a teacher after 13 years at Talladega and retired after 32 years as an educator.

Monk was the only surviving Mosley brother in April 2010.

Wallace and Ray RICHESON

'We all thought we had been jinxed'

Wallace Richeson and his buddies were more than a little nervous on their final B-17 bombing mission over Germany during World War II, according to a surviving member of the crew.

"We had already flown our required missions, but because of a paperwork mix-up, we had to go again," said turret gunner Dale Files. "We all thought we'd been jinxed, so we were a little anxious on that extra mission. But we made it, and we were all able to come home," Files added.

Richeson was a navigator in the 493rd Bomb Group, known as "Helton's Hellcats," with the Eighth Air Force in Europe. He went into the service soon after graduation from the University of Alabama, where he played tackle for the Crimson Tide 1939-41.

His younger brother Ray also served in the Army Air Forces during World War II, seeing duty as a B-24 bomber pilot with the 15th Air Force in North Africa and Italy. Ray returned from the war to letter at guard three years for the Crimson Tide (1946-48) and serve as team captain as a senior.

Wallace flew his first mission on October 5, 1944, to strike an ordnance factory in Muenster, Germany, and followed with 35 more throughout the winter, hitting such targets as oil refineries, tank factories and rail yards in Hamburg,

Wallace, left, and Ray Richeson

Frankfort, Cologne and other German cities. "Rich (Wallace Richeson) was a tall, big man, and you had to be a small guy to get into the plane," Files said. "But he showed up every day ready to go and got right in.

"We were hit by a lot of flak (antiaircraft artillery shrapnel)," Files said of their bombing runs. "We had a lot of planes shot down." The 493rd flew 158 missions and lost 41 planes, according to military records. "We lost two engines once coming out of Germany and were making little

Clockwise from top: Wallace Richeson (right rear) with flight crew; Wallace Richeson; Ray Richeson

headway, so we had to crash-land in Belgium," Files said. "Our navigator (Richeson) and the pilots got us into U.S.-held territory, so we were able to get back to England and fly again.

"On another close call, we were limping home and just made it across the English Channel by 30-40 yards," Files said. "We landed with our wheels up in deep mud and had to climb out the top of the plane. We jumped off into mud up to our knees and had a time trying to get away from the plane in that mud. We thought it might catch fire and explode," Files added.

Wallace Richeson earned the Air Medal for his service and returned to his home town of Russellville after the war and worked for Reynolds Aluminum until retirement. He died in 1998.

Ray Richeson received his wings on April 15, 1944,

and was assigned to the 464th Bomb Group for most of his overseas duty. The 464th flew combat missions in Italy and Europe from the summer of 1944 until the end of the war, losing 138 planes in 210 sorties. Richeson played football for the Army Air Forces Personnel Distribution Center Comets at Louisville in 1945 before returning to play for the University of Alabama 1946-48.

Ray Richeson was drafted by the Philadelphia Eagles in 1949, but played guard for the Chicago Hornets for one season instead.

Following his playing days at Alabama, Ray Richeson served as head football coach at Meridian (MS) High School and at Livingston State College in the mid-1950s before becoming an insurance agent. He served as president of the A Club Alumni 1967-68. He died in 2003.

Above: Scenes from the battlefronts around the globe.

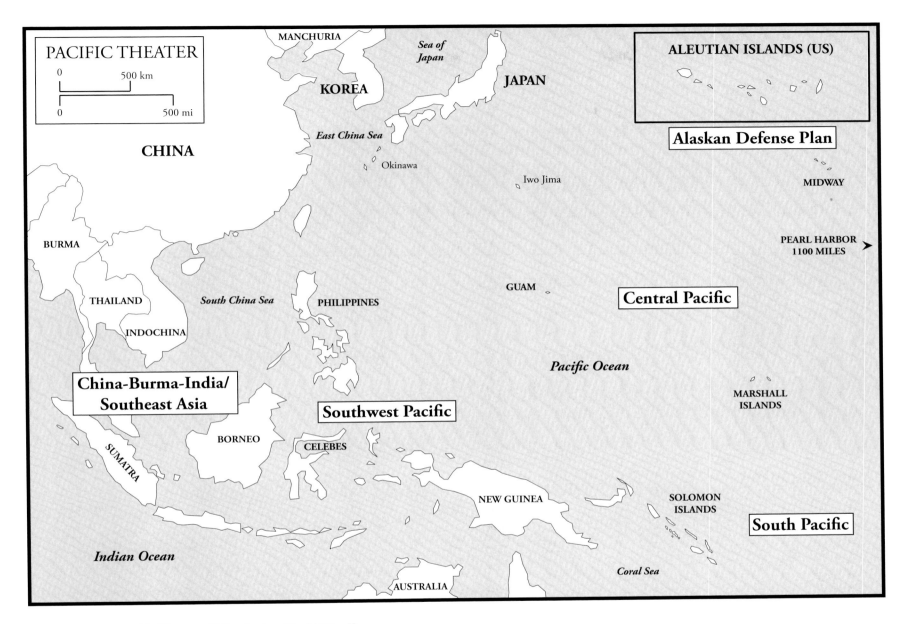

Map shows the Pacific Theater of War during World War II.

REFLECTING *the time*

"*I arrived in Tuscaloosa on Sunday afternoon, December 7, 1941. Everybody was fired up and wanting to join the service.*"

— *John "Studie" Staples*

Opposite: A football game program cover from 1944 depicted America's patriotism during World War II.

OFFICIAL 25c PROGRA

ALABAMA-TENNESSEE

GION FIELD   OCTOBER 20, 1945

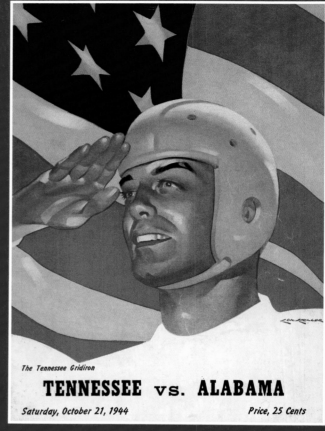

The Tennessee Gridiron

TENNESSEE vs. ALABAMA

Saturday, October 21, 1944   *Price, 25 Cents*

OFFICIAL PROGRAM

25c

ALABAMA
Pensacola Naval Air Station

DENNY STADIUM   NOVEMBER 24, 1945

War-time game programs often featured patriotic themes.

OFFICIAL 25c PROGRAM

ALABAMA-GEORGIA
LEGION FIELD   OCTOBER 27, 1945

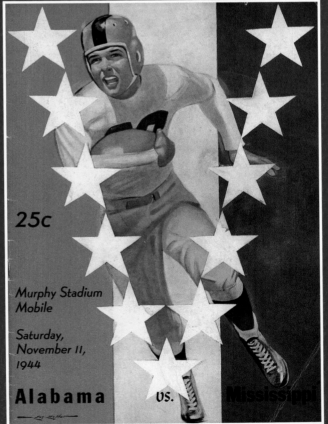

25c

Murphy Stadium
Mobile

Saturday,
November 11,
1944

Alabama   vs.   **Mississippi**

25c

ALABAMA
VS.
HOWARD

Legion Field
Saturday, Oct. 7, 1944

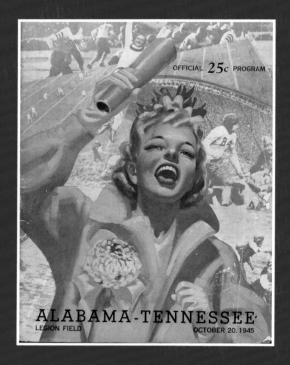

OFFICIAL 25c PROGRAM

ALABAMA-TENNESSEE

LEGION FIELD   OCTOBER 20, 1945

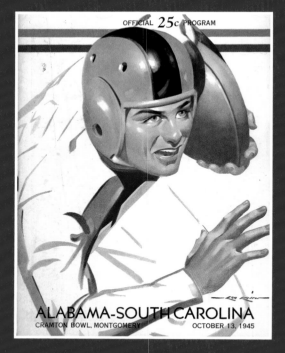

OFFICIAL 25c PROGRAM

ALABAMA-SOUTH CAROLINA

CRAMTON BOWL, MONTGOMERY   OCTOBER 13, 1945

ALABAMA vs. **SOUTH CAROLINA**

Saturday, Nov. 7, 1942

Denny Stadium

HOMECOMING

Price

25c

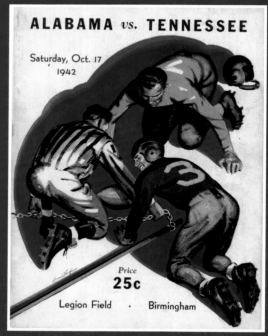

ALABAMA vs. **TENNESSEE**

Saturday, Oct. 17
1942

Price

25c

Legion Field · Birmingham

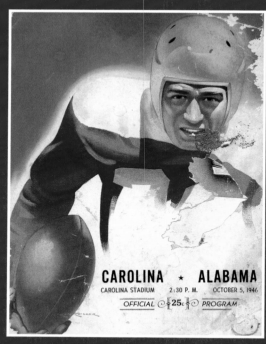

CAROLINA ★ ALABAMA

CAROLINA STADIUM   2:30 P. M.   OCTOBER 5, 1946

OFFICIAL 25c PROGRAM

THE TENNESSEE GRIDIRON

TENNESSEE vs. **ALABAMA**

SHIELDS-WATKINS FIELD   OCTOBER 19, 1946

OFFICIAL 25c PROGRAM

Colorful game programs depict support for Alabama football and the U.S.

Above: Former University of Alabama football tackle and B-17 pilot Tom Borders as depicted by artist Peter Hurd. Hurd painted Borders and several other U.S. pilots for Life *magazine in 1942–43. Borders died in action on December 26, 1942, when his plane was shot down on a bombing raid over Tunisia.*

Left: Recruitment posters from World War II.

Above: An American P-51 fighter plane takes off from an Iwo Jima airfield in 1945.

Right: U.S. B-17 bombers take off from a British airfield in this 1942 painting by artist Peter Hurd. Former University of Alabama football player Tom Borders, who was later killed in action, was the pilot of plane number 19100 (top foreground) and was one of the early American heroes of the war. Hurd painted several pilots and planes for Life magazine in World War II.

UNIVERSITY OF ALABAMA

ALUMNI NEWS

MRS. DEANY ROBERTS GARNER, LT. COMD'R. ROBERT N. BAVIER, JR., LT. (jg) MARY A. ROBERTSON

Volume 28   MARCH, 1945   Number 5

UNIVERSITY OF

ALABAMA
ALUMNI NEWS

Pfc. Leonidas Monroe Jones, '44

SERVICE ISSUE
Dedicated to the Alumni who gave their lives for our Country

Volume 28   MAY, 1945   Number 7

UNIVERSITY OF

ALABAMA
ALUMNI NEWS

DECEMBER 1942

Alabama Alumni News *covers from the World War II era.*

War-time images from the University of Alabama's yearbook, the Corolla.

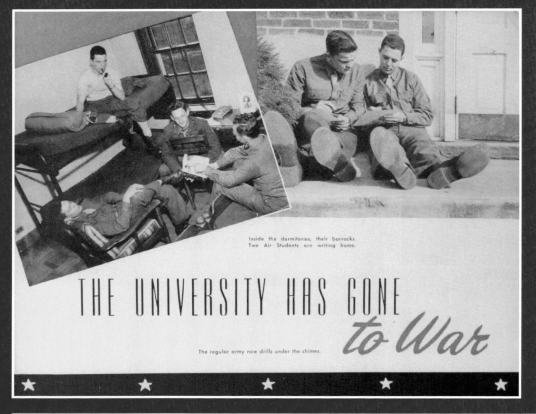

Inside the dormitories, their barracks.
Two Air Students are writing home.

THE UNIVERSITY HAS GONE
to War

The regular army now drills under the chimes.

★   ★   ★   ★   ★

To the tread of MARCHING FEET

War-time images from the University of Alabama's yearbook, the Corolla.

THE COROLLA 1943

World War II affected campus life in may ways.

To the Thousands . . .

COACHES *in service*

"Fight. Keep on fighting. The man that won't be defeated can't be defeated."

— Wallace Wade

Opposite: General Dwight D. Eisenhower briefs U.S. paratroopers before the D-Day invasion of France on June 6, 1944. (National Archives photograph)

Hank **CRISP**

'He would give a player the shirt off his back'

Henry G. "Hank" Crisp lost his right hand in a farm accident at age 13, but he never let the handicap slow him down as an athlete, coach or even in service to his country during World War II.

Crisp ranks among the University of Alabama's most versatile and honored athletic figures as head coach in basketball and track, assistant coach in football, athletic director and intramural sports director over a 46-year period.

Known for his toughness on the football field as an assistant under five head coaches, Crisp was just as well known for his compassion and willingness to help his players off the field. "He would literally give a player the shirt off his back, shoes from his feet or his last dime if he felt the boy was in need," Gadsden sports writer Jimmy Smothers once wrote of Crisp.

Despite the loss of his hand, Crisp was an outstanding athlete in prep school at Blackstone Military Academy in Virginia (1914) and at Hampden-Sydney College (1915-16) before going to Virginia Tech, where he became one of the best athletes ever at the school (1917-20). He worked his way through college at Virginia Tech by firing the gymnasium furnace.

Crisp earned letters in football, basketball and track at Virginia Tech, playing offensive

Hank Crisp (left) greets a Navy commander.

University chancellor Dr. George Denny praised Crisp at the 1939 celebration for his "hard work, loyalty, sacrifice, character, sportsmanship and persistence."

fullback and defensive tackle in football, guard in basketball and running the 440 in track. He earned All-South Atlantic honors and was elected captain of the football team as a senior.

Crisp came to Alabama as head track coach and assistant football coach in 1921. He was hired by athletic director Charles Bernier, who had been his coach at Hampden-Sydney and at Virginia Tech. Xen Scott was Alabama's head football coach at the time.

Crisp took on the added duty of head basketball coach in 1924 and held the position until 1942. His basketball teams won the Southern Conference title in 1930 with a 20-0 record and the Southeastern Conference championship in 1934 with a 16-2 mark. In 19 seasons as basketball coach, Crisp had an overall record of 266 wins and 129 losses. He continued as line coach under Wallace Wade (1923-30) and was largely responsible

for the rugged defensive units the Crimson Tide fielded in winning its first three national championships under Wade (1925, 1926 and 1930).

Crisp also served as athletic director 1931-39 and 1954-57 and as line coach under Frank Thomas 1931-41 and 1945, Red Drew 1950-54 and J. B. Whitworth 1955-57. He was also director of campus intramural sports 1954-67. Alabama football teams were 184-64-15 with Crisp as an assistant coach.

During almost five decades at Alabama, Crisp did whatever he was asked by the university in any sport and beyond. He earned the title of "Hustling Hank" by serving as coach and trainer, patching uniforms, repairing shoes and serving as team disciplinarian. He also became a second father figure to many of the players.

The North Carolina native was honored by the A Club at the 1939 A-Day game after 18 years with the athletic department. At the time he received a fishing boat, fishing tackle and a shotgun. He had first been honored in 1923 with the presentation of a car.

University chancellor Dr. George Denny praised Crisp at the 1939 celebration for his "hard work, loyalty, sacrifice, character, sportsmanship and persistence." Drew said at the time that Crisp was "the squarest shooter I have ever come in contact with."

Crisp did his part for his country when he left the University in 1942 to become a civilian employee with the Georgia Navy Pre-Flight School

Hank Crisp with Jim Whatley and Jimmy Walker (L-R).

Alabama coaches Crisp, Campbell, Drew, Bostick and Laney (L-R)

in Athens, teaching physical fitness and serving as trainer for the football teams. He remained with the Navy until the war ended and returned to coach Tide linemen again in 1945, helping the team to a 10-0 record, including a 34-14 win over Southern Cal in the January 1, 1946, Rose Bowl.

He went to Ole Miss as an assistant coach when Drew became head coach there in 1946, but returned in 1950 to serve eight more seasons as line coach for the Crimson Tide before finally giving up coaching after the 1957 season.

Crisp died January 23, 1970, just prior to his induction into the Alabama Sports Hall of Fame. He is also a member of the Helms Hall of Fame and the Virginia Tech Hall of Fame.

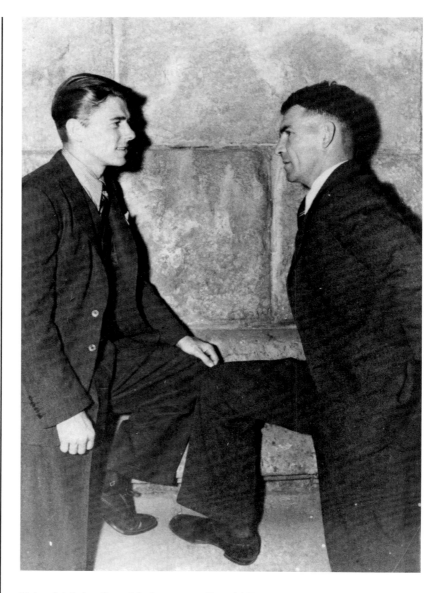

Crisp (right) talks with then-actor Ronald Reagan at the 1938 Rose Bowl.

Harold "Red" **DREW**

Tide coach served during two world wars

Harold "Red" Drew is legendary in University of Alabama athletic lore as a beloved, witty and even-tempered head coach in football and track and long-time assistant football coach spanning 35 years.

Drew also served as head football coach at four other colleges, extending his coaching career to almost 50 years before his retirement in 1965. The Maine native also saw military duty during two world wars, first as a Navy pilot in World War I and later as a physical fitness instructor and recreation director in World War II.

Drew grew up in Dwyer Brook, Maine, and was an outstanding athlete in high school and college. He lettered in football, basketball and track at Bates College then served as captain of the football team at Springfield College in 1917 before being called into service during World War I. While training as a pilot at Pensacola Naval Training Station, Drew became the first American pilot to bail out of a plane. After completion of training, he was assigned to fly

patrols over the Panama Canal Zone 1918-1919. He returned to Springfield for a final year of football in 1919 before earning his degree in 1920.

Drew served as head football coach and athletic director at Trinity College in Hartford, Connecticut, for three years before heading south to become head football coach and athletic director at Birmingham-Southern College in Alabama. He left Birmingham-Southern to become an assistant football coach under Frank Thomas at Chattanooga for two seasons, then became head coach at Chattanooga when Thomas went to Georgia as backfield coach in 1929. When Thomas replaced Wallace Wade as Alabama head coach in 1931, Thomas chose Drew to coach the Crimson Tide ends and serve as UA track coach, positions Drew held until he entered service again in 1942.

Drew conducted physical fitness training for Navy pre-flight cadets in Louisiana in 1942 and 1943 before being sent to the Pacific theater of war, where he served on Saipan as director of fleet recreation. Drew was a lieutenant commander when he left the Navy in the summer of 1945 following Japan's surrender to end the war.

Drew returned to Tuscaloosa in time to help the Crimson Tide to a 10-0 record in 1945, including a 34-14 Rose Bowl win over Southern Cal. Shortly after the bowl game, Drew was named head football coach at Ole Miss, a position he held for only one season before returning to Alabama as head coach in 1947 when Thomas stepped down due to illness. Drew was

head coach of the Crimson Tide 1947-53 and compiled a 55-29-7 record, including appearances in the Sugar, Orange and Cotton Bowls. His 1947 team was 8-3, the 1950 team was 9-2 and his 1952 team finished 10-2 after a 61-6 win over Syracuse in the Orange Bowl.

The 1948 Alabama team defeated Auburn 55-0 in the first game between the two in-state rivals since 1907. Drew's 1953 team won the Southeastern Conference championship with a 4-0-3 league record and earned a spot in the January 1, 1954, Cotton Bowl game.

Drew coached several Crimson Tide greats as a football assistant, including All-America ends Don Hutson (1934) and Holt Rast (1941); Paul "Bear" Bryant (1933-35); Tut Warren (1937) and Rebel Steiner (1945). As Tide head coach he had All-Americas Ed Salem (1950) and Bobby Marlow (1950-52) and All-SEC performers Harry Gilmer, John Wozniak, Ed Holdnak, Al Lary, Pat O'Sullivan, Mike Mizerany, Hootie Ingram, Jerry Watford, Corky Tharp, Salem and Marlow.

He was the Alabama track coach for 23 seasons, posting a career dual meet record of 84-26. Among Drew's top track performers were Charley Mosley and John Uelses. Mosley set individual Alabama records and scored the most points ever for an individual in an SEC track meet. Uelses won the SEC pole vault event as a sophomore and went on to become the first man to clear 16 feet in the event. Drew was inducted into the Alabama Sports Hall of Fame in 1971.

Drew (left) with UA Coach Frank Thomas.

Drew is survived by sons Harold Jr. and Robert and daughter Polly Jansen. Harold Jr. served in the Signal Corps in Europe during the World War II and Robert served in the Navy aboard a troop ship. Drew's son-in-law, Robert Jansen, served as a Navy officer aboard a submarine.

Wallace **WADE**

A front-line soldier in two world wars

Wallace Wade is remembered most as the head football coach who led the University of Alabama to its first three national championships and its first three Rose Bowl appearances.

Wade's legendary career did not start or end there, however.

Wade was Alabama's head coach 1923-30, and his teams had a combined record of 61-13-3 with four Southern Conference titles. After eight seasons at Alabama, Wade went to Duke, where his teams went 110-36-7 in 16 seasons, including two Rose Bowl appearances.

Alabama became widely known for its defensive play under Wade as his Crimson Tide teams recorded 47 shutouts in 77 games. Wade's 1924 Crimson Tide team went 8-1 and captured the school's first Southern Conference championship. The 1925 team allowed only one touchdown during its 9-0 regular season, and that came in a 50-7 rout of Birmingham Southern. The Tide defeated Washington 20-19 in the Rose Bowl to finish 10-0 and claim its first national championship along with a second Southern Conference title.

Above: Wade (left) with Frank Thomas.

Wallace Wade with the team at the 1926 Rose Bowl (above), with coaches (left) and kneeling for a photo.

The Crimson Tide allowed only 27 points in 1926 while going 9-0 in regular season play to earn its second Rose Bowl invitation. Alabama and Stanford fought to a 7-7 tie in Pasadena, but Alabama claimed another Southern Conference title and at least a share of the national championship.

Wade's 1930 Alabama team—his last—still holds the record for fewest points allowed in a season with 13. The Tide went 10-0 and again won conference and national titles by defeating Washington State 24-0 in the Rose Bowl.

Wade, a quiet man who believed in discipline and hard hitting, announced in April 1930 that he would leave Alabama when his contract expired after the 1930 season. Rumors persisted that he left because of criticism due to Alabama's 5-4-1, 6-3 and 6-3 records 1927-29. He told the 1930 team in preseason practice that he intended to win another championship in his final season, and he silenced his critics by delivering on his promise then quietly left town.

A Tennessee native, Wade had played guard for Brown University in the second Rose Bowl game ever in 1916, making him the first to appear in the Rose Bowl as a player and head coach when he carried the Tide to Pasadena after the 1925 season.

Wade joined the Army following his college playing career and served as a captain in the cavalry in France during World War I. Following the war, he coached two seasons at Fitzgerald and Clark Military School in his home state of Tennessee, compiling a 16-3 record and winning the state prep school championship in 1920.

As an assistant at Vanderbilt 1921-22, Wade helped the Commodores to an overall 15-0-2 record and two Southern Conference championships before being hired by Alabama

Wallace Wade (left) with Cecil Daniel

before the 1923 season.

Wade coached at Alabama through 1930 then led Duke 1931-41 before joining the Army again in March of 1942 at age 49 for service during World War II. He coached the West team of Army All-Star football players in 1942 as it played professional teams in charity games throughout the fall. He then trained as commander of the 272nd Field Artillery Battalion and led the unit into battle in Europe beginning in April 1944. He participated in the Battle of Normandy, Battle of the Bulge, the breaking of the Siegfried Line and the crossing of the Rhine River during the Ninth Army's drive through Germany, reaching the rank of lieutenant colonel.

Wade earned the Bronze Star and four battle stars and the French government presented him with its Croix de Guerre (Cross of War) with Palm, a high honor for heroism. His son, Wallace Wade Jr., served with the 9th Infantry Division during World War II.

Wade returned to Duke as head coach 1946-50 then served as commissioner of the Southern Conference 1951-1960 before retiring. He was inducted into the College Football Hall of Fame, the Alabama Sports Hall of Fame, Tennessee Sports Hall of Fame, North Carolina Hall of Fame, Brown University Hall of Fame and the Helms Hall of Fame. Three of Wade's former Alabama players—Fred Sington, Johnny Mack Brown and Pooley Hubert—are also in the National Football Hall of Fame.

Wade died at age 94 on September 23, 1986. His statue overlooks the Walk of Champions near the north entrance to Bryant-Denny Stadium along with those of other Alabama coaches who have led Crimson Tide teams to national championships. A street near Bryant-Denny Stadium is named Wallace Wade Drive in his honor and the Duke University football stadium also bears his name.

The HIGHEST PRICE

"I'm no hero; I just did a job and survived. The heroes were those who didn't make it."

— *John "Studie" Staples*

Opposite: Crosses mark the graves of fallen American soldiers at a military cemetery in France.
(National Archives photograph)

The *The* HIGHEST PRICE

Thirteen former players died during the war

More than 6,000 former University of Alabama students served in the U.S. armed forces during World War II and 343 of those lost their lives, according to University historical records. Over 300 former Crimson Tide football players were among those who served and 13 of the former players lost their lives during the war, eight in combat.

The following former Alabama football players and a manager are those known to have died in the line of duty during World War II:

BARTLE A. (BART) AVERY of Gloversville, New York, was killed during combat in Germany on April 6, 1945. He was a captain in the Army's 84th Infantry Division. Avery was a member of both the Alabama football and basketball teams 1940-42. He was awarded the Silver Star for "conspicuous gallantry in action" in addition to the Bronze Star and Purple Heart. Avery was married to the former Ellen Beale Daniel of Tuscaloosa. Avery's brother, Lt. Milton L. Avery, a co-pilot on a B-24 bomber, was also killed in action during the war when his plane was shot down over Hamburg, Germany, on June 4, 1944.

ROBERT D. (BOB) BIJUR of New York, New York, was a member of the Alabama football team 1939-40. He left school early to join the Royal Air Force during World War II. He was killed in Europe in August 1943 and is buried in England.

THOMAS H. (TOM) BORDERS of Birmingham, Alabama, was killed December 26, 1942, when his B-17 bomber exploded over Tunisia after being hit by German antiaircraft fire. Borders played tackle on Crimson Tide football teams 1937-40. Borders was the pilot of the first American plane to shoot down a German plane in World War II in August of 1942. He was awarded the Air Medal with two oak leaf clusters for extreme bravery in action.

BEN COMPTON of Greensboro, Alabama, died of a heart attack on October 18, 1946, while serving as liaison officer at the Tuskegee,

Alabama, Army Air Base. A University of Alabama lineman 1921-24, Compton was a major in the Army Air Forces.

CLIFF (SWEDE) HANSEN of Gary, Indiana, was killed in the crash of a bomber in Tennessee in March 1942. Hansen was an Army lieutenant. He played tackle at Alabama 1938-41, earning letters in 1940 and 1941. He played in the Tide's 29-21 win over Texas A&M in the January 1, 1942, Cotton Bowl.

ROBERT HUTSON of Pine Bluff, Arkansas, was flight officer on a troop transport plane when he was killed in a crash in the South Pacific on August 27, 1943. He was a younger brother of former Alabama All-America end Don Hutson. Robert played football and basketball as a freshman at Alabama in 1940 along with his twin brother Ray. The Hutson twins participated in spring football practice in 1941, but joined the Army Air Forces during the summer. Ray was a pilot during World War II and flew 77 missions over the "Hump" in the China-Burma-India Theater.

CRAWFORD H. (HAL) JONES of Tuscaloosa, Alabama, was killed by a German sniper on April 19, 1945. Jones was a first lieutenant in General George S. Patton's Third Army and died just three weeks before Germany surrendered to end the war in Europe. Jones was a sophomore quarterback on the 1942 Alabama football team. Hal's brother Harwell, who was on the 1928 Alabama football and track teams, also served in World War II.

HENRY EDWARD (RED) JONES JR. of Laurel, MS, was killed by a sniper near Harlange, Luxembourg, on January 2, 1945. Jones was a 6-2, 190-pound sophomore end on the 1942 Alabama football team and a member of the A Club. He reported to active duty with the Army on April 7, 1943, and arrived in Normandy in July of 1944. Jones was a platoon sergeant in the 320th Infantry Division at the time of his death.

WILLIAM F. (BILL) KRAUTWALD of Peoria, Illinois, was killed in action January 18, 1944, in the Asiatic Theater. Sgt. Krautwald was a 6-2, 227-pound tackle on the Alabama teams of 1939-40 and enlisted in the Army in 1941.

NATHAN MARX of Birmingham, Alabama, earned a letter as football manager in 1937 and was a member of the A Club. He was Navy lieutenant serving as a flight instructor when he was killed April 28, 1945, in a plane crash near Los Alamitos, California.

NEAL PATTON of Decherd, Tennessee, was killed December 14, 1942, when two Coast Guard patrol planes collided off the coast of California. Patton was a guard on the 1940 Alabama freshman football team.

Arlington National Cemetery is shown in an early morning sunrise.

JAMES L. (BABS) ROBERTS of Blytheville, Arkansas, died on December 22, 1944, after being accidently shot in a firing range accident at Fort Campbell, Kentucky. Roberts was co-captain of the 1942 Crimson Tide football team and also captain of the boxing team. A 1943 Alabama graduate, Roberts was a sergeant in the Army.

JOHN QUINCY (JOHNNY) ROBERTS of Birmingham, Alabama, was a member of the football, baseball and boxing teams at Alabama (1936-38) and served as president of the A Club. He died at the Battle of Midway on June 4, 1942, when he appeared to purposely crash his dive bomber into the deck of the Japanese aircraft carrier *Kaga,* helping to sink the ship. Ensign Roberts, a pilot from the aircraft carrier *USS Enterprise,* was posthumously awarded the Navy Cross and Purple Heart. The U.S. Navy destroyer escort *USS John Q. Roberts* was named in his honor.

JAMES EDWIN (JIMMY) WALKER of Tuscaloosa, Alabama,

was captain of the 1935 University of Alabama football and basketball teams and a two-time All-Southeastern Conference basketball player 1935-36. He was killed in an automobile accident while on duty in Brazil as a Navy lieutenant in 1943. He enlisted in the Navy in 1942 after serving as head basketball coach and assistant football coach at Virginia Military Institute for four years.

Coast guardsmen tend graves in the Pacific.

MARINES

"You didn't talk about the war. You didn't want to relive it. You just looked to the future."

— *John "Studie" Staples*

Opposite: Wrecked U.S. landing craft and other equipment litter the beach in the aftermath of fierce battle on the Japanese island of Iwo Jima in World War II. Mount Suribachi is visible in the background. (National Archives photograph)

Jack **ALAND**

'It was like stepping into another world'

Jack Aland carried the key to his parents' home in Birmingham with him during his service as a U.S. Marine during World War II. That key was a constant reminder of his goal of returning home safely from battles against the Japanese in the Pacific.

Aland, a husky 6-0, 217-pounder, was a former University of Alabama football player and a lieutenant with the Fourth Marine Division. He saw action in the Pacific assault landing on Iwo Jima, where he received a Purple Heart for his wounds and a commendation for his leadership.

Aland joined the Marine reserves in early 1942, shortly after the Japanese attack on Pearl Harbor that drew America into the war, and was called to active duty a year later following Alabama's 1942 football season. More than 90 percent of the players on Alabama's 1942 team went into service in early 1943, leaving the school with too few players to field a team in 1943.

Aland trained in the states for a year and was

commissioned a second lieutenant before being shipped out to join the Fourth Marine Division in the Pacific in 1944. The division had already seen combat in assault landings at Roi-Namur on Kwajalein Atoll, where it met little resistance; on Saipan, where the division suffered 5,981 casualties, and on Tinian, where it suffered another 1,800 casualties.

Aland joined the division in time for one of the most memorable battles of the war, which began with the February 19, 1945, invasion of Iwo Jima. Three Marine divisions (Third, Fourth and Fifth) numbering approximately 70,000 men fought on the small volcanic island and almost 7,000 of those were killed. Another 20,000 Marines were wounded and more than 20,000 Japanese were killed. The Fourth Division suffered 9,098 casualties on Iwo Jima, almost half the division, and Aland was among those wounded in the month-long battle when he was hit in the leg by shrapnel from a Japanese artillery shell.

"When we landed it was just like stepping into another

world entirely," Aland later wrote in a letter home of his experience on Iwo Jima. "From the time I set foot on that beach—covered with something I am not allowed to mention—until the island was secured it was the same thing everywhere you looked," he wrote. Aland was referring to the thousands of dead bodies that littered the ravaged beaches and hillsides. His mortar platoon arrived on the island in the late afternoon of the first day of fighting and provided fire support for the front-line Marines throughout the fighting.

Aland received a commendation for his service on Iwo Jima which said his "leadership and initiative served as an inspiration" to the men under his command. His letter home said "I am thankful to God that I can sit down and write a letter; in other words, just to be alive. Any Marine here today will say the same thing."

While on a troop ship headed for the Iwo Jima invasion, Aland became friends with Associated Press photographer Joe Rosenthal, who made the now-famous photograph of the U.S. flag being raised on Mount Suribachi. Rosenthal later gave Aland several censored photographs of the carnage on the island, and his family still has the photos. Aland also brought home a small Banzai flag marked by a bullet hole which he took off a dead Japanese soldier, according to his son Robert.

"He didn't talk very much about the war," Robert said of his father. "He would rather talk about Alabama football and teammates like Don Whitmire and Bobby Tom Jenkins."

Aland was discharged from the Marines following the surrender of Japan in September 1945 and he returned to Birmingham to be reunited with his parents and six older siblings. He worked in his family's department store (The

Marines in action in the Pacific.

New Ideal) and later opened his own store (Aland's) with his brother and brother-in-law. Aland died at age 86 on August 28, 2009. He was survived by his wife Ellen and children Jack Jr., Karen and Robert. Another daughter, Linda, is deceased.

Aland was a native of Birmingham and was a star football and track athlete at Ramsey High School. He won the state high school shot put championship as a senior in 1940 and earned a football scholarship to the University of Alabama. He was a member of the Crimson Tide team that went 9-2 in 1941 with a 29-21 victory over Texas A&M in the Cotton Bowl. Aland was also on the 1942 team that went 8-3 and defeated Boston College 37-21 in the Orange Bowl.

Aland was honored posthumously by the University Athletic Department before the Alabama-Tennessee football game in October 2009 as a Crimson Tide athlete and military veteran.

Warren **AVERITTE**

'They don't stop until you kill them'

Warren Averitte made the pages of *Look* magazine in May 1944 as a wounded and heavily bandaged U.S. Marine being led from the battle-scarred jungles of Bougainville during World War II.

Averitte lost his left eye during the six-day battle for Hellzapoppin Ridge on the Pacific island during December 1943, and was cited for bravery when he continued to lead his platoon in battle even after being seriously wounded. The dramatic photograph of Averitte with his head and eyes covered with field bandages was one of several featured in a four-page magazine article on the battle, which was named "Hellzapoppin" after a popular Broadway show of the era.

Marines from the Third Division invaded Bougainville on November 1, 1943, with the goal of establishing an airfield on the island. Although they were successful in that effort, the battle for total control of the island continued until August 21, 1945, well after the atomic bombs were dropped on Hiroshima and Nagasaki, Japan. The division had 400 men killed during dense jungle fighting against determined Japanese defenders. The Marines made extensive use of the famed Navajo "code talkers" for transmitting radio messages during the fighting on Bougainville, just as they had earlier on Guadalcanal.

Averitte, a native of Greenville, Mississippi, was a 1941 graduate of the University of Alabama and a three-year

Averitte (head bandaged) being led from jungle after being wounded.

letterman (1938-40) at center on the football team. He earned second-team All-Southeastern Conference honors in 1940. He was a member of the Alabama team that defeated Fordham 7-6 at New York's Polo Grounds on October 7, 1939, in the Crimson Tide's first televised football game. It was also only the second football game ever televised. Fordham had played Waynesburg College in the first televised game a week earlier.

Although his name doesn't show up in the records, Averitte said he played in the Crimson Tide's January 1, 1938, Rose Bowl loss (13-0) to California.

"I was a redshirt in 1937, but Coach Thomas took me to the Rose Bowl game and I even played," Averitte said. "They snuck me in so it wouldn't cost me any eligibility. You could change jerseys with another player and get away with it back then," he laughed. "I was even interviewed by a newscaster named Ronald Reagan. I remember he asked me how to pronounce my name. He was a nice guy."

Alabama was 9-0 in 1937 before the Rose Bowl loss and went 19-6-2 the next three seasons. Averitte played behind All-America center Cary Cox in 1938-39 and was the starter in 1940.

Averitte signed a $130 per game professional football contract with the Detroit Lions in early 1941, but did not report to camp. His contract signature was witnessed by Tide roommate and teammate Tom Borders, who was killed in action as a bomber pilot in World War II. Another of Averitte's roommates at Alabama was halfback Charley Boswell, who lost his eyesight in action in Europe.

"I knew I would be going into the service soon," Averitte, 92, said in March of 2010. "I think my draft number was two, so I went home and worked with Swift and Company for a few months after graduation before joining the Marines. Coach (Frank) Thomas was going to get me in the Air Corps, but I wanted to take my chances on my own two feet."

Averitte received his Marine training at Quantico, Virginia, and was commissioned a second lieutenant in June 1942. He then spent 13 months in the South Pacific before his

Averitte with wife Georgia on their wedding day.

head wound on Bougainville sent him back to the states for treatment. He was injured on December 17, 1943, as his 40-man platoon attacked more than 200 Japanese troops dug into a narrow ridge.

Then a first lieutenant, Averitte was commended for meritorious service in the attack, and his citation read in part: "Despite the fact that three of your key noncommissioned officers became casualties during the assault, you successfully maneuvered your troops into a favorable position and directed them in delivering effective fire at the Japanese emplacements. You continued to lead the platoon even after you had been wounded, remaining on the field until you had been temporarily blinded by blood flowing into your eyes. You protested your removal from the scene of action as you were being led to the rear. You displayed outstanding courage, leadership and devotion to duty." His Purple Heart citation was personally signed by Navy Admiral W. F. "Bull" Halsey.

"I got mad," Averitte said of his wound on Bougainville. "I didn't want to leave (the battlefield); I wanted to fight."

Averitte had seen his first action on Guadalcanal in August of 1942. "There was a little shooting going on there, too, and it got worse," he said. "I was a platoon leader, but they really led me. We didn't have time to properly train. They just threw us out there, but they had no choice. We just got out there and slugged it out. We didn't know how to fight in the jungle and the Japanese did. They were sneaky fighters; we had a tough time of it," he added.

The Marines attacked Japanese forces on Guadalcanal on August 7 and captured the airfield there, although the battle for total control of the island continued for several months. From Guadalcanal, the Marines moved on to attack the

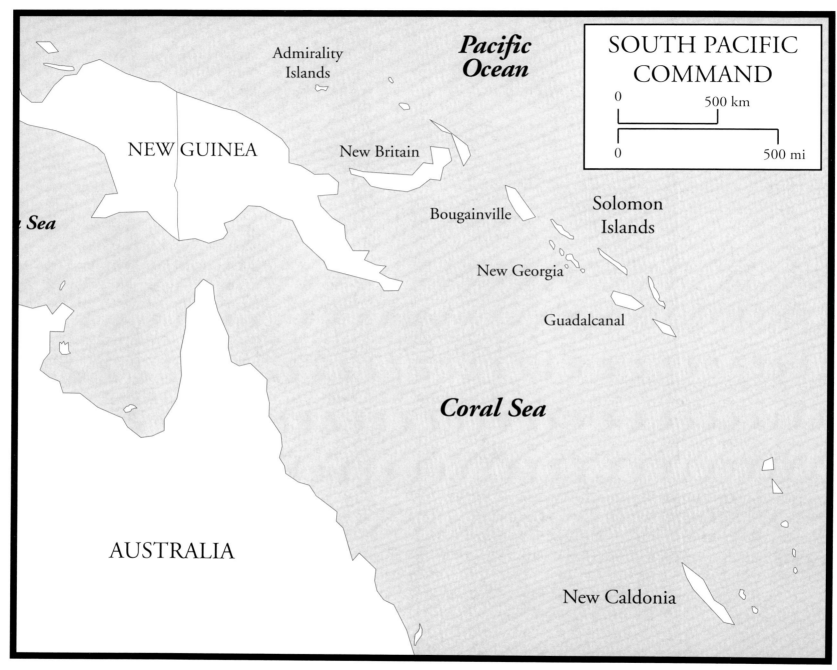

Map shows South Pacific Theater of war.

"We didn't have time to properly train. They just threw us out there, but they had no choice. We just got out there and slugged it out. We didn't know how to fight in the jungle and the Japanese did. They were sneaky fighters; we had a tough time of it."

enemy at Bougainville in November, and fighting continued there until the war ended.

"My outfit (Company A of the Third Marine Division) went on to Iwo Jima and almost got wiped out," Averitte said. "I heard from one of them later on; he was the only survivor I ever talked to."

Speaking of his war experiences, Averitte once said "You fight on your own with only your rifle, bayonet and helmet. The Japanese keep coming in at you and they don't stop until you kill them." He recalled one occasion when a Japanese soldier played a flute all night long before an attack. "He almost drove us crazy with his incessant music," Averitte said.

Describing the Japanese fighters on Bougainville, one Marine general said "They come in hard, walking on their dead, usually on a front not to exceed 100 yards. They try to affect a breakthrough which they exploit like water running from a hose. When stopped, they dig in like termites and fight to the death. They crawl up even the most insignificant fold in the ground like ants. And they use all their weapons with spirit and boldness."

After being wounded, Averitte was sent from Bougainville to the U.S. Naval Hospital in New Orleans, where he received extensive treatment, including the removal of his left eye. While there, he met and married Navy nurse Georgia Ann Harwell, who had cared for him in the hospital.

Following his recovery, Averitte returned to Greenville and coached high school football for six years, posting a 46-15-1 record. He then went to Columbia University, where he served as an assistant coach under Lou Little while earning his doctoral degree in physical science.

Warren Averitte as Tide center in 1940.

Little had been an ambulance driver in Europe during World War II along with former Ole Miss football player and assistant coach Buster Poole. Poole and Averitte had been friends since high school, and Poole recommended Averitte for the job at Columbia.

"Lou Little was the best football man and finest man I've ever known," Averitte said. "He was great with kids and the kids loved him. He got the most out of them. He was a highly respected, great guy."

After earning his doctorate at Columbia, Averitte was named professor of physical science at the University of Chattanooga in 1953 and held the position until his retirement in 1979.

Johnny AUGUST

All-America for sure if not for the war

When you name the great triple-threat halfbacks who played football under Coach Frank Thomas at the University of Alabama the list always includes Harry Gilmer, Dixie Howell and Joe Kilgrow, all three All-America Rose Bowl stars.

Had World War II not come along, the name Johnny August would almost certainly have been added to that exclusive list.

"The name Johnny August has been on the tip of every tongue in Tuscaloosa for many months as a second Dixie Howell. Or perhaps a super Dixie Howell," wrote *Birmingham Age Herald* sports writer Bob Phillips in September 1942. "August came down as a transfer from Ohio State with all-star stamped all over him and in a redshirt season against the varsity and a subsequent spring practice, he has consistently lived up to the high expectations of him ever since."

A University news release said August "sparkles in an open field with his blinding speed and elusiveness. Probably

Johnny August as an Alabama halfback.

the best passer on the squad, Johnny can also hold his own with the best Tide punters."

August, a native of Shadyside, Ohio, was well on his way to that anticipated stardom by mid-season in 1942. The Crimson Tide sophomore played his way into the starting left halfback spot for the last two games of the season in an era when sophomores rarely started for the talent-rich Alabama teams of the era.

"Johnny August found himself Saturday,' wrote Zipp Newman of the *Birmingham News* on November 8, 1942, following the Tide's 29-0 victory over South Carolina. "He punted well, passed well and seemed to run harder, picking up 59 yards," Newman said of August, who passed for touchdowns of 24 and 49 yards in the win.

"Johnny August is the apple of Thomas' eye for the key position in his backfield. After watching him in today's fierce scrimmage, it is easy to see why," wrote Raymond Johnson of the Nashville *Tennessean* prior to the Alabama-Vanderbilt game.

Johnny August (11) on his way to an Orange Bowl touchdown.

"The highlight of Saturday's performance was the brilliant playing of Johnny August," wrote Naylor Stone of Birmingham on November 22, 1942, following Alabama's 27-7 win over Vanderbilt in Birmingham. "This young man started clicking against South Carolina. Then against Georgia Tech he performed brilliantly. But he had his field day against Vandy, turning in his finest performance of the nearly finished campaign. He was brilliant in running back punts, passing and kicking, proving a brilliant triple threat all afternoon."

August rushed for 48 yards, returned two punts for 51 yards and completed two passes for 37 yards on one 43-yard

August walked away from the game as the star he had dreamed of becoming, and no player on the Alabama team had reason to expect a brighter football future.

scoring drive against the Commodores. "It was by far his best game of the season. He was running hard with the ball. He passed well and his kicking was a joy for the Crimsons to behold," wrote Newman in praise of August following the Vanderbilt game.

August, a 5-11, 175-pounder, started the next game against a Georgia Navy Pre-Flight team made up of former college and professional players and was injured in a 35-19 loss. He finished the 1942 regular season with 214 yards rushing on 52 carries, 247 yards passing on 16 completions in 26 attempts and a 39.6-yard average on 20 punts. He had started the season as a backup to senior Russ Mosley, who led the Tide in passing in 1942 with 352 yards.

August bounced back from his injuries against Georgia Pre-Flight to start and star in the Orange Bowl on January 1,

1943, as the Tide beat Boston College 37-21. August shared the headlines in the win by rushing nine times for 48 yards, including a 15-yard score, and throwing a 16-yard touchdown pass to Ted Cook. He also completed passes of 21 and 27 yards in the game and had one sure touchdown pass dropped in the end zone.

Sports writers praised August after the game, calling him a "sensational sophomore" while pointing to his "fancy capers" as a runner and skill as a passer. "He seemed to have Boston College men all around him, but he cocked his arm and let fly with all the coolness of Red Ruffing (New York Yankees Hall of Fame pitcher) himself," wrote Jack Bell of the *Miami Herald* on January 3, 1943.

August walked away from the game as the star he had dreamed of becoming, and no player on the Alabama team

Bama's halfbacks in 1947 included (L-R) Monk Mosley, Ed Salem, Johnny August, Harry Gilmer and Gordon Pettus.

had reason to expect a brighter football future. "August looked as calm and cool as Dixie Howell. He showed he is now ready to take over the left-half position," wrote Newman.

World War II had been raging for a year, however. America battled determined and fanatical enemies on two separate fronts, and it needed manpower. The draft age was 18, and within a few months the entire 36-man Orange Bowl traveling squad had gone into military service. By the summer of 1943, 57 of the 58 men on the 1942 varsity roster were in service, forcing Alabama, like many other colleges, to suspend football in 1943.

August joined the Marines and trained at Camp Pendleton, California; Parris Island, South Carolina, and Cherry Point, North Carolina, before shipping overseas. He also played one season of service football at Cherry Point while serving as a physical fitness instructor.

August was aboard a ship in the Pacific, on his way to join the Sixth Marine Division on Guam, when Japan surrendered on August 14, 1945, to end the war. He served as part of the occupation forces in northern China with the mission of accepting the surrender of Japanese forces before returning to the states for discharge in March 1946.

August returned to Alabama for the 1946 football season and seemed to pick up where he left off nearly four years earlier, according to sports writers.

"Johnny August, who looked like a Dixie Howell in his last game for Alabama before going into the Marines, came out to befuddle the Hurricanes," Newman wrote after August helped Alabama defeat Tulane 7-6 in the second game of the 1946 season. "Gilmer was Gilmer, but August's show of his old form must have been a great sight for Frank Thomas. He now knows that he has in Gilmer and August two of the finest triple threats in the country," Newman wrote.

"This August is the cat's whiskers when it comes to faking a pass and striking out like lightning off tackle. And he can cut around the flanks with the best of the ball toters," wrote Newman, who had touted August as "better than Gilmer" prior to the season. "Wait until you see him go. He can pass and run and everything. Just you wait and see."

The Johnny August story of a GI returning from service to find someone else playing in his old position or filling his job was repeated millions of times as veterans returned from World War II.

Stone wrote that August was "easily the Tide's standout" in the Tulane game.

Alabama edged South Carolina 14-6 in the rain and mud a week later with Gilmer and August each engineering touchdown drives. Gilmer intercepted a pass to end one Gamecocks drive and August quick-kicked 55 yards and later punted dead on the South Carolina one-yard-line as they shared the headlines.

But Gilmer, the leaping passer who was every schoolboy's hero at the time, was the Alabama star from that time on as August found playing time hard to come by. August, now 25 years old, did well when he played; he simply didn't play a lot.

After all, Gilmer was a two-year starter (1944 and 1945) for the Tide and a returning All-America performer who had finished fifth in the 1945 Heisman Trophy voting. He had led Alabama to a perfect 10-0 season in 1945, including a 34-14 win over Southern Cal in the Rose Bowl. Perhaps spurred on by the competition from August, Gilmer responded with another outstanding season in 1946.

Gilmer ended up leading the Tide in rushing in 1946 with 497 yards on 133 carries while passing for 930 yards and five touchdowns on 69 completions in 160 attempts. He also returned 37 punts for 436 yards, returned nine kickoffs for 230 yards, intercepted eight passes for 79 yards and punted 56 times for a 38.4-yard average.

August, meanwhile, rushed 45 times for 143 yards and one touchdown while completing three of 11 passes for 43 yards and one touchdown. He also returned 15 punts for 140 yards and punted 23 times for a 37.4 average.

It was the same story in 1947 when both players were seniors. Gilmer, a fan favorite, did most of the playing and led the team in passing with 610 yards and five touchdowns on 57 completions in 93 attempts. Lowell Tew, Gilmer and Billy

Johnny August on the move for Alabama.

Cadenhead were the team's leading rushers, and August saw even less playing time than in 1946.

It was obvious that the returning war veterans had a hard time getting into the lineup because the entire 1945 team had returned for 1946 and 1947, and Thomas (1946) and Red Drew (1947) were reluctant to break up a winning combination. The Alabama roster for 1946 included 36 returning servicemen while the 1947 roster listed 31.

"Johnny was a great back," said Don Salls of August in 2009. "He was light, fast, and really an unsung hero. I don't think he ever got the credit he deserved." Salls played with August in 1942.

Clem Gryska, an Alabama halfback 1945-48 who played with Gilmer and August, said they were much alike in many ways. "They had a lot of the same skills, mannerisms and stature," Gryska said. "Both were nonchalant off the field, but they went after it on the field. They could both throw and run."

August started at centerfield on the 1947 Alabama baseball team, helping the Tide to the Southeastern Conference championship and a spot in the NCAA Regional tournament.

August was drafted by the NFL's Cleveland Rams, but ended up joining the Brooklyn Dodgers of the All-America Conference in 1948. He passed for two touchdowns in his first preseason game and again appeared headed for stardom before an injury ended his career.

August returned to the University of Alabama, where he earned his degree in 1949 and married Alice Miller of Attalla, Alabama. They moved to Rome, Georgia, where August worked as an insurance agent and lived the quiet, peaceful, small-town-America life for which he and millions of others like him had fought. He died November 7, 1998, at age 77.

The Johnny August story of a GI returning from service to find someone else playing in his old position or filling his job was repeated millions of times as veterans returned from World War II. It was one of the many misfortunes of war, but one that few veterans dwelled on. Things at home had changed, and they had changed, too. For many, football was no longer the highest priority in their lives. Most were happy just to be home and they simply moved on with their lives, never looking back at the war or what might have been.

Johnny August, judging from the media accolades at the time, almost certainly would have been an All-America football player if not for the war. Perhaps he thought about that himself now and then as he recalled the 1942 season and his outstanding play in the Orange Bowl on January 1, 1943; perhaps not.

He was surely the typical, wholesome All-American boy of his generation—the generation that went to war and won and earned the honor of being known forever as America's greatest generation. Few of them ever had reason for regret.

Gregory "Gri" CASHIO

'I've never been as scared in all my life'

Gregory "Gri" Cashio never got to wear the white dress uniform that swayed him to join the Marines during World War II, but he always loved the Marines anyway.

Cashio was a member of the Marine assault troops in the invasions of Eniwetok, Guam and Okinawa as U.S. forces drove the Japanese back toward Japan following their December 7, 1941, attack on Pearl Harbor, Hawaii.

Cashio was one of six University of Alabama football players who joined the Marines during the Crimson Tide's final home game of 1942 as he interrupted his playing career for military duty. "Some of the Marine reservists came to a campus dance wearing their white uniforms and they couldn't beat the girls off with a stick. Gri joined up," said his widow Angela Cashio with a laugh. "He was proud to be a Marine, but he always said he never saw a white uniform again."

Cashio earned a football scholarship to Alabama as an All-State end at Gadsden High School and played on the 1942 Crimson Tide team that posted an 8-3 overall record, including a 37-21 win over Boston College in the Orange

Bowl on January 1, 1943. Cashio and the other five players who had been sworn into the Marines on November 28 departed for service immediately after the Orange Bowl game. Cashio spent just over three years in the Marines and returned to play guard for the Crimson Tide in 1946 and 1947, earning a letter on the 8-3 team that lost to Texas 27-7 in the Sugar Bowl game on January 1, 1948.

Cashio was a machine gunner assigned to the Sixth Marine Division's 22nd Marine Regiment. He saw his first action just over a year after leaving the University as U.S. forces took Eniwetok Atoll in February 1944. He fought in the invasion of Guam in the summer of 1944 and in the battle for Okinawa from April 1-June 21, 1945. Okinawa produced the highest number of allied casualties in the Pacific theater, with over 12,000 killed and nearly 40,000 more wounded during the 82-day battle. Battles in the waters surrounding Okinawa saw another 4,907 U.S. soldiers killed and 4,874 wounded, primarily from kamikaze attacks on Navy ships. One of the most famous U.S. casualties at Okinawa was war correspondent Ernie Pyle, who was killed by Japanese machine gun fire on Ie Shima.

Cashio, a master sergeant, was missing for almost

three weeks during one of the invasions, according to his wife, but he survived the battles with only scratches and bruises and served in the occupation of China before his discharge in 1946. He earned the Asiatic-Pacific Campaign Medal with two stars, the American Campaign Medal, the World War II Victory Medal and the Good Conduct Medal. "As far as I am concerned, every Marine in those battles deserves them all," Cashio's wife said of his military decorations.

The following excerpts from a letter home to his parents in early 1944 offer a first-hand glimpse at Cashio's war-time experiences:

"I have been in two landing operations against the Japanese since I have written to you….

Cashio (right) with Marine buddies in the Pacific.

It's only by God's grace that I am here tonight writing to you. Mother, I've never prayed so hard and so much in my life as I did in those operations. I made vows and promises to God and to the Blessed Mother that if I came out of these battles I'll never break them…I wish I could tell you what islands that we took but I can't. All I can say is that we have been in battle. It's horrible but it's what one expects when he is part of it. I've seen a lot of brave men, some of the bravest in the world. That's what you can say about the United States Marine Corps personnel.

"I've never been as scared in all my life as I have been on these two operations. It wasn't being scared to fight the Japanese; it was a certain kind of fear that is unexplainable. Once you get over this fear it's something out of this world. I've also spent some rugged nights in this war, the worst of

all, but best of all is that I am here writing to you now. Of course I've had some close calls and I am lucky to be here," Cashio wrote.

Cashio returned to the University and served as an assistant coach with the Alabama freshmen in 1949 as he worked toward his master's degree. He later coached football at Talladega, Thompson, Lake City, Florida, and Shades Valley high schools. During eight seasons at Shades Valley, Cashio's teams won three county championships. He coached a number of outstanding players during his career, including future Alabama players Dave Sington and Lauren Stapp; Bill Clark of Army; Lewis Akin of Vanderbilt and George Gregory of Ole Miss. While at Thompson High, Cashio coached Jim "Peanut" Davenport, who later played baseball for the San Francisco Giants. Following his coaching career, Cashio served as president of American Materials and Supply Company prior to his untimely death at age 47. He was an active University of Alabama alumnus and served as president of the A Club.

Cashio's survivors included his wife Angela and children Tony Cashio, Frances Patton, Margie Costanzo, Richard Cashio, Mary Grace Kaufmann, Angela Bennett and Gregory Cashio.

Cashio's brother Sam served in the Navy during World War II and saw duty in the Pacific aboard the USS Crescent. The two brothers saw each other twice during the war.

Eli **KALUGER**

He survived the Mosquito Bowl and the war

Eli Kaluger never played in a varsity football game for the University of Alabama, but he saw plenty of combat action during World War II.

The Shadyside, Ohio, native came to Alabama in 1940 as a transfer from Miami of Ohio. Kaluger joined the Marines on April 2, 1942, however, only a few months after his brother Mike had survived the Japanese surprise attack on Pearl Harbor on December 7, 1941.

By August of 1942, Kaluger was in the South Pacific, where he fought in the first major U.S. offensive of the war as the Marines attacked Japanese forces on Guadalcanal. Before the battle for the island ended in February 1943, 650 Americans and 25,000 Japanese had died. Kaluger was among 1,278 U.S. troops wounded during the fighting when he was shot in the shoulder by a sniper.

Kaluger received the Purple Heart and recovered from his wounds to fight in several other battles with the Sixth

Marine Division, including Guam and Okinawa. His division had 1,700 killed and 7,400 wounded on Okinawa. Following the surrender of Japan in August 1945, the division spent several months in Tsingtao, China, assisting with the Japanese surrender there before Kaluger returned home.

The Marine corporal did play one final football game while in the Marines, however. He was in the infamous "Mosquito Bowl" game on Guadalcanal on December 24, 1944. The game featured the hardened Marines of the 4th and 29th regiments in tee shirts, cut off pants and combat boots. The game was watched by 10,000 troops and broadcast over Armed Forces Radio throughout the South Pacific as regimental bands played in the background.

Many of the players were injured in the scoreless tie, prompting the division commander to ban further football games in his division. Two months later the division was part of the 60,000-man allied assault on Okinawa. Many of the Mosquito Bowl players were either killed or wounded

Marines display a bullet-riddled Japanese flag.

there as U.S. forces suffered an estimated 50,000 casualties, including 12,000 killed, during the 82-day battle.

Rather than return to Alabama after the war, Kaluger chose to give professional baseball a try and batted .272 in 338 at-bats in the Texas Lone Star League in 1947. He also tried professional boxing briefly before returning to Shadyside to work in a tractor factory until retirement. He died in 1995.

Kaluger's three brothers also served in the military during World War II. Charles served in the Army and was killed at Luzon on February 23, 1945; Mike was in the Navy,

and Nick served in the Army in Europe.

Johnny August, another Shadyside, Ohio, native, came to Alabama with Kaluger in 1940 and remained on the football team through the 1942 season. As the starting left halfback, August led the Crimson Tide to a 37-21 win over Boston College in the January 1, 1943, Orange Bowl before joining the Marines.

Bill **SHOUSE**

'My best friend was killed the first night'

Like most young American men coming of age during World War II, Bill Shouse couldn't wait to get into the fight, and he joined the Marines as soon as he graduated from West High School in Nashville, Tennessee, in 1942.

After being trained to fly Marine planes equipped with new, secret radar capability, Shouse was sent to the Pacific in January 1944. "I went over on the smallest troop ship I ever saw. I was seasick the whole time and had to sleep on deck," he said.

"I was in the first twin-engine night-fighter squadron the Marines ever had," Shouse said. "We trained in Cherry Point, North Carolina, and I was crew chief—the same as co-pilot— in a four-man crew."

Shouse met the famous flyer Charles Lindbergh while in training, along with ice skater and movie star Sonja Heine. "She wanted to get into the plane and look around, but I refused to let her in," Shouse said. "We had that new secret radar that England had given us and I had been told that no one was to know about it, so I did what I was told and kept her out. I thought I had gotten myself into trouble, but the colonel told me later that I had done the right thing," Shouse said.

Shouse was a staff sergeant assigned to Group Four of VMFN Squadron 531 on Bougainville Island in the South Pacific. "We were to fly night patrols over Rabaul, a big

A U.S. warplane attacks an enemy target.

Texas, to train in new planes. We were there when the war ended."

Shouse was offered a commission to remain in the Marines, but turned down the offer after receiving word from his mother that he had football scholarship offers from both Alabama and Vanderbilt waiting for him at home. He eventually picked Alabama, reported for spring practice in 1946 and lettered at end his first three seasons (1946-48). Alabama went 8-3 and lost to Texas 27-7 in the Sugar Bowl in 1947 in its best season during that period.

"We played both offense and defense back then, and we had no face masks. I ended up with 103 stitches in my face as a player," Shouse said. An injury kept Shouse out of action as a senior. He married his wife Eleanor in 1948 and graduated in 1950. He soon started a career in trucking service sales and was still at it at age 89 in 2009. "Eleanor drives me around to see a few special customers and friends," he said of his continuing work in Birmingham.

distribution and refueling center for the Japanese," Shouse said.

"My best friend, Pete Barber of Knoxville, was killed the first night our planes went up. We sent up three planes and lost all three and all 12 men that first night," he said solemnly.

There was still heavy fighting on Bougainville when Shouse and his squadron arrived and it continued until the war ended with the Japanese surrender in August of 1945. "Every afternoon at five o'clock they would shell us," Shouse said. "But they were pushed back far enough by our troops that the shells didn't reach our planes." Shouse spent a year flying night patrols over the Solomon Islands four nights a week, shooting at whatever enemy movement he saw. He dodged enemy planes and antiaircraft fire well enough to come home without a scratch.

"We lost all our planes," he said. "They were all shot up, so they sent us back to Eagle Mountain Lake,

Bill Shouse as a UA football player.

"I never gave the war another thought after it ended and I got to Alabama to play football," Shouse said. He said Alabama football taught him about hard work and brought him many long-lasting friendships. "It was wonderful," he said of his days at the University of Alabama.

John "Studie" STAPLES

'The island was covered with dead soldiers'

John Staples, like many others, had his University of Alabama football career interrupted by World War II. He was sworn into the Marines at halftime of Alabama's final home football game in 1942 and 27 months later was involved in one of the bloodiest battles of World War II.

Staples landed on the Japanese island of Iwo Jima on his 23rd birthday, February 19, 1945, and he earned the Bronze Star for heroism there as part of a 70,000 Marine force assigned to take the island. Four days after his arrival, Staples was a witness as the Marines raised the first American flag on Mount Suribachi, although the fierce fight for control of the island's strategic airstrips would go on another month.

"Everybody saw it," Staples said of the flag raising event. "All the ships fired off shots and everybody cheered, but the battle was far from over."

A photograph of a reenactment of the original flag raising, taken by Associated Press photographer Joe Rosenthal, appeared in practically every American newspaper, won a Pulitzer Prize and became the model for the Marine Corps Memorial at Arlington National Cemetery. The costly victory on Iwo Jima became symbolic of America's determined march toward victory in the Pacific theater and was an inspiration to the entire country. The heroic actions of the Marines on the island have been featured in several movies and books.

Staples received an annual reminder of the Iwo Jima D-Day landing for more than 60 years from Marine buddy Bill Justice, who called Staples on his birthday each year and played the Marine Hymn on his harmonica. "He was two days late the last time (February 2009) and I was a little worried," Staples said.

John Staples in an Iwo Jima bunker.

Staples revisited Iwo Jima in 2005 along with his son John and found it much different from the first time. "It was so devastated then," Staples said of the island after the 1945 battle. "Now it's all overgrown and simply an airstrip. It brought back some memories, of course, but I didn't dwell on them. It was a long time ago, but you never forget," he said.

The airstrips on Iwo Jima, located approximately 700 miles from Japan's main island, were considered critical to U.S. forces as a fighter base and stopover point for crippled bombers returning from flights over Japan.

Staples, a second lieutenant with the Fourth Marine Division, was among the 30,000 Marines to wade ashore on the first day of battle, and as many as 40,000 more

Above: Staples (left) with Marine pal George Watkins.
Left: Staples on Mount Suribachi, Iwo Jima.

would follow before the fighting ended. An ordnance officer, Staples earned the Bronze Star with "V" for valor for "heroic achievement" from February 19-March 22, 1945, while "neutralizing and disposing of unexploded bombs and clearing mine fields and booby traps." His citation said Staples "braved enemy mortar and artillery fire to clear roads and other areas" for the movement of men and supplies.

"I'm no hero; I just did a job and survived," Staples modestly said of his duty on Iwo Jima. "None of us who left there were heroes. The heroes were those who didn't make it. But I'd like to think we saved a lot of lives by clearing the mines and disposing of the bombs," Staples said. "You just had to know what you were doing," he added of his dangerous task of disarming mines and booby traps and defusing unexploded bombs.

"I came ashore on the afternoon of February 19, my 23rd birthday, and the island was covered with dead soldiers, wreckage and unexploded bombs," Staples said of his Iwo Jima experience. "Our planes had bombed the island for days and our ships had fired artillery at it from point-blank range for four days before the landing," Staples said. "Everything was turned to black dust, but as it turned out they hadn't killed a pickup truck load of Japanese because they were all underground," Staples said. "We went in thinking the Japanese had either left or been killed. We thought we would mop things up in a few days, but it took a month and thousands of lives. No one realized what fierce fighters the Japanese were; they were suicidal," he added.

An estimated 21,000 Japanese soldiers were dug in on the island, living in a network of tunnels and fortified bunkers, and they battled the Marines for a month before victory was finally declared on March 22. The Marines used flame throwers to clear the tunnels, and only 1,083 Japanese were taken prisoner, most of those weakened by starvation and thirst. The Marines suffered some of their worst losses of the war on Iwo Jima, with almost 7,000 killed, 19,000 wounded and more than 2,500 scarred by battle fatigue.

Although there was wide celebration when the first American flag was raised on the volcanic mound called Mount Suribachi four days after the initial Marine assault on February 19, Staples said there was no celebrating when the fighting finally ended. "Too many men were killed," he said solemnly. "In war, you see how many of the enemy you can kill. Maybe it's wrong, but that's how it is."

U.S. Navy admiral Chester Nimitz called all the Marines who fought on the island heroes, saying "Among the

Staples with wife Jean in 1944.

Americans who served on Iwo Island, uncommon valor was a common virtue."

Staples said he and his squad made it only 20 yards onto the beach the first day before digging in for the night. "There were dead Marines on the beach and floating in the water and boats and equipment scattered all over the place and the Japanese were firing artillery shells and mortars at us from all sides," he said. "One of my Marines, a 16-year-old boy, was throwing up from the shock and said he couldn't take it, but when we left the island a month later he had become a hardened Marine. I prayed all night," Staples said of his first night on the island. "I prayed for myself and for my men; I promised the Lord everything."

Staples and his squad moved forward the following morning to begin clearing mine fields and defusing the many unexploded bombs that littered the island. "Ten percent of our bombs were duds, and they were all over the island," Staples said. "We had to defuse them and clear the Japanese minefields. They had three different patterns for laying mines, and there was no way you could get through an area without hitting one," he added. "We probed into the sand

gently; we didn't just jab in there. We found 175 in one field and had to defuse them all while under fire from snipers. "I was scared, but I just prayed and went on and did my job," Staples said. "It was dangerous if you didn't know what you were doing. You sure didn't have anybody looking over your shoulder telling you how to do your job." The hundreds of bombs and mines were hauled to the beach, taken out to sea

Staples (right) with his bomb disposal squad on Iwo Jima.

and dumped overboard at a minimum depth of 15 fathoms, he said.

When the island was finally secured and safe for U.S. occupation, Staples was shipped back to Hawaii for additional training in anticipation of the invasion of Japan. The surrender of Japan following the bombings of Hiroshima and Nagasaki in August 1945 ended the war, and Staples was sent to Japan for several months to dispose of unexploded bombs and munitions there. He was discharged in time to return to the University of Alabama in 1946 for his senior

season on the football team.

"Your priorities were a little different after the war," Staples said of himself and his many war veteran teammates at Alabama in 1946. "Chances are you had been in a spot where your life was on the line. You didn't have that in football, so football was a lot easier after the war. You didn't talk about it (the war). You didn't want to relive it. You just looked to the future," he said.

Staples (lower right) directs squad in removal of dud bomb.

Despite a three-year absence from football, Staples was among the regulars and earned his second letter as a senior in 1946. After earning his master's degree at Alabama in 1948, Staples served as an assistant coach at Blytheville, Arkansas, for two years with former Alabama halfback Russ Mosley, and their 1949 team won the state championship. Staples was recalled to military service for two years during the Korean War and reached the rank of major. He moved to Florida

in 1953 as head coach at Lakeland High School for two years before becoming personnel director for Polk County Schools for 14 years. He served 12 years as director of teacher education, certification and staff development for the Florida Department of Education before his retirement in 1981.

Staples died at age 87 on November 23, 2009. He is survived by daughters Rebecca, Donna, Susan and Sally and son John. His wife of 52 years, the former Jean Freeland of Birmingham, died in 1996. Staples met Freeland at the University of Alabama and they were married in March, 1944, two days after Staples received his Marine commission.

Staples' older brother Ralph served in the Army during World War II and was among the troops who landed at Normandy on D-Day, June 6, 1944. John and Ralph once operated the "Spudnut" shop on University Boulevard while John was in graduate school. "Sputnuts" were donuts made from potato flour, Staples explained.

Staples grew up in Owensboro, Kentucky, where he picked up the life-long nickname of "Studie" and played end on his high school football team. "I never dropped a pass," Staples joked. "That's because they never threw me one." Although he claimed that he was not a good football player, Staples and an Owensboro teammate were offered scholarships to a junior college in Ellisville, MS, following their senior season.

"That was the roughest football I ever played in my life," Staples said of his junior college experience. "Being in the military was hard work, and playing football at Alabama was hard, but no football ever compared to what we went through at that junior college," he said. "After a week or two, the other boy from Owensboro woke me up in the middle of the night and said he was going home, and it didn't take much to talk me into leaving with him. I only had enough money for a bus ticket to Birmingham, so I hitch-hiked the rest of the way home," Staples added.

Staples arrived home tired and hungry, but got little sympathy from his father, who was more than a little disappointed that Staples had given up a chance for a college education. "I asked Mama what I should do and she said that I'd better get out and get a job or go back to the junior college and see if they would take me back," Staples said. "The next morning Mama gave me a brown bag with three peanut butter and jelly sandwiches and three quarters and I started hitch-hiking back to Mississippi. That doesn't sound

like much, but my mother never had three quarters that I knew about," Staples said.

Staples switched from end to guard in junior college and was recruited by Alabama after the 1941 season. "I arrived in Tuscaloosa on Sunday afternoon, December 7, 1941," Staples said. "Everybody was fired up and wanting to join the service," Staples said of mood of the UA campus on his arrival.

As a 5-10, 180-pound junior college transfer, Staples was a part-time starter at guard in 1942 between All-America center Joe Domnanovich and All-America tackle Don Whitmire. Their play helped Alabama to an 8-3 overall record, including a win over Boston College in the Orange Bowl.

Staples and Crimson Tide teammates Gri Cashio, D. Joe Gambrell, Kenny Reese, James Gunnin and Frank Killian were all sworn into the Marine Corps at halftime of Alabama's final home game of 1942, a 35-19 loss to the Georgia Navy Pre-Flight team on November 28. They were allowed to play in the Orange Bowl on January 1, 1943, before reporting to duty. Staples started the bowl game and threw key blocks on two Alabama touchdown runs in the game as the Tide defeated Boston College 37-21. Staples also played football during the 1943 season while training at Cherry Point, North Carolina, along with Whitmire, who had joined the Navy.

The estimated 70,000 Marines (Third, Fourth and Fifth Divisions) who fought on Iwo Jima were under the command of Lieutenant General Holland M. "Howlin' Mad" Smith, an Alabama native who earned a law degree from the University of Alabama in 1903. Smith, who has been called the father of modern U.S. amphibious warfare, was commander of the Fleet Marine Force in the Pacific theater.

Staples (inset) revisits Mount Suribachi.

Above: Marines storm ashore in one of many Pacific landings.

Above: U.S. troops raise the American flag on Iwo Jima in this famous Associated Press photograph by Joe Rosenthal.

Right: Map shows large expanse of Central Pacific battle zone.

Opposite page: War-weary Marines pose for a photograph on the Pacific island of Bougainville.

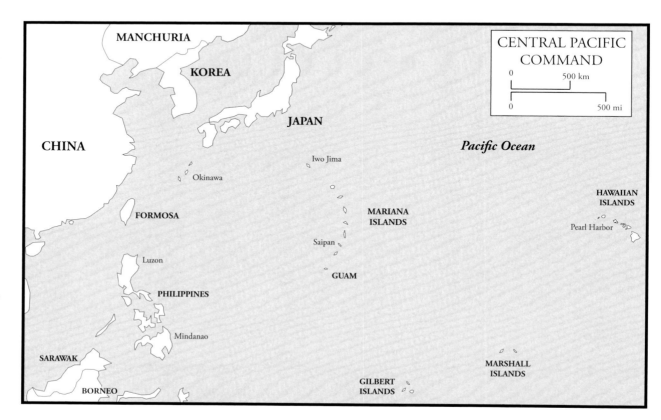

CENTRAL PACIFIC COMMAND

0   500 km

0   500 mi

MANCHURIA

KOREA

JAPAN

CHINA

Pacific Ocean

Iwo Jima

Okinawa

HAWAIIAN ISLANDS

FORMOSA

MARIANA ISLANDS

Pearl Harbor

Saipan

Luzon

GUAM

PHILIPPINES

Mindanao

SARAWAK

MARSHALL ISLANDS

BORNEO

GILBERT ISLANDS

NAVY

"A German sub could have taken us with a pocket knife."

— *Paul "Bear" Bryant*

Opposite: U.S. warships head into battle in this Pacific Theater convoy during World War II. (National Archives photograph)

W.C. BATY

'He didn't enjoy talking about the battles'

Dr. W. C. Baty Jr. saw the worst of World War II as a battlefield surgeon during three major Marine invasions in the Pacific, and the experience was something he never liked to remember or talk about.

Baty was a Navy commander serving as division surgeon with the Fourth Marine Division during bitterly opposed amphibious assault landings at Kwajalein, Saipan and Tinian during 1944-45. His division suffered more than 17,000 total casualties during those battles, and Baty was responsible for the care and treatment of those casualties.

Baty served aboard the battleships *USS Arkansas* and *USS New Mexico* and destroyers *USS Gilmer* and *USS Berry* during Pacific assault landings.

"He didn't enjoy talking about the battles," said Baty's son Bill (William C. Baty III). "He was reluctant to even answer our questions if we asked."

Bill Baty's very first memory is of December 7, 1941, the day the Japanese

attacked U.S. ships at Pearl Harbor, Hawaii, killing approximately 2,400 Americans and destroying a number of U.S. ships and planes. He was five years old at the time.

"We (Dr. Baty, his wife Sylvia and their three small children) were living in a tent on the island of Samoa at the time," said Bill Baty. "My very first memory is of that day because my father left immediately for another assignment and we were left on the island for several months." Mrs. Baty and the children, ages one, five and seven, finally returned to the states on a troop ship with armed Navy escort as American families were evacuated from Pacific bases in the wake of advancing Japanese forces.

"We had to hide in the jungle many times on Samoa when air raid sirens went off," said Bill Baty. "And on the ship coming home we had drills every day where we had to put on life vests and go to assigned lifeboat stations. There was always a fear of Japanese

Top: Baty (left) in the Pacific. Below: In his jeep "Sylvia."

submarines."

After arriving in San Francisco, the Baty family made its way to Bessemer to visit with Dr. Baty's family for several months before joining Mrs. Baty's family in Puerto Rico for the duration of the war. They did not see Dr. Baty again for almost three years.

Baty had as many as 100 doctors and 1,000 corpsmen under his command in the Pacific, and his job was to prepare them for the missions ahead as they headed into battle. "He taught battlefield surgery to medics, set up hospitals and treated the wounded," said Baty's daughter Janelle Avery of Tuscaloosa. "He was also responsible for the burial of thousands of Japanese soldiers killed in the battles." Baty was also known for being in the thick of the action, even picking up wounded soldiers and transporting them to aid stations in his jeep, named "Sylvia" for his wife, according to Mrs. Avery.

Baty spent more than 30 years in the Navy, serving aboard several ships, as Chief of Staff at the Quantico, Virginia, Naval Hospital and on the staff of the San Diego

Naval Base Hospital among many other assignments. He retired as a Rear Admiral in 1959 after receiving the Bronze Star with combat V, Legion of Merit with combat V, Asiatic-Pacific Campaign Medal with three stars, Presidential Unit Citation with one star, American Campaign Medal, American Defense Service Medal and National Defense Service Medal. Ten of his 30 years were spent on foreign soil or at sea. Although Baty was in the Navy, he considered himself a Marine because he was assigned to the Marines for 20 of his 30 years in service. "He even asked to be buried in his Marine Corps uniform," Bill Baty said.

A native of Bessemer, Baty moved to Tuscaloosa after his military retirement and served as the University of Alabama football team physician 1959-71, rarely missing a football game or practice. He also served on the staff of the UA Student Health Center for more than two years and as the Tuscaloosa County Health Officer for ten years before health problems forced him to retire.

Baty played football at Alabama 1920-23 and was called the best defensive back in the South in numerous newspaper stories during his senior season. Baty was "feared for his unerring and merciless tackling," according to the 1922 Corolla. "The gamest, scrappiest, pluckiest little half that ever wore a Crimson jersey," said the 1923 Corolla of the

Baty had as many as 100 doctors and 1,000 corpsmen under his command in the Pacific, and his job was to prepare them for the missions ahead as they headed into battle.

160-pound Baty. Birmingham sports writer Zipp Newman once called Baty "the toughest player for size I ever knew." As a freshman with the Crimson Tide, Baty played against his older brother Jim when Alabama defeated Birmingham Southern 45-0 in 1920.

Baty was a member of the 1922 Alabama team that upset the University of Pennsylvania 9-7 before 25,000 fans in Philadelphia to gain the Crimson Tide its first national attention. He played his first three seasons under Xen Scott and his final year under Wallace Wade. Alabama was 28-10-4

during Baty's four years on the team.

While a student at Alabama, Baty was a member of Black Friars, Jasons, Arch and Phi Gamma Delta fraternity. He also served as vice president of the student body. The same adventurous spirit that led him to a Navy career also led him to summer employment in the wheat fields of Kansas and Oklahoma during his college years. "He and Clarence (Turkey) Johnston hitched rides on freight trains together and slept in hay barns during the summers," Mrs. Avery said. "They did it to earn money for college, and I think for the adventure of it, too."

Baty earned himself a room-and-board scholarship to Alabama by being selected All-State fullback twice at Bessemer High School, where he was captain of the unbeaten 1919 team. He graduated from the university in 1924 and entered Harvard Medical School, where he also played professional football on weekends to earn money for college expenses.

"He played football under an alias (George Copeland) while he was in medical school at Harvard," Mrs. Avery said. "He used his middle name (Copeland) and the name they called the cadaver (George) they used in medical school to make up his alias." Baty played for the Providence Steam Roller in the National Football League and made the newspapers from time to time with his play.

Baty transferred to George Washington University after two years at Harvard and played more college football there under another alias until being exposed. He made newspaper headlines in his first game with George Washington in 1927 as a "mystery man" addition to the squad.

Baty earned his medical degree from George Washington in 1929 and went directly into the Navy, where he remained until 1959.

"He loved football," Mrs. Avery said of her father. "He never missed an Alabama game after he retired, and he saw as many as he could when he was in the Navy." "I guess I never had as much fun doing anything as I had playing football," Baty once said. "I just really enjoyed it."

Recurring problems from illnesses contracted in the Pacific bothered Baty in his later years, and he died in 1977.

Top: Baty at retirement.

Above: Baty in a bunker in the Pacific.

Left: A medic treats a wounded
GI in the field.

Young **BOOZER**

'He was always moving forward'

Young Boozer was a rare individual, gifted and successful in every endeavor undertaken, including athletics, business and civic activities. His list of achievements would fill a volume, and perhaps should.

Boozer gained notoriety at the University of Alabama as much as an outstanding student as he did as an outstanding athlete, and his siblings did the same. "They made some waves at the university as students and athletes," Young J. Boozer III said of his father and his father's younger siblings Wilmer, Rebecca and Frances Boozer.

"He was always moving forward," Boozer said of his late father's philosophy for success. "He never looked back."

Boozer's "waves" on the football field included lettering at halfback 1934-36 as he played alongside such Crimson Tide legends as Don Hutson, Dixie Howell and Paul Bryant. Boozer roomed with Bryant, in fact, and they remained close friends for life. Boozer, known for his speed, once scored three touchdowns in one game. He intercepted a pass and knocked down another one in the Tide's 29-13 Rose Bowl win over Stanford to cap a 10-0 national championship season in 1934.

Boozer was among the regulars in 1935-36 and frequently reeled off exciting runs as he helped the Tide to 6-2-1 and

Boozer (left) served aboard the USS Monrovia (inset).

held islands. The ship, which earned seven battle stars during World War II, also returned battle casualties from the front to U.S. hospitals in the Pacific.

After discharge from the Navy as a lieutenant senior grade, Boozer served as deputy director then director of the U.S. Savings Bonds division of Alabama and served as general manager of Dixie Sporting Goods in Birmingham. He went on to serve in several high profile business positions, including president of Cotton States Life Insurance Company, senior vice president of Federated Guaranty Life Insurance Company, senior vice president of Alabama Farm Bureau Insurance Companies and secretary-treasurer and director of Southland Insurance Company.

Boozer was active in numerous organizations, including the Alabama Safety Council, National Kidney Foundation, State Cancer Society, Tombigbee Girl Scouts, Alabama Alliance of Business and Industry, Alabama Chapter of the Leukemia Society of America, Salvation Army, Alabama Heart Association, YMCA, United Fund and American Legion. He was also an active member and junior warden of Christ Episcopal Church in Tuscaloosa. He died in June 2000.

Boozer was inducted into the Alabama Sports Hall of Fame in 1993 and was selected for the 1961 Sports Illustrated Silver Anniversary All-America Award. In 1989 he received the UA National Alumni Association's Paul W. Bryant Athlete-Alumni Award, which is presented to a former Alabama athlete who has distinguished himself in personal and professional accomplishments, in character and in his contributions to society after leaving the University.

While Boozer served in the Pacific, his brother Wilmer, a 1941 UA graduate and lieutenant in the Army Air Forces, was killed in a plane crash in December 1944 while serving as a test pilot at Robins Field in Georgia. He had received an Army commission in the infantry through ROTC and transferred to the Army Air Forces.

8-0-1 records. He also played baseball for the Tide, using his speed to fill the centerfield spot and leading the conference in hitting two seasons, once with a .452 average. His play helped the Tide baseball team to two conference championships.

In the classroom, Boozer was an honor student, served as president of the Cotillion Club, president of the College of Commerce junior class and secretary-treasurer of the A Club. A member of Sigma Nu, he was also tapped into the honorary organizations of Omicron Delta Kappa and Jasons, received the Interfraternity Council Service Award as the student who had done the most for the student body and University in his four years, and was named one of only 29 "Outstanding Men" by the University. He graduated in 1936 and went into banking in his home town of Dothan.

Boozer joined the Navy in 1943 and served until June 1946, spending 28 months of his tour in the South Pacific. He served aboard the attack transport ship *USS Monrovia,* delivering men and equipment for troop assault landings at Tarawa, Kwajalein, Saipan, Guam, Luzon and other Japanese-

Boozer joined the Navy in 1943 and served until June 1946, spending 28 months of his tour in the South Pacific.

Paul *"Bear"* **BRYANT**

'Soldiers were praying, and I was leading 'em'

Paul "Bear" Bryant was on cloud nine on the morning of December 7, 1941, as he drove from Arkansas toward home in Nashville, Tennessee, where he was an assistant football coach at Vanderbilt University.

Bryant was itching to become a head coach after four years as an assistant under Frank Thomas at Alabama and two seasons under Red Sanders at Vanderbilt. He felt certain that he had just landed the head coaching job at the University of Arkansas after a meeting with Arkansas Governor Homer Adkins.

"I was 28 years old and couldn't have been more filled with myself," Bryant wrote in his autobiography *Bear* of his feeling on that December Sunday. But as he arrived in Nashville he heard the shocking news that Japanese warplanes had bombed the U.S. Pacific Fleet headquarters at Pearl Harbor, Hawaii, killing more than 2,300 servicemen and sinking or damaging 18 ships.

Bryant's hopes of returning to Arkansas, where

Bryant enlisting in the Navy , 1942.

he had grown up on a family farm, quickly vanished, just as the dreams of millions of other Americans did that day as the U.S. was suddenly thrust into World War II.

The U.S. declared war on Japan the following day and within a few months American forces were fighting against Japan throughout the Pacific and against Germany in North Africa and Europe. The war did not end until late summer 1945 following two devastating U.S. atomic bomb

attacks on Japan.

Bryant, who had played football at the University of Alabama 1932-35, was anxious to join the fight from the first day, and especially so after hearing a speech by former Navy football coach Tom Hamilton a few weeks later at a meeting of the American Coaches Association in Detroit. Hamilton told the coaches that they would soon be needed by the Navy to teach physical fitness and athletic skills to combat pilots in order to improve their judgment, reaction time, agility, etc., as well as teach swimming and other sports which could be helpful to the pilots.

"I took the train back to Washington and went to work the next day and who should be there but Bear Bryant," Hamilton later wrote. "I heard your talk and I'm ready to go to war," Bryant was quoted by Hamilton as saying. Hamilton urged Bryant to return to Nashville, saying that the program had not yet started and that he would make sure Bryant was among the first selected.

Two weeks later, Bryant showed up at Hamilton's desk again, anxious to get started. "I haven't heard from you," Bryant reportedly said. "I have left home. I'm not going back. I can't go back now; I've told all my friends that I've gone off to war," Bryant added. "So he lived in our home for about three weeks and we put him to work answering the phone and working as a civilian until we could finally process him and get him in the Navy," Hamilton wrote of Bryant.

Bryant officially entered the Navy in early 1942 and was sent to the Naval Academy at Annapolis, Maryland, for training before being commissioned a lieutenant junior grade. He was selected for duty as a physical fitness instructor, like scores of other coaches at the time, including several of his former teammates and fellow coaches at Alabama.

Bryant was assigned to the coaching staff at the Georgia Navy Pre-Flight School in 1942 and finished his Navy career as head coach of the North Carolina Navy Pre-Flight football team in 1945. He also spent 14 months in North Africa (1943-44), serving as a physical fitness instructor and overseeing aircraft maintenance. "He (Bryant) knew how to get the very best effort from his men while still keeping their admiration and respect," wrote retired Rear Admiral M. H. Tuttle, who was Bryant's commanding officer in Africa, in a later statement.

Although Bryant was never involved in actual combat during the war, he was involved in what could have been a major disaster at sea while sailing from New York to North Africa in early 1943 aboard the *USAT Uruguay,* a former cruise ship which had been converted to a troop transport ship.

"I was sick before we got out of the harbor," Bryant wrote in *Bear.* "But I was alert enough to get friendly with an officer, and he gave me permission to stay topside with him. I dreaded going down into that hold to sleep. The smell of people sick was bad enough, but I knew a submarine would get us and I'd be the first one in that cold water. I made up my mind if I was going in I wanted to be high so I could be the last," he wrote.

Several days out—on February 12—the *Uruguay,* packed with 5,000 servicemen, was rammed by another ship. The collision tore a 70-foot hole in the *Uruguay,* killing 13 men and injuring 50 more. "I was playing poker at the time and I grabbed my canteen and my machine gun and ran topside," Bryant wrote of the incident. "I got as far up from the water as I could. There were soldiers all around me praying, and I was leading 'em."

Only heroic action by the crew kept the ship from sinking, and after a few days it was able to return to Bermuda for repairs before proceeding to North Africa. "We lay dead in the water about three days," Bryant wrote. "A German sub could have taken us with a pocket knife." Bryant, still anxious to get close to the action, hitched a ride on another ship from Bermuda to North Africa, according to his autobiography. "I kept telling them I was available and they ignored me," he wrote. "Eventually they put me on a tanker for Africa, one that was loaded with ammunition, the last thing I wanted on.

"I never did fight anybody," Bryant added. "I was really no more than an errand boy for the next year and a half, helping look after the navy planes on patrol."

When he returned from North Africa, Bryant was assigned to the North Carolina Navy Pre-Flight program at Chapel Hill as head football coach in the summer of 1944. The assignment became a stepping stone to his first head coaching job. Bryant used his connections with his former commanding officer (Rear Admiral Tuttle) to get incoming Navy flight trainees with football backgrounds assigned to North Carolina. Bryant later used many of these same players as the core of his team when he became head coach at the University of Maryland in the fall of 1945.

Maryland had won only one game in 1944, but Bryant's hand-picked squad went 6-2-1 in 1945 and put him in the national spotlight at age 32. School president H. C. Byrd

Bryant (above left) as an Alabama football end.
U.S. ships burn at Pearl Harbor (below left).

threw a banquet for the team in the spring and announced that Bryant had a lifetime contract. But Bryant resigned in anger and took the head coaching job at Kentucky a month later after Byrd, himself a former Maryland head coach, fired one of Bryant's assistants and reinstated a player Bryant had kicked off the team while Bryant was out of town.

Bryant spent the next eight seasons at Kentucky, posting a 60-23-5 overall record and winning three out of four bowl games. The 1946 Kentucky team went 7-3, becoming the first Wildcat team to win seven games since 1912, and Bryant was rewarded with a pay raise and a long-term contract. The 1947 Kentucky press guide spoke of him in glowing terms, calling him "a tireless worker, patient teacher and in a class by himself as a recruiter. Paul Bryant is home folks, destined to become one of the greatest coaches of football," the article,

Bryant and teammates heading to the Rose Bowl.

Texas A&M—and he took it.

Bryant wasted no time impressing the thousands of cadets who greeted him on his arrival at the all-male school in College Station, Texas. As he walked to the microphone to address the students and Aggie supporters for the first time, Bryant took off his coat and tie, threw them to the ground and stomped on them. Then he rolled up his sleeves and told the crowd he was ready to go to work. "Those Aggies went crazy," Bryant wrote in *Bear.* But that was only the start. Bryant's reputation soon soared, for better or worse, when he trimmed the returning Aggie football squad of 115 to 27 players during a rugged pre-season training camp held in the boiling desert heat at Junction.

With only a handful of players returning, Texas A&M posted a 1-9 record in 1954, producing the only losing season for Bryant in his 38 years as a head coach. The Aggies then went 7-2-1 in 1955 and 9-0-1 in 1956 as conference champions and Bryant was chosen Southwest Conference Coach of the Year in 1956.

Texas A&M went 8-0 and was ranked No. 1 in the nation to start the 1957 season, but when word leaked out that Bryant planned to leave A&M to become head coach at Alabama after the season, the disappointed Aggies lost three straight games (7-6 to Rice, 9-7 to Texas and 3-0 to Tennessee in the Gator Bowl) to finish 8-3. The Aggies were 24-5-2 during Bryant's last three seasons, and halfback John David Crow won the Heisman Trophy as a 60-minute player in 1957 to become Bryant's only Heisman Trophy winner.

Crow gained just over 500 yards rushing, but he was also outstanding as a pass receiver, punt returner and defensive back. Bryant, noted for rare high praise for individual players, endorsed Crow for the Heisman by saying that he had "led the league in running over people" and said that if Crow didn't win it "they ought to stop giving it."

Bryant was furious with Alabama insiders who failed to keep his return to his alma mater secret, saying it had cost his Texas A&M team a national championship, and Aggie supporters were unhappy that Bryant was leaving. What should have been a triumphant return to Tuscaloosa

written by long-time *Birmingham News* sports writer Zipp Newman, prophetically concluded.

Bryant led the Wildcats to their first and only Southeastern Conference championship in 1950 with an 11-1 record. He was named SEC Coach of the Year and Kentucky's Citizen of the Year for his 1950 coaching feat.

But Bryant grew restless after playing second fiddle to legendary Kentucky basketball coach Adolph Rupp for eight seasons and finally asked the Kentucky governor to help him get out of his contract as head football coach in February 1954. At the time he left Kentucky, he had only one job offer—

Paul "Bear" Bryant (seated center) signs a contract as University of Alabama head football coach in December 1957 while Ernest G. Williams, Fred Sington, Paul W. Bryant Jr. (rear) and Mary Harmon Bryant look on.

had turned bittersweet for Bryant by the time he arrived in Tuscaloosa in late December, but he did return.

Bryant had gained the reputation for rebuilding football programs at his first three coaching stops, and no program needed rebuilding more than that of Alabama. The Crimson Tide had gone 4-24-2 in three seasons under J. B. "Ears" Whitworth, including a 40-0 loss to Auburn in its closing game of the 1957 season.

Bryant held rugged practices during the spring of 1958 at Alabama just as he had on his arrival at Texas A&M, and many players left Alabama just as they had at Texas A&M. The remaining players performed beyond expectations in

the fall, however, going 5-4-1 with their worst loss by only 10 points (13-3) to LSU. The Tide was on its way back, with 7-2-2 and 8-1-2 records the next two seasons proving the point.

Bryant had promised his incoming freshmen in 1958 that they could win a national championship in 1961 if they did all he asked, and they delivered with an 11-0 national championship season, the first of six for Bryant during his 25 years at Alabama. The Tide also won national titles in 1964, 1965, 1973, 1978 and 1979 under Bryant. Bryant teams won 13 conference championships during his tenure at Alabama, and his teams lost only five conference games during his last 12 years as head coach. Three of those SEC losses came in his final season of 1982, when the Tide went 8-4.

Bryant had a record of 232-46-9 in 25 seasons at Alabama and an overall record of 323-85-17. He had won more games than any other Division I coach at the time he retired. He had also won more national championships (six) than any other coach, carried his teams to more consecutive bowl games (24), won more conference championships (15) and been named national coach of the year more times (three) than any other coach. He was named SEC coach of the year 10 times and SEC Coach of the Century.

Bryant's teams averaged 8.5 wins per season over his 38-year coaching career. His Alabama teams averaged 9.3 wins per season over his 25 years and his teams averaged 10.3 wins per season over the final 12 seasons. Bryant's teams were the first to win 100 games in a decade (103-16-1) during the 1970s. His Alabama teams were 25-0 in homecoming games and 72-2 in Bryant-Denny Stadium, including an NCAA record 57 straight wins from October 26, 1963, until November 13, 1982.

Bryant was an inaugural inductee into the Alabama Sports Hall of Fame in 1969 and was inducted into the Arkansas Hall of Fame in 1964. He was named to the Sports Illustrated Silver Anniversary All-America team in 1960 and inducted into the National Football Foundation College Football Hall of Fame in 1986. He received the Stagg Award from the American Football Coaches Association in 1983 in recognition of his outstanding service to the advancement of football and was presented the Presidential Medal of Freedom in 1983.

Bryant retired after the 1982 football season, ending his career with an emotional 21-15 win over Illinois in the Liberty Bowl. He died unexpectedly just over a month later—January 26, 1983—following a heart attack at age 69. His death stunned football fans throughout the state and nation, and thousands of people lined the streets and highways to view his funeral procession as it moved slowly down what is now Paul W. Bryant Drive past Bryant-Denny Stadium and made its way from Tuscaloosa to Birmingham. "We love you Bear" banners stretched across highway overpasses; interstate traffic came to a standstill; many people along the streets and

roadways wept openly and others stood in dazed silence as his hearse passed.

Bryant had returned Alabama football to national prominence and kept it there for 25 seasons. Alabama's record for the 25-year period was the best in the nation, and not only had his teams won an amazing six national championships, they had been in the final running for just as many more. He taught his teams to expect to win, and they almost always did. Bryant led Alabama football back to national prominence and in doing so gave the team, school, state and South a source of pride during the racially troubled 1960s.

Bryant came from humble beginnings in rural Arkansas, growing up on a farm near Fordyce, where he played football

Bryant remains a legendary symbol in University of Alabama football lore and the school football stadium bears his name along with that of Dr. George Denny, who was president of the university when the stadium was built in 1929.

for the Fordyce High School Redbugs. He earned All-State honors at tackle while playing on unbeaten teams in 1929 and 1930 and once wrestled a carnival bear to earn his nickname. Bryant was recruited to play football at Alabama by a Pine Bluff pool hall operator named Jim Harland. Alabama assistant coach Hank Crisp went to Arkansas to sign Bryant and a Fordyce teammate in the summer of 1931.

Bryant once talked of leaving Alabama in his early days as a player—quitting something for the first time in his life—until he heard from Collins Kilgore, a cousin in Fordyce, who sent Bryant a telegram saying "Go ahead and quit just like everybody predicted you would." "I wasn't about to quit after that," Bryant said in telling the story many times through the years.

Bryant played end at Alabama, lettering 1933-34-35. He often called himself "the other end" because he played opposite All-America end Don Hutson from Pine Bluff. Alabama went 7-1-1, 10-0 and 6-2-1 during Bryant's playing years, winning two SEC titles and the national championship in 1934 with a 29-13 win over Stanford in the Rose Bowl. Bryant gained fame as a player in 1935 by playing one of his best games ever with a broken leg against Tennessee as the Tide upset the Volunteers 25-0. He served as president of the

Bryant (right) with Navy pal.

A Club in 1936.

Bryant married campus beauty Mary Harmon Black while in college at Alabama and joined the Crimson Tide coaching staff in the summer of 1936 after spending the spring as a coach at Union College in Jackson, Tennessee. Alabama went 29-5-3 during the four years (1936-39) Bryant was an assistant coach. He was an assistant at Vanderbilt 1940-41 before entering the Navy for World War II.

Bryant remains a legendary symbol in University of Alabama football lore and the school football stadium bears his name along with that of Dr. George Denny, who was president of the university when the stadium was built in 1929.

A larger-than-life statue of Bryant stands near the Walk of Champions at the north entrance to Bryant-Denny Stadium today along with statues of other football coaches who have led University of Alabama teams to national championships. The Paul W. Bryant Museum on Paul W. Bryant Drive near the UA athletic complex pays tribute to Crimson Tide football history through the years and Bryant shared in much of that history as player, assistant coach and head coach.

As a player and coach, Bryant became known as a winner, the label he enjoyed most, and his ever-present name and statue on the University of Alabama campus are constant reminders of his winning standards.

Bryant left a lasting legacy for his former players by establishing a scholarship fund for their children and hundreds have benefited from it through the years.

Paul W. Bryant Jr., a University of Alabama graduate and prominent Tuscaloosa businessman, currently serves on the University System Board of Trustees and as chairman of the Crimson Tide Foundation.

Bill CADENHEAD

'I knew if we got hit I'd probably die'

You can find Bill Cadenhead's footprints in the sidewalk at Denny Chimes as the University of Alabama's most valuable football player in 1948 and one of the Tide's captains in 1949, but he went halfway around the world before putting them there.

He came to the University of Alabama as a freshman twice before playing in a game, and in between spent 36 months in the Navy during World War II.

Cadenhead first came to Alabama as a freshman football signee from Greenville, Mississippi, in December 1942, only to find most of his teammates and other athletes moving out of the athletic dormitory as he was moving in. They were all on their way to military service, so Cadenhead returned home to Mississippi to join the Navy himself.

"I wanted to get in on the war," he said. "But I don't want to sound too patriotic. I would have chosen football over the Navy, but it looked like we'd have no football team in 1943 anyway," he added. More than 90 percent of Alabama's 1942 varsity squad actually went into military service in the first few months of 1943 and the school, like many others, was

Captains Cadenhead (left), Doug Lockridge (1949)

unable to field a football team in 1943 due to the lack of players.

"I didn't think the war would last long," Cadenhead said. "I figured we could sink that little island of Japan in a few weeks." Cadenhead was rejected on his first try at enlistment because he had the measles, but he made it on his second try and was sent to San Diego, California, for training. His football talents were soon spotted there and he ended up playing football in 1943 after all as a member of the base team.

"We had a good year," Cadenhead said. "We beat Southern Cal and UCLA and had a 7-2 record." Both losses were to the March Field Army team which featured former Crimson Tide star halfback Jimmy Nelson. Cadenhead played tailback and made the All-Coast team with an average of eight yards per carry and eight touchdowns. "We had four All-America linemen, so the backs had a pretty easy time of it," he said.

"Right after the football season ended I volunteered for submarine duty," he said. "I chose submarine duty because I didn't want to get maimed or injured for life. I knew if we got hit I'd probably die. To me it was all or nothing."

After submarine training, Cadenhead was assigned to

the *USS Croaker* for duty in the Pacific theater over the next 16 months. The *Croaker* put to sea in July 1944 and earned a Navy Unit Citation for sinking a Japanese cruiser on August 7. It sank five Japanese freighters and damaged another before returning to port in Australia. The *Croaker* also patrolled waters in the Sea of Japan and the Luzon Straits. Cadenhead also served aboard the *USS Tuna* near the Philippines then served aboard the *USS Cobbler* off New England before his discharge as a seaman first class in March 1946.

"On one occasion we could feel the depth charges exploding, but they didn't know where we were, so we weren't too concerned," Cadenhead said of his combat experiences. "And a few times we saw planes and had to dive."

"I enjoyed my time in service," Cadenhead said. "I got to see a lot of places I wouldn't have seen otherwise, like Australia, the Panama Canal, Hawaii, San Francisco, San Diego, Subic Bay, Connecticut and a few other places."

Cadenhead returned to the University of Alabama in the summer of 1946 and played on the varsity football team as a freshman that fall, even though the squad was loaded with returnees from the unbeaten (10-0) 1945 team that defeated Southern Cal 34-14 in the Rose Bowl. He caught the attention of Tide coaches early with "his never-say-die running, speed and piston-like knees" and even started the 1946 season opener against Furman.

"I was lucky," Cadenhead said modestly of his playing time at right halfback in 1946. "Most of the returning servicemen didn't get half a chance. I played a lot because Lowell Tew got hurt and I had four years left. I got more of a chance than most of them (returning war veterans)," he added. Cadenhead, at 5-11, 180 with 10-flat speed in the 100, played regularly on both offense and defense his first three seasons. Although a knee injury slowed him as a senior in 1949, he started every game and played full time on defense.

Cadenhead lettered all four seasons and regularly drew media praise for his "fine defensive work" and "power running." He earned the nickname "Lightning" with

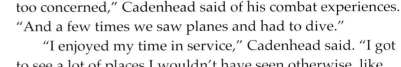

his speed. He gained 168 yards on 54 runs as a freshman. He added 282 yards on 76 carries and caught 11 passes for 129 yards as a sophomore. He gained 275 yards on 65 plays as a junior, averaging 4.3 yards per carry. He also intercepted several passes, including one from Kentucky quarterback George Blanda in 1947 and another from Mississippi State's Shorty McWilliams. He led Alabama's 10-0 win over Tennessee in 1947 by scoring the only touchdown on a Statue of Liberty play and making a diving tackle to stop a would-be UT touchdown.

Cadenhead recalled many of his experiences in the Alabama athletic dorm, especially those including tackle Charlie Compton. "He was something else," he said of Compton. "He would shoot his 22 rifle down the hall to get our attention if we got too loud," Cadenhead laughed. "It was nice to get married and move out of the dorm."

Although there were numerous war veterans on the 1946-48 Tide football teams, Cadenhead said they never talked about their war experiences. "We wanted to put it all behind us," he said. "Football was my main concern, at least until I met Rachel (his wife for more than 61 years)."

Cadenhead passed up an offer of $3,600 a season to play professional football with the Detroit Lions after his senior season in 1949, choosing instead to take the head coaching position at Coffee High of Florence in the fall of 1950 at the same pay. Rachel took a teaching job at Coffee Junior High for $1,800 a year at the same time. Cadenhead coached at Coffee for five seasons before going into the insurance business, where he remained until retirement at age 72.

Cadenhead was still an active man of many talents at age 85. He was still attending Alabama football games in addition to being an avid gardener and producing beautiful needlepoint and embroidery work. He took up stitching while in college at Alabama when Rachel began embroidering dish towels, pillow cases, etc. prior to their wedding.

"I got into it because we couldn't afford to do anything else," Cadenhead said. "We had no money and no car." He did have to do a little explaining to roommate Bob Hood and best friend Monk Mosley in the athletic dorm, however. "I told them the sewing was therapy for the stress of submarine duty," Cadenhead laughed. "They would just pat me on the head after that and leave me alone."

Cadenhead met Rachel in an unusual way soon after his return to the University of Alabama in 1946. "Shorty Erwin

USS Croaker

and I were hitchhiking in front of the Supe Store, trying to get a ride downtown to a movie, when a girl named Martha Sue Fletcher and Rachel stopped to give us a ride," Cadenhead said. "Martha Sue and Shorty knew each other, so we all went to see 'The Postman Always Rings Twice' together. Rachel and I were married two years later on June 5, 1948," he added with a proud smile. Rachel joined the players' wives and girlfriends on a train trip to the January 1, 1948, Sugar Bowl game, and both recalled the trip with happiness, despite the outcome of the game (27-7 loss to Texas). "I guess ours was a storybook romance if you can have one on a limited budget," Cadenhead said.

Rachel dropped out of college to work for a year and save money for their wedding "and to buy a little car," but returned to earn her teaching degree. Billy earned his master's degree in 1950.

Cadenhead's entire family—father, mother, two brothers and Bill—all took part in the war effort. His older brother John, who attended Alabama on a football scholarship as a freshman end in 1939, was a pilot in the European theater and survived to fly again after being shot down over France. His brother Bobby, who played center at Mississippi State, was a pilot in North Africa and Italy and remained in the military until retirement. His father worked as a boilermaker repairing ships in Hawaii during the war and his mother worked at the Greenville, Mississippi, Air Force Base.

Rachel's brother Hugh Patillo graduated from the U.S. Military Academy and served in Korea and Vietnam. He also served as an ROTC instructor at Alabama before his retirement. Her brother Ralph attended the University of Alabama two years before joining the Air Force. His plane was shot down over Vietnam and he was later declared killed in action.

John "Mac" FORNEY

His job was saving lives in the bloody Pacific

John "Mac" Forney, a center on the 1920 University of Alabama football team, saw the human pain and suffering of World War II first-hand as a Navy surgeon with the Seventh Amphibious Forces in the Pacific theater of operations.

Forney was a Tuscaloosa physician and surgeon before the war, treating patients from his office in what is now the University Club on University Boulevard while living just a few blocks away at No. 2 Pinehurst.

His full name was John McLaughlin Forney Sr., and he earned the rank of commander while serving in several front-line positions during the war, including chief of surgery on the hospital ship *USS Bountiful*, chief surgeon during bloody assault landings on half-a-dozen Pacific islands and chief medical officer at several Navy bases.

His son, John M. Forney Jr., graduated from Tuscaloosa High School in the mid-1940s and enlisted in the Navy. He served as a seaman first class in occupied Japan for six months before returning to the University of Alabama to earn

a degree. He later served on the radio broadcast team for Alabama football for 30 years (1954-1984) and is remembered as a fan favorite during the Paul "Bear" Bryant coaching era.

Forney spent three years in the Pacific treating the wounded from some of the most intense fighting in history, including the invasions of Leyte, Mindoro, Lingayen and Corregidor. Medical teams from the *USS Bountiful* treated casualties from battles in the Philippines, Ulithi, Iwo Jima and Okinawa, the latter two being the most costly in terms of American lives in the war with 6,821 Marines killed on Iwo Jima and 12,000 GIs killed on Okinawa. More than 57,000 more American soldiers were wounded in the two battles.

The *USS Bountiful* also received more than 264 injured Navy personnel from the aircraft carrier *USS Bunker Hill*, which had another 372 killed during a Japanese kamikaze attack in May, 1945. Hospital ships followed closely behind Army and Marine units as they fought their way across the Pacific, taking island after island for airstrips from which to launch

The USS Bountiful *(foreground) off the island of Iwo Jima.*

bombing raids on other islands on the way to Japan.

Forney received the Bronze Star for exceptional service and was credited with not only saving many lives but also with "making possible the transportation of casualties over greater distances than had been attempted before." Dr. Forney also received five unit citations with the Navy "V," the Navy and Marine Corps Medal for treating wounded under fire and the Navy Commendation Medal.

Forney graduated from the University in 1922 and attended Rush Medical School in Chicago. He later married Kathleen Foster of Tuscaloosa, whose brother Richard served as president of the University of Alabama 1937-41. Forney's father, Jacob Forney, was an educator who once taught at Jacksonville State Teachers College and later served as the first professor of education at the University of Alabama.

Forney's grandfather was Major General John Horace Forney, a graduate of the U. S. Military Academy who resigned as an instructor at West Point in 1861 to join the Confederate Army. He served in battles in northern Virginia and First Manassas and was wounded at Dranesville, Virginia. He later served as a division commander at Vicksburg, where he was captured in the surrender of that city and where his statue stands today.

Following his service in World War II, Dr. Forney moved his practice to Birmingham for several years, then to New York City. He is survived by seven grandchildren, including John M. Forney III of Birmingham.

Herb **HANNAH**

'If you're going to do something, do your best'

Herb Hannah must have had that special "something" football coaches look for in athletes, considering the many obstacles he overcame on his way to success in life.

The son of a Limestone County, Alabama, sharecropper, Hannah was a 20-year-old high school senior when the Japanese bombed Pearl Harbor on December 7, 1941, to bring the United States into what was already a world-wide war.

And as horrible as the war was, it likely helped Hannah and thousands like him escape the poverty of their youth. It certainly hastened his exit from high school and eventually led him to the University of Alabama, where he, his younger brother and three sons all played football.

Hannah immediately tried to join the Marines when the news of Pearl Harbor broke, but was rejected because he had no high school diploma.

Although he was president of the Beta Club, it didn't look like Hannah was going to graduate because he had too many absences due to working on the farm. Determined to get into the fight, he talked his teachers into that diploma in May of 1942 and went back to join the Marines. "There was a long line at the Marines desk and a short line for the Navy, so he took the short line and joined the Navy," his son David said in recalling some of his father's "war stories."

By the fall of 1942, Hannah was a seaman refueling

ships on a dock at the Panama Canal in South America. "He tried to get transferred to a ship going through the canal once, but didn't get his transfer in time. That ship was later torpedoed and all the men lost," David said.

Hannah's work ethic was quickly spotted by an officer who suggested he apply for officer candidate school. He passed the test and was soon assigned to the Navy's Pre-Flight training program in Athens, GA, where his life took a dramatic turn. Not only did he earn his commission and wings in Athens, he also met his future wife, Geneva "Coupe" Watkins, who was teaching secretarial science at Georgia. Hannah also played football for the Georgia Pre-Flight team, although he had played only one year of six-man football in high school. One of his coaches at Georgia was Hank Crisp, the long-time Alabama assistant, and Crisp took note of Hannah's size and football ability. "Coach Crisp told Dad that if he made it through the war to look him up," Hannah's son John said.

The war took top priority, however, and Hannah became a TBM (Torpedo Bomber) pilot assigned to the South Atlantic, Caribbean and Gulf Coast regions, flying from coastal bases and the aircraft carriers *USS Kearsarge, USS Ranger* and *USS Franklin D. Roosevelt* in search of German submarines for the remainder of the war and well afterward. "I think he only chased one submarine the whole time," David said.

That didn't mean there had not been submarines to chase before lieutenant Hannah arrived on the scene, however. Official military records show that 92 Merchant Marine and warships were sunk and 882 lives lost in the Gulf of Mexico area from February 1942 through December 1943, with most

coming in 1942. The area included waters surrounding Florida, the Bahamas, half the island of Cuba and the entire Gulf of Mexico to the Yucatan peninsula.

More than 50 ships were sunk in the Gulf of Mexico during that period, and 25 more were sunk along the coast of Florida from Key West to Daytona Beach, according to Navy reports. The Navy estimated that from 10-20 German submarines operated in the Gulf area, sinking oil tankers, supply ships and warships departing these areas. There was similar enemy submarine activity off the northern U. S. coast as scores of other U. S. and British ships were lost. Several ships were even torpedoed within sight of East Coast cities such as New York and Boston. The German submarines were finally pushed back as the U.S. increased its manpower and military capability and went on the offensive.

Hannah was encouraged by Navy friends from South Carolina to play football at Clemson after his discharge in early 1947. Clemson coach Frank Howard showed little interest, however, and Hannah took Crisp's advice and came to the University of Alabama instead. He joined the team during the summer as a 26-year-old freshman, and soon earned a half scholarship to go with his GI Bill benefits.

"Herb was a big guy (the tallest and heaviest on the Tide roster at 6-3, 220) and he always looked like he wanted to hit somebody," said Clem Gryska, Hannah's teammate at Alabama 1947-48. "He was a tough player," Gryska added. "Downfield blocking is his forte and a thing of beauty to watch," Alabama's 1950 football media guide said of Hannah.

Hannah spent four seasons with the Crimson Tide, earning letters 1948-50, and went on to play a year of

Tide's Ed Holdnak, Herb Hannah, Floyd Miller, Bill Cadenhead, Red Noonan and Pat O'Sullivan (L-R) await action.

professional football with the New York Giants as the oldest NFL rookie ever at age 30 in 1951. Hannah didn't return to pro football in 1952, choosing instead to "get a real job," according to son Charley. He coached football at Cedartown and Canton, Georgia, for four years, but sought higher income for his growing family and went into agricultural products sales. He eventually founded Hannah Supply, a successful wholesale farm and animal supply business which

he operated for many years before his retirement. He died in May of 2007 at age 85.

"He had a slogan, 'If you're going to do something, do your best'," Charley said of his father. "And he felt that you ought to give back, too. He said, 'If you're climbing a mountain, you should always reach down and pull others up with you'." And Hannah did just that by helping and encouraging family members in many ways, according to Charley.

"He was a special guy in a lot of ways," said Charley. "He was the middle child in a family of nine children, and it takes someone with special determination to lead a family out of the poor circumstances they had seen. He expected you to take on your part, but he always tried to provide opportunities and encouragement. He believed in giving someone a fighting chance, but he expected that extra effort from you, too," Charley added.

Bill, the youngest son in the Hannah family, followed in brother Herb's footsteps by playing football at Alabama, too. He was a freshman in 1952 under Drew, but joined the Marines for a tour before returning to Alabama to play under Coach J. B. "Ears" Whitworth in 1957 and under Coach Paul "Bear" Bryant in 1958 and 1959. Bill was an assistant football coach at Cal State Fullerton when he died in a plane crash on November 13, 1971, along with fellow assistants Joe O'Hara and Dallas Moon.

Herb's sons John, Charley and David followed him to Alabama, too, taking the Hannah tradition to new heights.

John, a 6-3, 260-pound offensive guard (1970-72), was All-Southeastern Conference in 1971 and 1972, All-America in 1972, and won the Jacobs Trophy in 1972 as the SEC's

Hannah (left) with fellow pilot.

best blocker. He was widely honored as the nation's offensive lineman of the year as a senior and has been elected to the Alabama Sports Hall of Fame, the College Football Hall of Fame, UA's Team of the Century, ESPN's All-Time College Football Team and the NFL Hall of Fame. He played professionally with the New England Patriots 1973-85 and is recognized as one of the all-time great NFL offensive linemen. John also earned three letters in track at Alabama while setting school records in the shot and discus events.

Charley, at 6-6, 250, lettered at defensive tackle for Alabama 1974–76. He played professionally with Tampa Bay 1977-82 and Los Angeles 1983-88 after his Alabama career, during which he earned the Billy Neighbors Most Improved Defensive Lineman Award twice and All-SEC honors in 1976.

David, 6-4, 220, was one of only three freshmen to letter in 1975, and he went on to earn All-SEC honors in 1979 as he helped Alabama win national championships in 1978 and 1979 as a defensive tackle. A knee injury slowed him as a senior and kept him out of professional football.

Herb Hannah's rise from poverty to military, college and professional success and the ensuing accomplishments of his family members offer an example of the classic American success story. The Allied victory in World War II preserved the American way of life that allowed such successes.

Bobby Tom JENKINS

War detoured All-America fullback to Navy

Although World War II caused Bobby Tom Jenkins to take a detour from the University of Alabama to the U. S. Naval Academy, it could not keep him from earning the All-America honors for which he seemed destined as a high school star. Robert Thomas was his given name, but Jenkins earned football stardom at Talladega High School as Bobby Tom by scoring 156 points, rushing for 1,450 yards and gaining 2,350 all-purpose yards as a senior in 1940. He was captain of the football team, a straight-A student and class valedictorian.

Bobby Tom Jenkins (16) on the run in January 1, 1943 Orange Bowl.

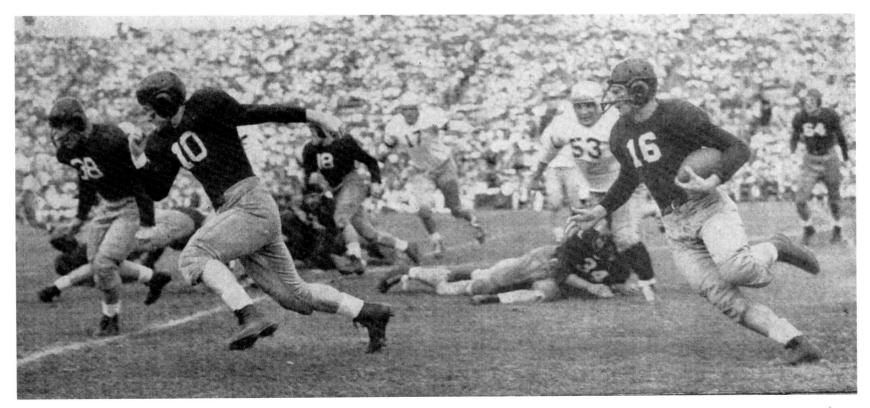

At 6-0, 182 pounds, he was a highly sought-after football recruit.

In signing Jenkins to a scholarship, Tide head coach Frank Thomas said, "I believe he is one of the finest high school prospects ever to enroll at the University."

Jenkins spent two years at Alabama and showed flashes of stardom from the start as he impressed coaches and sports writers with his speed, power and passing prowess. As a sophomore fullback playing behind Don Salls in 1941, Jenkins scored on a 38-yard run to help beat Tennessee 8-0 then capped the season by scoring two touchdowns in the Tide's 37-21 Orange Bowl win over Boston College.

Jenkins joined the Army Air Forces in the spring of 1943, however, when the draft age of 18 was in effect, and never played for Alabama again. He spent only six months in the military before receiving an appointment to the Naval Academy, where he joined the football team in the fall as a third-string halfback. He quickly moved up to first-team status after returning a punt for a 70-yard touchdown in the team's season opener and was a star for the next two seasons.

Jenkins led Navy to 9-1 and 8-2 records in 1943 and 1944, earning All-America honors in 1944 in a national backfield that included himself, Glenn Davis and Doc Blanchard of Army and Glenn Horvath of Ohio State. Jenkins was described by the press as "a human dynamo," "190 pounds of fluid force," "virtually unstoppable" and "the piston-legged personification of power" in press accounts of his play.

"Bob Jenkins is All-America far beyond the game of football," said Navy coach Oscar Hagberg at the time.

"He is the All-America boy, a great competitor, clean and hard hitting, a fine student and modest."

A knee injury kept Jenkins out of football in 1945. He graduated from the Academy in January 1946 and started a four-year-tour of Navy duty. He served two years on the destroyer *USS Soley* then helped with the mothballing of ships at Newport, Rhode Island, for the remainder of his tour while also coaching the Navy Prep football team.

Jenkins returned to his home state briefly in 1950 before being called to service again for the Korean War (1951-53). Following military duty, Jenkins operated a machine tool business in Birmingham for many years. He was active in the Birmingham Monday Morning Quarterback Club and served as its president in 1982. He was inducted into the Alabama Sports Hall of Fame in 1983.

Jenkins' former Alabama teammate Don Whitmire took a similar route to the Naval Academy after the 1942 season, and the two were roommates at Annapolis in 1944 and 1945. Whitmire, a native of Decatur who earned All-SEC and All-America honors at Alabama in 1942, earned All-America honors at tackle for Navy in 1945.

Two other members of Alabama's 1942 squad gave Georgia Tech a boost while playing for the Yellow Jackets under the Navy's V-12 program. End Phil Tinsley and lineman Bill Chambers both earned All-Southeastern Conference honors at Tech in 1943 and Tinsley earned All-America honors in 1944 while helping Tech win the SEC championship. Chambers lettered at UCLA 1946-47 after active Navy duty during the war.

Ben *McLEOD*

He helped win championships in three sports

Ben McLeod had plenty of memories of University of Alabama athletics, and with good reason. He had memories of championship seasons in football, basketball and baseball to recall.

McLeod came to Alabama on a basketball scholarship in the fall of 1932 after leading Geraldine High School to consecutive state championships in 1931 and 1932. While at Alabama 1932-35, he earned eight letters in three sports, even though he had never played baseball before college. He was a part of five Southeastern Conference championship teams and the unbeaten 1934 national championship football team that defeated Stanford 29-13 in the Rose Bowl on January 1, 1935.

McLeod received the UA National Alumni Association's Paul W. Bryant Alumni-Athlete Award in 2008 in recognition of his professional accomplishments and contributions to society since his graduation in 1937. He was also honored at the time as the oldest living A Club member. "I appreciate it, but I think they've overdone it a little," he said at the time.

One of McLeod's fondest memories was the trip to the Rose Bowl after the 1934 season when the Crimson Tide team featured such stars as Dixie Howell, Don Hutson, Bill Lee and Paul "Bear" Bryant. McLeod played end as a backup to Bryant, and said he only played a few minutes in the game, although the train ride and entire Rose Bowl experience before more than 80,000 fans left a lasting impression. "What I remember most about it is Dixie Howell running and Don Hutson catching passes," he said.

McLeod was one of the Tide's stalwarts on the basketball team during his career as he teamed with All-SEC stars Jim Whatley and Jimmy Walker to lead the squad's attack. "Mac is one of the best ball handlers on Southern courts," said the 1935 Corolla of McLeod. He played both infield and outfield in baseball and batted over .300. He was named UA's "Athlete of the Year" in 1935.

Following college, McLeod served as head football coach at T. R. Miller High School in Brewton for five seasons (1937-

41), posting a 23-3-2 mark his last three seasons. The 1941 team went 8-0 and allowed only seven points all season.

McLeod joined the Navy when the U.S. entered World War II and played football for the Pensacola Naval Air Station Goshawks football team during training, even playing against his alma mater in 1942 as the Crimson Tide beat the Goshawks 27-0.

McLeod served eight years active duty with the Navy, including time as a physical fitness instructor at Pensacola NAS and Great Lakes NAS and sea duty in the North Atlantic. McLeod also served as athletic director at Pensacola NAS one year. Following his discharge, McLeod remained in the Navy Reserve for 25 years while serving as recreation director at the base. He retired from the Navy Reserve in 1972 as a full commander.

McLeod's son Ben was a part of two national football championships at Alabama under Bryant (1964-65) and lettered at defensive end in 1965. He later coached for several years and now operates a charter fishing boat out of Pensacola.

McLeod played baseball, basketball and football at Alabama. He is No. 39 (front row) in the team photo.

Hugh Barr **MILLER** Jr

'I thought I would be dead by then, but I rallied'

Hugh Barr Miller's extraordinary World War II experience reads more like a movie or television miniseries script than real life, but it was real, and frighteningly real at that.

Miller miraculously escaped a series of life-threatening events while missing in action for 43 days in the South Pacific before returning home as one of the U.S. Navy's most decorated and honored heroes of the war.

Miller suffered internal injuries while helping rescue two shipmates during the sinking of the destroyer *USS Strong* in the Solomon Islands in July of 1943. He spent four days adrift in the Kula Gulf, watching many of the men with him die or drift away before reaching land.

He then spent 39 days on the Japanese-held island of Arundel—the last 32 of them injured, weak and alone—during which he was credited with killing as many as 15 enemy soldiers as he fought to stay alive in the hope of eventual rescue.

Miller earned the Navy Cross, the Navy's highest

decoration for heroism, for his efforts, which included gathering valuable intelligence information before his dramatic rescue on August 16.

Eleanor Roosevelt, wife of then-president Franklin Roosevelt, presented Miller with the Navy Cross and Purple Heart with cluster as he recuperated from his wounds in a Navy hospital. Miller's Navy Cross was one of only 2,889 awarded during World War II.

"My football training under Wade (Alabama football coach Wallace Wade) plus my experience since boyhood in the hunting and outdoor life of Alabama undoubtedly are responsible for the fact that I am alive today," Miller said after his rescue.

Navy Admiral William F. "Bull" Halsey awarded Miller the Navy Cross soon after his rescue and later requested that the award be changed to the Congressional Medal of Honor, citing numerous factors for the later recommendation.

"It is recommended that Lieutenant (now Commander) Hugh Barr Miller Jr. be awarded the Medal of Honor for conspicuous gallantry and intrepidity in combat with the enemy at the risk of his life, above and beyond the call of duty," Halsey wrote in his recommendation to the Secretary of the Navy on May 7, 1956.

Miller's son, Landon Miller of Tuscaloosa, said that Congress and President Dwight Eisenhower approved Halsey's recommendation for the Medal of Honor for Miller, but that the medal was never awarded for some unknown reason. Several newspaper accounts verify approval of the medal, but Miller died in 1978 without having received the medal.

A 1932 University of Alabama graduate and the smallest member of the 1930 Crimson Tide Rose Bowl football team at 5-7, 140 pounds, Miller repeatedly defied all odds during his survival after being seriously wounded during the sinking of the *Strong*. Miller served as stores and gunnery officer on the ship, which was sunk by a Japanese torpedo on the night of July 4, 1943, costing 46 U.S. servicemen their lives.

Miller, a 33-year-old lieutenant, was among the last men off the ship as he helped evacuate the ship and took time to cut two men free of tangled lines. Miller and the two men were seriously injured when the destroyer's depth charges exploded, breaking the ship in half and sucking them deep underwater. After surfacing, Miller and the two men were able to reach a floater net and clung to it throughout the night.

"Throughout the night we picked up other people, some injured and some not injured," Miller later wrote of the incident. "By daylight we had become a group of two floater nets and two broken rafts. That first day I sent three officers ashore on one of the broken rafts with the only paddle we

USS Strong

had to try to get assistance to us; our position was approximately in the middle of Kula Gulf. No assistance arrived," Miller continued in his after-action report.

"The next day I sent ashore a group of four men on the other broken raft, but no assistance was gotten as a result of their efforts," Miller said. At least five of the survivors, meanwhile, had died while adrift. The remaining six men, concentrated on one floater net, finally drifted to land on July 9, according to Miller's official report. Two more men, both seriously injured, died by July 13, leaving only four survivors.

Miller, himself still weak, bleeding internally and unable to walk without assistance on July 15, feared Japanese patrols would soon find them, so he ordered the three able-bodied men to move on without him in an effort to reach safety. Miller gave one of the men his shoes and sheath knife and kept only two Japanese beer bottles of water, a small broken knife blade and six coconuts for himself as he awaited what he thought was certain death. The three uninjured men set out toward the other end the island in search of friendly natives, not knowing that the area was occupied by as many as 1,000 enemy soldiers, and were never heard from again.

"I was so uncomfortable that I didn't try to conserve this water and I exhausted my supply before the morning of the 16th of July," Miller wrote. "I thought I would be dead by then, but I rallied. The day of the 16th…I became determined to live.

"Late in the afternoon of the 17th I was still without water and quite uncomfortable. I prayed for rain and in my prayers promised that if I could get rain I would get up and help myself," Miller continued. "That night there was a very hard rain." Miller satisfied his thirst, filled his two beer bottles and got up on the morning of July 18 to try to return to a spring more than a mile away that the men had seen on their arrival on the island.

"I could only move very slowly and it took me about a half day to cover two-thirds of the distance," Miller wrote. "At this point I had to cross an open salt flat which was dry at that time of day at low tide. When I was in the middle of this salt flat, a Japanese Zero tried to strafe me. He missed me but one bullet splattered when it hit a rock and two pieces of steel hit me." Luckily, Miller's injuries—one in the neck and one in the wrist—were minor, and he finally reached the spring by late afternoon.

Comic book depiction of Miller.

"The next day I got up and got a coconut and opened it by beating the husk off on a sharp coral rock. That day, which was the 19th of July, I was able to eat the meat of the coconut, which was the first solid food that I had been able to retain since the ship went down," Miller said. "From then on, there was plenty of fresh water and coconuts and my strength was on the upgrade."

Miller was on the northeast end of Arundel Island, and although there were no permanent Japanese installations nearby, enemy patrols covered the area frequently, forcing Miller to move his camp several times before finally settling on a safe, secluded spot in the jungle about 100 yards from the spring. Miller was able to stay in that camp for the remainder of his stay on Arundel Island.

"The same day I made my permanent camp I attracted the attention of a low-flying American TBF plane. I had felt that my one chance of escape would have to be to attract the attention of an American plane and that they would send some kind of boat to get me. I knew where I was and that it would be too hazardous an operation to rescue me, but I never lost hope for my eventual rescue," Miller continued. "This plane circled a dozen times very low and looked me over very carefully, often being so close that I could see the plane crew so well that I could almost identify them if I saw them again. I don't know what they reported, but I never received any assistance from any report they ever made."

Japanese barges and boats carrying reinforcements to nearby New Georgia Island moved past Arundel Island nightly, according to Miller's report. "The night of the second or third of August, what I thought was an American PT boat drifted quietly down Hathorn Sound and hid against the mangrove trees....When the Japanese barges loaded with soldiers came by them, they cut these barges to pieces with

Miller (center) receives medals from Eleanor Roosevelt and Admiral Halsey.

Miller (right) being interviewed after his rescue.

their 50-caliber machine guns and did one fine job of killing the Japanese," Miller wrote. "Apparently not knowing whether there were enemy troops behind them in the woods, as a precautionary measure they (the men on the PT boat) sprayed the woods with a Tommy gun. This Tommy gun very nearly got me and kept me so in hiding that I was unable to make any efforts to reach them.

"The next morning I chanced detection by going out on the edge of Hathorn Sound and robbing a dead Japanese soldier of his shoes, socks, bayonet, grenade carrier, two hand grenades and five cans of horrible Japanese tinned beef," Miller wrote. "This tinned beef was almost impossible to eat, but I ate it every other day for lunch and it undoubtedly added to my strength."

Later that day, Miller attracted the attention of another American plane, which circled several times and dropped a small package containing a small bottle of iodine, a bandage and one chocolate ration D. "This ration D was the only square meal I had in 43 days," Miller wrote.

"The Japanese, having determined that I was on Arundel

Island as a result of my robbing this dead soldier, sent a five-man patrol after me the following night," Miller wrote. "I saw them coming in the moonlight in the woods and retreated in front of them for 100 yards to my camp. They did not hear or see me at any time. When it became evident that they were going to walk right into my camp, I decided to try out one of the two hand grenades that I had. When they were 30 yards from me in the position that I wanted them in, which was in a close group, I tossed a grenade in the middle of them and killed all five."

The next morning Miller found that the rifles of all five Japanese soldiers had been destroyed by the grenade blast, but he was able to recover six more grenades, bayonets, five more tins of canned meat and other items.

"I buried this party and planted plants over the level graves so that there is no way of ever finding them," he wrote. "I used the Japanese uniforms for underclothes to replace my greasy underclothes and used some of their soap to get the fuel oil (from the explosion of the *Strong*) off me which I had been unsuccessful in doing up to that time. Within the next three days, several other dead soldiers drifted ashore and I robbed their bodies and increased my supply of Japanese personal effects and hand grenades. I never did get any firearms."

Despite being armed with only a few grenades, Miller began to stalk the Japanese rather than try to simply avoid discovery. "My dad's philosophy of life was 'If you're on offense, they're on defense'," Landon Miller said in explaining his father's actions.

"On three different nights between the 9th and 14th of August, I slipped a mile and a half up the beach and heaved

Miller's rescue finally came on August 16, when he heard what he knew to be the sound of a low-flying American plane.

long-range hand grenades into Japanese machine gun positions. I know from the blood and some equipment that I found the next day that I got some each time, but every night when the boats completed their run they picked up these machine gun crews, so I do not know how much damage I did on those three occasions," Miller said.

"Almost every day there were patrols which I eluded. The last night I was there, the night of the 15th of August, they were within 30 yards of me and had they come any closer they would have gotten some more of their very good hand grenades, but they passed on by," Miller added.

Miller's rescue finally came on August 16, when he heard what he knew to be the sound of a low-flying American plane. "I rushed out on my salt flat and waved a towel and attracted the attention of the pilot," Miller wrote. "He circled me once, sized up the situation, flew to Munda and reported it. Within an hour, although there were enemy planes in the air, Major (Vernon) Patterson reached me with his rescue expedition," Miller wrote. The rescue team also included Major Goodwin Luck (pilot) and master sergeant John Happer in a small, twin-winged J2F Navy Duck.

The rescue plane landed near the island and Patterson went ashore in an inflatable raft to pick up Miller and the military papers he had collected from the dead Japanese soldiers. The papers, just as Miller had suspected, provided valuable military intelligence to U.S. forces.

Miller's Navy Cross citation, signed by Halsey, praised Miller for "extraordinary heroism" aboard the *Strong* and during his 43 days of peril. The citation read, in part:

"Lieutenant Miller, while extricating two comrades entangled in a line on the ship's side, was forced with them beneath water by the pull of the sinking vessel. Although injured and dazed by several underwater explosions, he clung tenaciously to the two men, fought clear of the

powerful suction and continued to hold them above water until he could place them in a net. In charge of survivors grouped together on a floating net, he finally reached a small island dangerously near enemy positions. Unwilling to allow his weakened condition to retard the progress of his companions, Lieutenant Miller ordered them ahead, and in spite of a lack of food and water, regained enough strength to wage a lone battle against enemy units with weapons retrieved from the bodies of dead Japanese. Menaced by constant fire from hostile scouting parties, he maintained himself for 39 days, gathering valuable information concerning enemy positions until he was finally rescued by friendly aircraft."

Miller received the award, along with the Purple Heart with cluster, from Mrs. Roosevelt and Halsey while recuperating at a Navy hospital on New Caledonia on September 15, 1943.

"It took him a long time to get over that," Landon Miller said of his father's grueling jungle ordeal. "He would wake up dreaming about it a lot. They call it post-traumatic stress syndrome now."

Miller expressed his gratitude while describing his daring rescue in a letter to Major Luck's family on September 2 while recuperating from his wounds.

"I was several miles behind the Japanese lines and there were Japanese planes in the air at the time," Miller wrote. "Despite this and despite the fact that they did not know whether I was an apprentice seaman or an officer or what, this small expedition set out without fighter plane coverage to get me. All they knew was that I was an American in a dangerous spot and in trouble." Noting that the men flew a small, slow plane within range of powerful Japanese guns, he said the men landed in the water in front of him and "calmly inflated a boat, came ashore and got me. Because they could see that I was weak, they would not allow me to cover the last 30 yards of water, which would have been dangerous for me, but made me wait until they could come and get me—at all times considering only my safety while they risked their own skins—and they flew me out to Munda.

"The appreciation which I feel toward them for saving my life cannot be put into words, but more important than that is the purely impersonal courage and daring which they displayed and which surely is the reason why a fighting Marine is superior to any other fighting man alive. Though one can never tell, I sincerely hope that they will be decorated for this act of bravery.

"Your Major Luck piloted the plane. When I last saw him on August 18, I promised to wire a message to you when I reached the States. It appears that I will be a month or so getting back and that is the reason I am writing. He was in the best of health and spirits when I left Munda. You may be perfectly sure that the Luck family may feel free to call on me at any time for anything. I can always be reached through my home address of 1925 8th Street, Tuscaloosa, Alabama. Sincerely, Hugh Barr Miller Jr."

Miller's heroic survival was reported in newspapers throughout the country and was also featured in *True, Male, Bluebook* and *Life* (Nov. 8, 1943) magazines, in the book The *Best 100 True Stories of World War II* and in several comic books. His story was also featured on the television series "Navy Log."

Miller returned to the U.S. soon after his rescue and received a hero's welcome wherever he went. He toured the country on War Bond drives, a regular routine with war heroes at the time as the government tried to boost morale on the home front and raise money for the war effort.

Following his Pacific ordeal, Miller served at the Dam Neck, Virginia, Naval base and at Pensacola Naval Air Station, where he helped establish the Navy's Judge Advocate General's Corps (JAG). He remained on active duty with the Navy for 34 years and retired in 1969 with the rank of captain. In addition to the Navy Cross and two Purple Heart awards, Miller received the Meritorious Service Medal, Asiatic-Pacific Campaign Medal, American Campaign Medal, American Defense Service Medal and the National Defense Service Medal.

Miller was the featured guest on the television show "This Is Your Life" on January 30, 1957, when he was invited to Hollywood to discuss a possible movie about his remarkable World War II survival. Miller was joined on the show by his family, former Alabama coach Wallace Wade, the former captain of the *USS Strong* and two of the Marines who had rescued him from Arundel Island. The host of the popular television show that night was actor Ronald Reagan, the future governor of California and president of the United States, who was filling in for regular host Ralph Edwards, who was sick.

Wade made his entrance onto the show by reciting a phrase he often used to urge his football teams to victory, saying "Fight. Keep on fighting. A man that won't be defeated can't be defeated." The familiar phrase had inspired Miller often during his dark nights in the jungles of Arundel Island.

Miller was born January 19, 1910, in Tuscaloosa, but grew up on a family farm in Hazlehurst, Mississippi, where his father was a well-known attorney. Miller learned to stalk, shoot and trap wild game as a youngster under the guidance of Jim Michael, a laborer on the farm, and those hunting skills proved critical to Miller's survival on Arundel Island.

"God and Uncle Jim walked by my side all the time," Miller said later in recalling the man who had taught him "the sounds and signs of the woods."

Miller lettered at quarterback and placekicker on the Alabama football teams of 1929-30 after participating in football and track as a freshman in 1928. He was a member of the Crimson Tide's 1930 unbeaten team that won conference and national championships. The team posted a 10-0 record, including a 24-0 win over Washington State in the January 1, 1931, Rose Bowl. Miller drop-kicked a 40-yard field goal in a 43-0 win over Howard College on September 27, 1930. The kick is believed to be the longest drop kick in school history. Miller passed up his final year of football eligibility to enter law school in 1931.

After earning a law degree from the University in 1933, Miller returned to Mississippi, where he practiced law until joining the Navy in 1939. He served as a staff officer at the Key West Naval Base for a short time before being assigned to the *Strong* as assistant gunnery officer in 1940.

Miller died in 1978, leaving surviving sons Landon and Fitzhugh Miller. His oldest son, Hugh Barr Miller III, died in a civilian plane crash in 1965.

Landon Miller was a scholarship football player at Alabama 1963-65 and also served in the Navy. He saw submarine duty off the coast of Vietnam in the late 1960s and is a retired Navy commander. Landon Miller is currently completing work on a detailed biography of Hugh Barr Miller Jr., focusing mainly on first-hand accounts of his World War II experiences.

"He didn't like to talk about his World War II experience,

but when he met people it always came up," Landon Miller said of his father.

The Miller family has numerous historic ties to the University of Alabama. Hugh Barr Miller's maternal great grandfather, Landon Cabell Garland, was the third president (1855-1865) of the University. Garland also served as a colonel in the Alabama Militia and later became the first chancellor of Vanderbilt University.

Miller's maternal grandfather, Burwell Boykin Lewis, was the eighth president of the University, serving 1880-1885. Frank Rose, UA president 1958-1969, was Miller's cousin. Miller's grandmother, Bertha Lewis Miller, was the first woman professor on the University faculty, and his mother was a member of the UA faculty during World War II.

Garland's wife Louisa is credited with saving the University of Alabama President's Mansion from destruction on April 4, 1865, when Union troops led by Major General John Croxton burned most of the buildings on campus near the end of the Civil War. Mrs. Garland's determined pleas persuaded the troops to put out the fire they had already set to the mansion and spare the landmark. A historical marker commemorating Mrs. Garland's heroic action stands near the mansion today.

Miller's paternal grandfather, Robert Miller, rode with Confederate General Nathan Bedford Forrest's Cavalry during the Civil War and Burwell Boykin Lewis also served in the Confederate Army. According to Landon Miller, the Miller family tree also includes Patrick Henry and Henry (Light Horse Harry) Lee of American Revolutionary War fame, Confederate Civil War general Robert E. Lee and Louie Napier, a Frenchman who served with George Washington during the Revolutionary War.

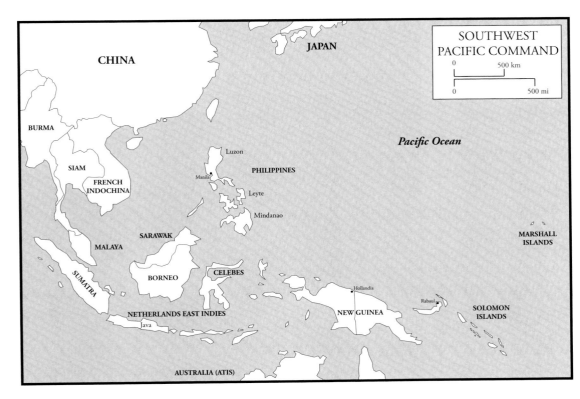

Lionel "Red" **NOONAN**

'Atticus Finch is alive and well in Judge Noonan'

Lionel W. "Red" Noonan was one of the lucky ones, you might say, because he didn't see action overseas during World War II. The Navy found he had special skills needed in training others instead.

A Mobile native, Noonan graduated from Murphy High School in December 1942 and joined the Navy shortly afterward. During recruit training, his outstanding skills as a gymnast and boxer caught the eyes of the instructors and he was assigned to their staff for the duration of the war.

Noonan taught judo and hand-to-hand combat to Navy and Marine recruits headed for battle throughout the world. He also played football and served as a training instructor at Camp Peary, VA, and as an instructor in the V-12 program at the University of Virginia, reaching the rank of petty officer.

Noonan had studied tumbling and acrobatics for several years while living in New Orleans as a youngster, and even performed at the 1934 Chicago World's Fair. He also performed at an exhibition game between the New York Yankees and New Orleans Pelicans in 1935 during which he met Yankees great Lou Gehrig, he said.

During recruit training, his outstanding skills as a gymnast and boxer caught the eyes of the instructors and he was assigned to their staff for the duration of the war.

Noonan on Navy duty in Virginia and climbing stadium steps on his hands.

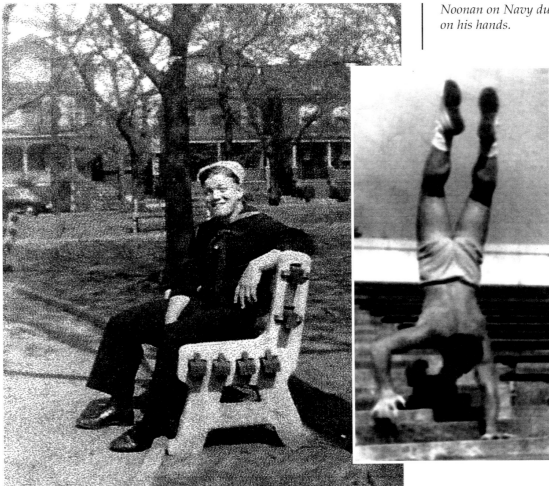

and stayed after the ball carriers until he brought them down," Noonan said.

Noonan also recalled playing a game at Boston College in a cold rain with the temperature around 33 degrees. "We just had our regular uniforms and at halftime they coated us with grease to fight the wind and keep the warmth inside our bodies," he said. Alabama lost that 1946 game 13-7 and finished the season at 7-4. Noonan carried the ball 31 times for 94 yards and a touchdown as a senior in 1949.

Noonan graduated in 1950, but stayed on to earn a master's degree and a law degree while serving as a graduate assistant football coach for three years. He and his wife Ruby lived in Friedman Hall during much of that time.

Noonan was voted friendliest student on campus in 1948, indicative of the outgoing personality that helped him achieve success later in life. He served as president of the A Club and president of the Law School Student Government Association and was selected for Jasons and Omicron Delta Kappa (ODK) and Who's Who in American Colleges and Universities.

He returned to Mobile following law school and in addition to practicing law he taught at Spring Hill College in Mobile, served two terms as a state senator and 18 years as Probate Judge of Mobile County. He also served on the Senior Bowl Committee, Junior Chamber of Commerce, as president of the Mobile Chapter of the UA Alumni Association and as a member of the Alabama Sports Hall of Fame Board of Directors among numerous other civic affiliations.

"A lot of opportunities presented themselves," Noonan said modestly of his successes. "And it didn't hurt that I

Noonan, a 5-10, 200-pounder who had twice earned All-City honors (once at fullback and once at tackle) in high school, was recruited by then University of Alabama head coach Frank Thomas after the war, and he joined the Crimson Tide in August 1946. He lettered four years as a fullback and linebacker (1946-1949). The football press guide once called Noonan "the squad's finest physical specimen…always good for short yardage and a real power runner."

"I played with some great people," Noonan said of his Alabama football days. "Some I remember best are Charlie Compton, Vaughn Mancha and John Wozniak. Compton played with reckless abandon. He was all over the field

"Watching him preside in Probate Court over the years, I have never seen a man more courteous and patient to lawyers and litigants alike, particularly in often unseemly and ugly fights over estates of departed loved ones."

had played football at Alabama. That experience provided me with a lot of friends throughout the state. I met a lot of wonderful people."

Noonan, who retired as Probate Judge in 2001, also served as president of the UA Law School, the state Probate Judges' Association and the Alabama Bankers Association Trust Division. He also received the G. Marie Daniels Leadership Award from the Mobile Bar Association and was elected to the Mobile Sports Hall of Fame and the Murphy High School Hall of Fame.

One special tribute to Noonan came shortly after his retirement when Mobile Bar Association president Donald Briskman wrote the following for the association's monthly bulletin:

"Atticus Finch is alive and well in Judge Lionel W. "Red" Noonan. Watching him preside in Probate Court over the years, I have never seen a man more courteous and patient to lawyers and litigants alike, particularly in often unseemly and ugly fights over estates of departed loved ones. His unfailing courtesy and kindness have led me to believe that never was there a job more suited to a man or a man more suited to a job than Red Noonan as Probate Judge." (Atticus Finch was portrayed as a highly principled attorney in the popular novel *To Kill a Mockingbird*, written by Monroeville, Alabama, native and UA law school graduate Harper Lee.)

The 1946 Alabama football team included many World War II veterans.

Howard **PIERSON**

'They went after our carriers with kamikaze attacks'

Howard J. "Oscar" Pierson lists combat service in three wars on his 33-year military resume, starting as a "deck ape" on the battleship *USS Iowa* at the battle of Okinawa during World War II.

"As millions of others, I was a high school dropout," Pierson said of his decision to leave school at age 17 and join the fight. "You had to have a parent's signature, and my mother tearfully let me go," he said.

Pierson saw action in World War II, Korea and Vietnam and flew combat-ready bombers during the Cold War in a career that started in 1944 and finally ended with his retirement in 1979.

Pierson joined the Navy in the summer of 1944, and after training at the Sampson (NY) Naval Training Station, was sent to San Francisco, where he boarded the *Iowa* and sailed for the Pacific battlefront on March 19, 1945.

Pierson's first action came quickly as the *Iowa* immediately joined the U.S. assault on the island of Okinawa, where 107,000 Japanese and over 12,000 U.S. soldiers died in 81 days of fighting during April, May and June.

The Battle of Okinawa involved the largest amphibious assault in the Pacific theater, with more than 102,000 Army troops and 81,000 Marines involved. In addition, hundreds of U.S. and allied ships supported the attack.

"I was just a seaman," Pierson said. "They called us

deck apes; they didn't give 17-year-olds a lot of responsibility back then." His assigned battle station was on an antiaircraft gun battery, and from that vantage point he saw first-hand the terror of hundreds of Japanese kamikaze attacks on the Navy fleet during the battle.

"Our ship was shelling the island and helping fight off the enemy planes," Pierson said. "They went after our carriers with kamikaze attacks, and they did it with intent and intensity," he said.

Japanese forces fought to the death in defending the island, just 340 miles from the Japanese mainland, and flew nearly 2,000 kamikaze missions against U.S. ships, sinking dozens, including 12 destroyers, damaging scores of others and killing over 5,000 American sailors. In addition to the kamikaze air attacks, the Japanese employed suicide attacks by speedboats and mini submarines in the battle.

The *Iowa* shelled numerous other Japanese islands and supported carrier operations in the Pacific until the war ended in August 1945 following U.S. atomic bomb attacks on Hiroshima and Nagasaki, Japan. The *Iowa* entered Tokyo Bay with the occupation forces and served as Admiral William F. "Bull" Halsey's flagship during the surrender ceremony. The surrender took place on

Left: Pierson as a 17-year-old "deck ape" in 1945.

Below: Griffith, Holdnak and Pierson (L-R) drove to Tuscaloosa in a Model A Ford.

the battleship *USS Missouri,* since that was President Harry Truman's home state, on September 2, 1945. The *Iowa* received homeward-bound GIs and liberated prisoners of war before departing for the U.S. on September 20.

After only 14 months of service, Pierson returned home to Succasunna, NJ, in the fall of 1946 to complete his last year of high school. "I was just three days too old to play football again," he said. "I was 19 and I thought I was a real salty veteran. My drill was to go to high school, go to Kitty's Tavern and drink beer then work the night shift at Hercules Powder Company from midnight to eight. When you're 19, you can do that for a little while, so that was my pace."

Pierson graduated from high school in the spring of 1947, however, and soon found his way to Tuscaloosa, where he eventually played football for the University of Alabama 1948-49 after an unusual start.

"I was friends with Eddie Holdnak, who had played a year at Columbia and who had a scholarship offer to Alabama," Pierson said. "We had played football together at Roxbury High School in 1943 before I went into the Navy. I had a Model A Ford and he asked me to drive him down to Tuscaloosa. So he, another friend named June Griffith and I headed south. That was some trip!

"When we got there, Coach (Red) Drew told Eddie, Griff and me to get some equipment and go out back. Man, that practice field looked like the Normandy beachhead! There were hundreds of young men in a massive cloud of dust banging into each other in basic football drills, coaches screaming vulgarities and blowing whistles, and generally all-around bedlam. It turned out to be a tryout, because afterward Coach Drew asked me if I would like to stay and play football," Pierson, who was 6-4, 210 at the time, said. Griffith wasn't offered a scholarship to Alabama, but ended up playing football at Gettysburg College, according to Pierson.

Pierson stayed at Alabama through the opening game of the 1947 season before being called home for a family emergency which kept him out of school the rest of the fall. He returned in early 1948 and earned a spot on the traveling squad as a sophomore.

"I played in 1948 and 1949 and made only a modest contribution to the team, but I did catch a touchdown pass (30 yards from Ed Salem) against Auburn in 1948, when we won 55-0," Pierson said proudly. The December 4, 1948, game was the first meeting between Alabama and Auburn since 1907, when the series was suspended because of bad blood between the teams. Pierson was also on the track team at Alabama and earned a letter in the discus event. Pierson and his 100-year-old father attended the 1998 Alabama-Auburn game to celebrate the 50th anniversary of the 1948 game. A number of other former Tide players also returned for the game, including halfback Ed Salem and center Mike Mizerany. Alabama won the 1998 game 31-17.

Pierson especially remembers the first time he suited up for a varsity game. "I shall never forget the Tulane game (Sept

"That moment is in my heart forever. I didn't have the maturity at the time to realize what I was becoming a part of, but I later grasped the magnitude of the legacy and tradition of Alabama football, with names like Bear Bryant, Dixie Howell, Johnny Mack Brown, Don Hutson and Holt Rast."

Japanese kamikaze attacks took a heavy toll on U.S. ships in Pacific battles.

25, 1948, in New Orleans) when manager Fred Posey laid out that beautiful, new, polished crimson jersey for me," Pierson said. "That moment is in my heart forever. I didn't have the maturity at the time to realize what I was becoming a part of, but I later grasped the magnitude of the legacy and tradition of Alabama football, with names like Bear Bryant, Dixie Howell, Johnny Mack Brown, Don Hutson and Holt Rast."

Pierson easily recalled his Alabama teammates and his time with the Crimson Tide football team. "I remember Charlie Compton well," Pierson said of the former Crimson Tide tackle who had earned the Distinguished Service Cross in Europe during World War II. "He would go to practice without pads; he was tough. Al and Ed Lary were good friends, too," he said. "They introduced me to Dixie with their fiddles and guitars; leg, chest and mouth slapping;

grits, greens and hambone. White lightning rounded out my Southern indoctrination," he added. Pierson also listed Salem, Herb Hannah, Charles Davis, Clem Gryska, Butch Avinger, Walter May and Holdnak, who went on to earn first-team All-Southeastern Conference honors at guard in 1949, among his favorite teammates at Alabama.

"Our GI Bill money allowed for multiple beer runs to the county line," Pierson said. "Avinger would always ask me at the first of the month, "Did our check arrive yet?'"

He also recalled Carl Crumpler, a member of the Crimson Tide basketball team in the late 1940s, as a close friend. Crumpler and Pierson went through flight training together and Crumpler was later shot down on a bombing run over

North Korea and spent five years as a prisoner of war. They have remained close friends since.

Pierson was enrolled in Air Force ROTC while at Alabama and received his commission in 1950. He went into the service soon afterward without playing his senior season of football or receiving his degree because of the Korean War. He earned his wings as a pilot in May 1952 and was soon sent to Japan, where he flew B-29 bombers in bombing missions over North Korea until the war ended in 1953.

"When the Korean War began, the military air thinking was like that of World War II: Keep bombing like we did---in formation, daytime, good aiming---and destroy the Koreans," Pierson said. "The bad news is, they didn't count on the Russian MIG jets. If you're flying reciprocal-engine aircraft and you get jumped by MIGs, you're in deep trouble. So we started out losing a lot of planes.

"The good news for me was I got there when they said, 'Let's just fly at night in a bomber stream,' and they did individual aiming and bombed respectively and the loss rate went way down. There were no night fighters in Korea to threaten us." After the Korean "Police Action" ended in 1953, Pierson attended navigator/bombardier training to fly the new six-engine, swept-wing B-47 bombers.

Pierson remained in the Air Force and later served four one-year tours in Vietnam, where he flew C-123, A-37, A-1, F-5 and OV-10 aircraft as a fighter pilot and forward observer. As a forward air controller, he was the last U.S. pilot to fly out of Cambodia. He ended up flying over 1,000 sorties in Korea and Vietnam combined, with over 10,000 flight hours as a command pilot. Pierson also served as an advisor to the South Vietnamese Air Force and the Royal Thai Air Force and proudly wears their wings also.

"I was determined to take on the communists," Pierson said of his service in Vietnam. "I had seen them in Korea."

He flew armed B-47 and B-52 bombers with the Strategic Air Command during the Cold War era until his retirement as a lieutenant colonel in May 1979. "In the 1950s and 1960s

Pierson served as a fighter pilot in Korea and Vietnam.

Japanes kamikaze pilots terrorized U.S. ships in the Pacific.

we were standing alert and flying missions all over the world carrying nukes (nuclear bombs)," he said. "I had a B-52 crew with ten megatons—ten megatons—ready to go to Moscow. A ten megaton bomb on Moscow would have killed two million people."

Pierson's combat decorations and awards include three Distinguished Flying Crosses, three Bronze Stars, 39 Air Medals, Meritorious Service Medal, Airman's Medal for Valor and the Vietnam Gallantry Cross. He is a member of the Air Commando Hall of Fame, Order of Daedalians and the Military Order of the World Wars. He serves as chaplain of the Air Commando Association, the Forward Air Controllers Association and the Military Officers Association of Marin County, CA.

Pierson said he flew military fighters, bombers and trainers "with one, two, four, six, eight and sometimes no engines" during his distinguished combat career. He also played football in Japan in 1953, earning a spot on the All-Far

East Air Force team.

In 1980, Pierson returned to the University to complete work for his B.S. degree in education, which he received in 1981 on the same day that then-Alabama head coach Paul "Bear" Bryant received an honorary doctorate degree. Pierson conducted motivational seminars in Dallas, earned a master's degree in communications from the University of Arkansas, and worked as a consultant with American Airlines seven years before finally retiring in the 1990s. While in Arkansas, he was inducted into the Arkansas Boys State Hall of Fame.

Pierson, now 83, married Gilberta Guth, the widow of his pilot classmate Joe Guth, in 2002. They have a blended family of eight children, 12 grandchildren and three great-grandchildren and reside in Northern California.

"I still marvel at the University of Alabama's influence on my life," Pierson said. "What a blessing it has been. The championship spirit has prevailed at the University in every athlete, coach, student, alum and fan. Bama's legacy will sustain forever. Roll Tide!"

Johnny **ROBERTS**

'He gallantly gave his life for his country'

Johnny Roberts was an adventurous and athletic young man who always wanted to be in on the action, whatever and wherever that might be.

He was an all-around athlete at West End High School in Birmingham and earned All-State and All-County honors in football and a scholarship to the University of Alabama in the fall of 1934. He stuck with the team for four years and lettered at fullback as a senior on the 1937 squad that went 9-0 and won the Southeastern Conference championship before losing to California 13-0 in the January 1, 1938, Rose Bowl.

Roberts also lettered on the 1937-38 baseball and boxing teams and served as president of the A Club 1938-39, proving his popularity among his fellow athletes.

According to press reports from the era, baseball was Roberts' best sport. He played with the varsity for three seasons, starting at third base in 1937 and at center field in 1938. He helped the Crimson Tide win the Southeastern Conference championship in 1938 as one of the team's leading hitters and base runners while batting in the cleanup position. He was also named to the 1937 National Amateur All-Star baseball team.

Roberts was a member of Theta Chi fraternity, the Cotillion Club, Spirit Committee and Interfraternity Council and served as assistant freshman football coach in 1938 and freshman boxing coach in 1939.

He graduated with a degree in education in May 1939 and played professional baseball that summer with the Pensacola Pilots of the Southeastern League, hitting .279 in 97 games as an outfielder on a team that also included Alabama natives Harry Walker and Bobby Bragan.

With war clouds looming, however, Roberts again couldn't wait to get into the action. He joined the Navy in October 1940 and reported for flight training at Pensacola Naval Air Station in January, 1941. He earned his wings in September and was flying bombers from Norfolk, Virginia, to California when the Japanese bombed Pearl Harbor on December 7, 1941, to draw the United States into World War II.

Roberts was sent to Hawaii and soon assigned to Scouting Squadron 6 as a dive bomber pilot aboard the

aircraft carrier *USS Enterprise*. He died heroically on June 4, 1942, during the Battle of Midway when he appeared to purposely crash his plane into the deck of a Japanese aircraft carrier during the decisive Pacific battle.

Roberts was awarded the Navy Cross, the Navy's highest decoration, and Purple Heart posthumously for his actions and the U.S. Navy destroyer escort *USS John Q. Roberts* was later named for him.

The Navy Cross citation praised Roberts for "extraordinary heroism," saying that "Ensign Roberts, with fortitude and resolute devotion to duty, pressed home his attacks in the face of a formidable barrage of antiaircraft fire and fierce fighter opposition. His gallant perseverance and utter disregard for his own personal safety were important

Roberts (holding eight ball) with A Club members, circa 1939.

contributing factors to the success achieved by our forces and were in keeping with the highest traditions of the United States Naval Service. He gallantly gave his life for his country."

The Battle of Midway marked a turning point in the war in the Pacific as U.S. forces sank four Japanese carriers and a heavy cruiser to weaken the enemy fleet and end the enemy's expansion into the Northern Pacific. Japanese losses included more than 3,000 men killed and 228 aircraft destroyed. U.S. losses included the carrier *Yorktown*, the destroyer *Hammann*, 145 aircraft and 340 men.

Details of the death of Roberts and the events leading up to it were documented by author Clark Lee in *They Call It Pacific*, a book of eye-witness accounts of the war in the Pacific published by Viking Press in 1943. Lee wrote vividly of Roberts and

his close friend and fellow pilot Carl Pfieffer, who also died at the Battle of Midway.

"Roberts played football for Alabama and he looked it. The first things you noticed were his sloping shoulders and his strong, powerful neck. He was only a little above middle height but he looked as strong as a bull," Lee wrote of Roberts. "His reddish-brown hair was cropped short when he joined the Navy and he grew a little mustache like the rest of the boys in his squadron. When you looked into his eyes they made you suddenly remember Captain Arthur Wermuth (heroic defender against overwhelming enemy forces) out on Bataan and Lieutenant John Bulkeley (Medal of Honor winner who evacuated General Douglas MacArthur from Corregidor) at the helm of the PT boat roaring up toward Subic Bay. He had the same look in his eyes.

"J.Q. (John Quincy was his full name.) didn't care about details. All he worried about was getting into action. Roberts and Pfeiffer were the most talkative members of their

bombing squadron. They were always talking about what they would do to the Japanese," Lee wrote. "J.Q. used to read about those Japanese pilots doing suicide dives into our ships…Those stories made J.Q. mad as hell.

"'Do those damn Japanese think they are trying to teach Americans what it is to be heroic?' J.Q. would ask the boys. 'They're not going to teach me anything. When we get our first crack at them I'm going to dive down and lay my egg right on the middle of

Roberts as a boxer and baseball player at Alabama.

the deck of their biggest carrier. And if I miss I'm going to keep right on diving down into the funnel and set that ship on fire'," Lee quoted Roberts as saying. "And I'll be right behind you, J.Q.," Pfeiffer reportedly said.

"The skipper of their squadron didn't like the way J.Q. and Pfeiffer looked when they said that. He told them, 'Look, boys, you don't have to do that. If you miss, why, hell, come back for another bomb and go back and don't miss the second time.'

"But J.Q. would say, 'Captain, I've only got one life to live and one death to die. If I live I've got a girl I want to marry. If I die I've made up my mind to die for my country and nobody can talk me out of it.' And Pfeiffer would say, 'I'll be

A Navy plane like Roberts (inset) piloted flies over the USS Enterprise.

right behind you, J.Q.'."

Scout planes from the *Enterprise* were searching for Japanese Admiral Isoroku Yamamoto's fleet on June 4, 1942, and they found it. It was the same Japanese fleet that had attacked U.S. ships and installations at Pearl Harbor and Midway seven months earlier. American intelligence had intercepted messages indicating the Japanese planned to attack and occupy Midway, a tiny atoll 1,300 miles northwest of Oahu, Hawaii, with hopes of further crippling the U.S. Pacific Fleet in the process. The U.S. had established a Naval Air Station on Midway in 1940 and Henderson Field

The USS John Q. Roberts was christened in March 1945.

"J.Q. never tried to pull out of his dive. He kept right on going down and flew his plane right into the *Kaga's* funnel. Pfeiffer was right behind him. There was a big sheet of flame and two big explosions that tossed the other planes around in the sky," Lee's account read.

Roberts was reported missing in action the following day but was not counted killed in action until a year later. His gunner on the dive bomber, Thurman R. Swindell, also died in the crash.

"The boys who used to fly with J.Q. and Pfeiffer and Johnny Butler (another pilot who was shot down by a Japanese Zero in the same attack) often talk about those three. They miss them a lot. But they reckon that when the Japanese hear about J.Q. and his buddies they won't try to teach Americans any more lessons in how to be heroic," Lee concluded.

Dr. John Ramsey, a University of Alabama history professor (1935-77) who served as a senior historian with the Army Air Forces during World War II and who had known Johnny Roberts as a student, once commented on Lee's account of Johnny's final actions by saying "I don't know how much Lee got from hearsay or how much he invented, but certainly anyone who knew Johnny Roberts as we did will agree that he was quite capable of doing exactly what Lee says he did."

In addition to the Navy Cross and Purple Heart, Roberts' was awarded the American Defense Medal, the Asiatic-Pacific Campaign Medal and the ribbon of the Presidential Citation awarded the *USS Enterprise*.

Roberts' mother, Mrs. Deany Roberts Garner, his sister Edna Roberts and other relatives attended the christening of the *USS John Q. Roberts* at the Charleston Navy Yard in March 1945. His father, Grover Roberts, was deceased. Roberts was born September 2, 1915, in Marshall County, Alabama.

there served as a base for American bombers and fighter planes. By decoding Japanese messages, however, outnumbered U.S. forces were able to launch their own surprise attack on the approaching Japanese ships and claim a decisive though costly victory. It was the first defeat ever for the Japanese Imperial Navy.

Pilots from Scouting Squadron 6 off the *Enterprise*—Roberts among them—arrived on the battle scene at mid-morning on June 4 and attacked the Japanese carrier *Kaga*, according to military records, as Japanese fighter planes swarmed in defense of the Japanese ship.

"The first pilots to dive got hits and flames shot up from the *Kaga's* deck," wrote Lee. "Then J.Q. Roberts dived and his bomb missed the deck and struck the water right alongside the carrier. Pfeiffer was right behind J.Q. and his bomb hit in the same place. The other pilots were just above them in their dive and they saw it all.

Nick *TERLIZZI*

He organized the 1943 Tide 'Informals'

Nick Terlizzi is one of only a few former University of Alabama football players to have played in 1943 as a member of the campus football team known as "the Informals."

Alabama was unable to field an official football team in 1943 because practically all the varsity and freshmen players from 1942 had joined the military service for duty in World War II. There were only 856 male students registered for classes in the fall of 1943 along with 1,367 women. Although there were an additional 2,600 male Army trainees on campus, they were not allowed to participate in organized athletics.

Terlizzi, who came to Alabama from New Jersey in 1942 determined to be a part of the Crimson Tide football tradition, organized what was first called "Terlizzi's Victory Team" by the student newspaper *Crimson White*. The squad was made up of incoming freshmen, a few draft deferred upper classmen and even a former Tide cheerleader.

Tide head coach Frank Thomas lent his support to "the Informals" by allowing them to use Alabama uniforms, practice facilities and even Denny Stadium for their games.

"Coach Thomas was great about it," Terzilli said. "Our coaches were Al Alois, Mitch Olenski and John Gresham (members of Alabama's 1942 team) and we played Marion Military Institute (twice) and Howard College."

The Informals also played a scrimmage game against the Campus Stars, a team made up of soldiers assigned to the Army Specialized Training Program on campus. The Campus Stars featured several former Alabama players, including All-America center Joe Domnanovich, All-Southeastern Conference back Russ Craft, Sam Cain, Al Alois, John Gresham, Ray Cox, Andy Bires, Joe Chorba, Olenski and Joe Shepherd. The Campus Stars defeated the Informals 21-12.

The Informals defeated Marion Military Institute 19-13 in a road game and 31-12 at home before losing to Howard College 42-6 in a War Chest Charity Game at Denny Stadium. Howard College was loaded with experienced college players, many of them in the Navy V-12 program. Unlike the Army, Navy trainees on college campuses were allowed to participate in varsity athletics at such schools as Howard College, Georgia Tech and North Carolina.

The charity game drew a large crowd to Denny Stadium and raised $2,000 for the Alabama War Chest Fund. The halftime show featured the Tuscaloosa High School band, two campus military bands and several military units.

"We had lots of fun," Terlizzi said of the informal 1943 football season.

The Informals featured a pair of freshmen All-State backs in Barton Greer of Murphy High School in Mobile and Frank McAlpine (a later Tide varsity player) of Greene County High in Eutaw. Other members of the team included former cheerleader Whitey Blanciak, Joe Marion, Shorty Lackey, Dwight Evans, Sal Seapellati, Joe Triolo, Bob Wooleridge, George Kachickas, Bob Okin, Carl Licht, Hudson Conway and Tom Edwards.

McAlpine, Greer, Marion and Blanciak were the offensive stars of the squad and Terlizzi stood out at tackle, although he had not played football as a freshman at Alabama in 1942.

"I came to Alabama because I had heard about Johnny Mack Brown and Alabama's Rose Bowl teams," Terlizzi said. "That tradition is what drew me there. I had planned to play football, but I started out in engineering and had too many labs as a freshman. I did go to a lot of practices, though, and got to know Coach Thomas. He got me a job as a lifeguard at Queen City Pool in the summer."

Terlizzi joined the Navy in early 1944 and was sent to the Naval Training Center at Sampson, New York, where he played on the 1944 base football team.

"They asked for volunteers for the football team and not many of us signed up at first," Terlizzi said. "But when they said those who didn't play football would be sent overseas about 300 signed up," he added. "Our coach was Jim Crowley, who had played in the same backfield with Coach Thomas at Notre Dame," Terlizzi said.

The Sampson Naval Training Center team in 1944 featured a number of former college and professional players and played such teams as the Green Bay Packers, New York Giants, Cleveland Rams, Boston Yanks, Villanova, Cornell and Colgate.

Terlizzi spent less than two years in the Navy before being discharged soon after the war ended in August of 1945. He returned to Alabama in the fall and changed his major to education so he could play football.

"Our line at Sampson in 1944 was bigger and better than the one we had at Alabama in 1945, but that Alabama backfield of Harry Gilmer, Lowell Tew, Norwood Hodges, Hal Self and those guys was something else. They were a great bunch of backs," Terlizzi said. "Gilmer and Tew were among the greatest ever in my book."

Terlizzi recalled that he played tackle behind Tom Whitley. "He (Whitley) weighed only about 179-180 pounds, but what he lacked in size he made up for in quickness. He was quick and he was a fighter," Terlizzi said.

Terlizzi earned a letter in 1945 as the Crimson Tide went 10-0 for the season, won the SEC title and defeated Southern Cal 34-14 in the Rose Bowl on January 1, 1946.

"The year 1945 was the greatest year of my life," Terlizzi said. "We had a great bunch of guys and went to the Rose Bowl. Gilmer had a great game out there and I got to play about the last five minutes of the game. It was a lot of fun.

"We came back into Tuscaloosa by train at about 3 o'clock in the morning and I didn't expect to see anyone, but there was a big crowd waiting for us and cheering for us. I couldn't believe it. It's something I'll never forget and it makes me love Alabama to this day," he added.

Terlizzi also played for the Tide in 1946 before earning his degree and returning to New Jersey, where he went into construction work with his father.

"Coach Thomas was a great man," Terlizzi said. "He was like a father to me. He stressed speed with his teams. He was always running us a lot after practice and because of that we usually wore teams down."

Terlizzi maintained his love of Alabama football through the years and his two children (Nick and Dianne) both hold master's degrees from the University.

At age 89 in March of 2010, Terlizzi said he was still cheering for the Crimson Tide and trying to keep in touch with as many of his former teammates as possible.

Jimmy **WALKER**

'There can be no compensation for his loss'

Jimmy Walker might well be the only University of Alabama athlete to ever serve as captain of both the football and basketball teams.

From all indications, however, that was simply what one would expect of Walker, who excelled in everything he ever attempted.

Walker served as captain of his baseball, basketball and football teams at Holt High School in Tuscaloosa County, making history there as one of the school's all-time great athletes.

At Alabama, Walker was a three-year starter at forward on the basketball team and earned All-Southeastern Conference honors in 1934 and 1935. The 1935 Corolla said Walker "had few equals in regard to smoothness and cleverness" and had a "knack for hitting the basket" in addition to his outstanding defensive play. He teamed with center Jim Whatley, also a football player, to lead the Crimson Tide to the SEC championship in 1934.

Walker led the Crimson Tide in scoring in 1935 with 127 points for the season as team captain. During his three-year career as a basketball starter, he helped the Tide win 48 consecutive home games. He was selected to the Kellogg All-America basketball team in 1935, and his certificate bore the signatures of legendary sports figures Glenn "Pop" Warner, who won more than 300 games as coach at several colleges; Coach Frank Thomas of Alabama, and Elmer Layden, one of Notre Dame's famed "Four Horsemen."

Walker played end on the Crimson Tide football teams of 1933-35. He served as team captain in 1935 when he started opposite Paul "Bear" Bryant after playing behind Bryant and All-American Don Hutson the two previous seasons. He was a member of the Tide's 1933 SEC championship team (7-1-1) and the 1934 team that went 10-0, including a 29-13 victory over Stanford in the Rose Bowl, to claim SEC and national championships.

Alabama was 6-2-1 in 1935.

Following graduation in January 1936, Walker rejected professional football (Boston Redskins) and basketball (Boston Celtics) offers to follow his dream of coaching. He spent two years as head football and basketball coach at El Dorado, Arkansas, before joining the coaching staff at Virginia Military Institute as head basketball coach and assistant football coach under former Alabama football great A.T.S. "Pooley" Hubert.

Walker spent four years at VMI, leading the basketball teams to a 27-28 overall record. He drew praise for his coaching efforts when his 1940-41 team posted a 10-6 record to give the school its first winning season in 13 years. One sports writer called Walker "the outstanding basketball coach in the state" of Virginia after his teams regularly upset such powers as Virginia and William and Mary. "Molding a winner from boys who were not varsity players in prep school is a coaching masterpiece. That's what Jimmy Walker has done," one newspaper report stated.

Walker's promising coaching career ended soon after the start of World War II, however. He joined the Navy in 1942 and spent time as a physical fitness instructor and coach at the Georgia Navy Pre-Flight School before being assigned to sea duty in the Atlantic. He was later stationed in Recife, Brazil, as a lieutenant with the Navy's Fourth Fleet.

Walker was seriously injured in an accident in Recife in December of 1943 when the car in which he was riding blew a tire and collided with a streetcar. He died a few days later at age 31. His body was finally returned to Tuscaloosa for burial in 1948.

Walker's sister, Mae Walker Gilchrist, was the first family member to hear of Walker's death. She was working in Washington, D.C., during the war and heard her brother's name called by well-known commentator Walter Winchell on his afternoon radio show.

Bryant wrote to Walker's mother on January 9, 1944, offering his condolences when he learned of his former teammate's death.

"It is with a heavy heart that I sit down and attempt to write this letter," Bryant began. "To all of us who were close to Jimmy, there can be no compensation for his loss, but we will do everything in our power to even the score with interest. Those of us who played and lived with him know that in that last game he was as valiant and courageous as he had always been in lesser games. Please accept what I can so poorly put into words, my heartfelt sympathy. Very sincerely, Paul Bryant."

The letter was written on Bryant's official Navy stationery. Bryant was on duty in North Africa at the time.

Pooley Hubert paid tribute to Walker in a letter to friends in Tuscaloosa shortly after his death, writing:

"The loss of Jimmy Walker was a terrible blow to us at the Institute and everybody in this community. Jimmy was the type of boy who had no enemies. Everybody loved him, and as I walked through town the next day everybody extended their sympathy…I do not know how we are going to replace Jimmy. I doubt that it can be done. He was an excellent football coach and his basketball teams were

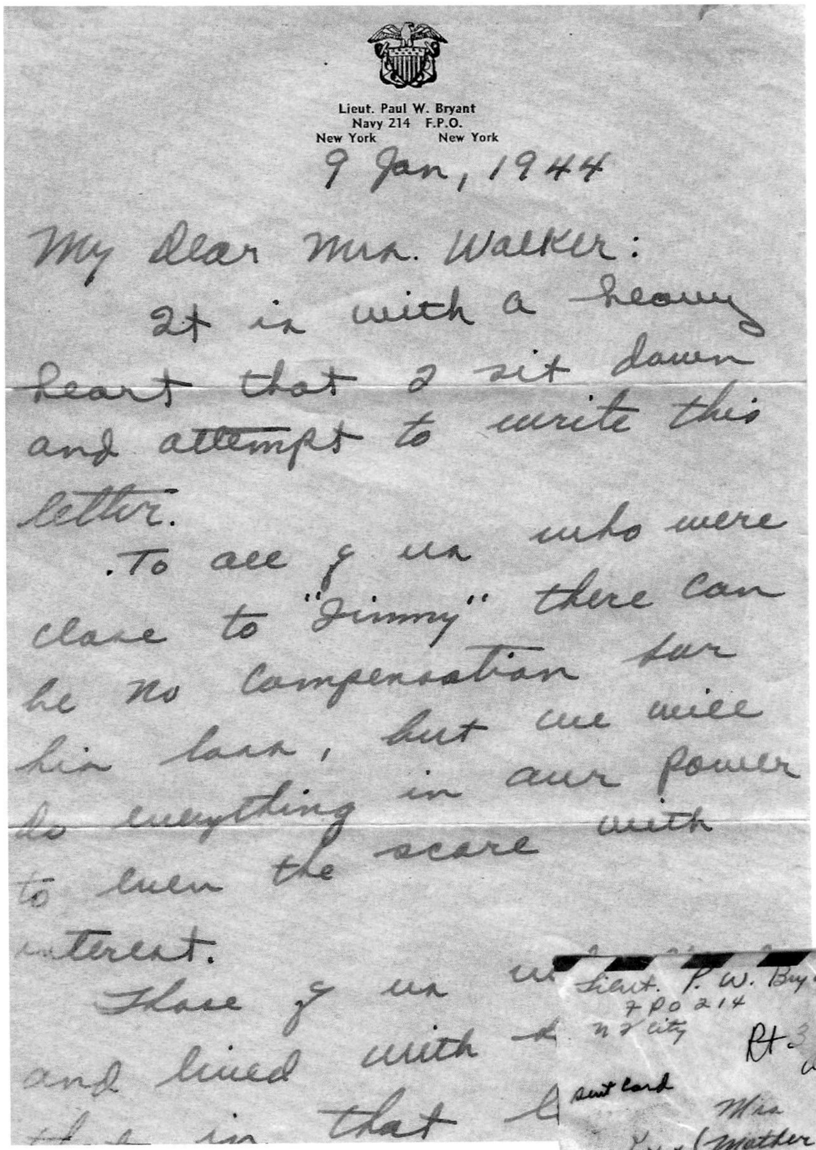

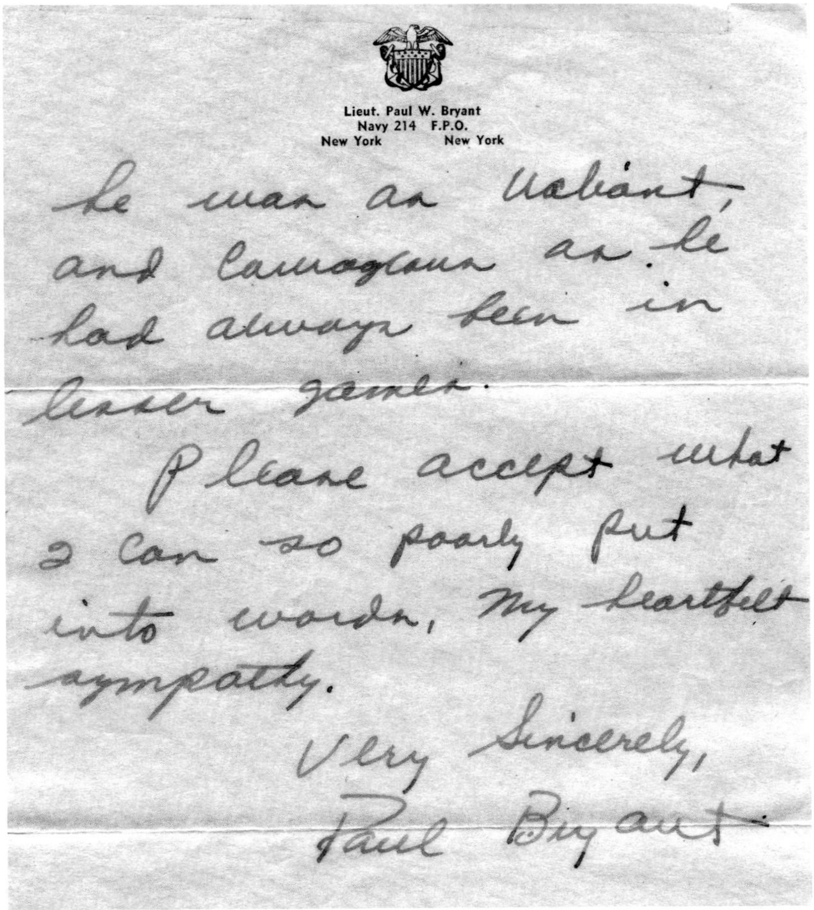

Lieut. Paul W. Bryant
Navy 214 F.P.O.
New York   New York

9 Jan, 1944

My dear Mrs. Walker:

It is with a heavy heart that I sit down and attempt to write this letter.

To all of us who were close to "Jimmy" there can be no compensation for his loss, but we will do everything in our power to even the score with interest.

Those of us who and lived with h___ ___ in that h___

[continued] he was an valiant, and courageous as he had always been in lesser games.

Please accept what I can so poorly put into words, my heartfelt sympathy.

Very Sincerely,

Paul Bryant

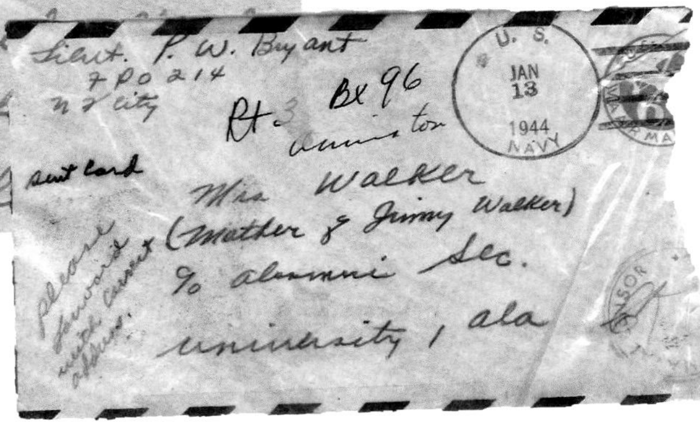

outstanding. The kids he coached were very fond of him. He was more than a coach to them.

"There is one thing certain, the boys he coached have benefitted by his association and are better men because of it. Jimmy went into the service to give his all if necessary, and he gave it. No man can do more. He has not died in vain and he will be remembered always by us with love," Hubert added.

Walker had written a letter of condolence to the mother of a shipmate from Tuscaloosa shortly before his death. The letter, which arrived after Walker's death, said "…I know that he did his best and gave his all for his country and his loved ones back home…I know you will feel that he gave all he had to help protect you and other mothers back home…I am happy on my way and hope for a chance to do more and more for my country and people. We all hope the war will be over soon, but hoping won't end it so we will have to keep blasting the enemy until they realize that the United Nations doesn't intend to stop until they have had enough."

A dive bomber prepares to take off from a U.S. carrier.

Scenes from Pearl Harbor, Hawaii, December 7, 1941.

DUTY ROSTER

"That generation, whatever the challenge, just went and did it and went on. They didn't talk about it a lot. They came home and went about their lives."

— *Joe Mosley*

Opposite: The British ocean liner Queen Mary steams into New York harbor in late 1945, returning more than 10,000 U.S. servicemen home after duty in Europe during World War II. (National Archives photograph)

WWII DUTY ROSTER

Former players, coaches and managers who served

Jack W. Aland

Alfred F. Alois

Warren Averitte

More than 300 former University of Alabama football players and coaches are known to have served in the military during World War II. Many others likely served, but are unlisted due to incomplete records. Additions or corrections to the following list are welcomed for future reference in the Paul W. Bryant Museum. Please email information to bryant-info@ua.edu or call 1-866-772-2327.

ABSTON, BILL, Peterson, AL. Halfback 1947-49. Served in the Navy and later as an officer in the Alabama Air National Guard.

ACKERMAN, EDWARD, Verona, NJ. Freshman football 1925. Army major.

ADAMS, GEORGE A., Montgomery, AL. Guard, 1935.

ALAND, JACK W., Birmingham, AL. Tackle 1940-42. Served in the Marines as an officer on Iwo Jima. (See story page 164)

ALBRIGHT, GEORGE V., Tuscaloosa, AL. Halfback 1944-46. Triple-threat back who threw three touchdown passes in a 63-7 win over Howard College in 1944. Navy.

ALOIS, ALFRED F., Schenectady, NY. Halfback 1940-42. Army captain. Served with Corps of Engineers in France, Okinawa and Philippines. Graduated from UA with an ROTC commission in March 1944. Retired from General Motors in Texas.

ANDERSON, VERNON L., Mobile, AL. Freshman football 1942. Army.

ANDERSON, FREDERICK F., Birmingham, AL. Center 1938. Army Air Forces.

ANGELICH, JAMES D., Indiana Harbor, IN. Halfback 1933-35. Navy lieutenant in North Africa.

ARTHUR, PAUL T., Birmingham, AL. End 1948-49. Marines.

AUGUST, JOHN C., Shadyside, OH. Halfback 1942, 46-47. Also lettered in baseball 1947. Star of January 1, 1943, Orange Bowl win over Boston College. Gained 214 yards rushing, passed for 247 yards and punted for a 39.6 average in 1942. Sergeant with 26th Marine Corps Regiment in the Pacific during WWII. Insurance agent in Rome, GA, following graduation from UA in 1949. (See story page 170)

AVERITTE, WARREN, Greenville, MS. Center 1937-40. Second-team All-SEC 1940. Saw combat action as a Marine lieutenant at Guadalcanal and Bougainville. Received a Purple Heart for serious wounds on Bougainville. Coached high school sports in Greenville before earning a doctorate from Columbia University. Professor of physical sciences at University of Chattanooga 1953-1979. (See story page 166)

AVERY, BART, Gloversville, NY. Quarterback 1941-42. Also played basketball. Earned Silver Star, Bronze Star and Purple Heart as Army officer with 84th Infantry Division in Europe. Killed in combat April 6, 1945.

AVERY, DON, Alhambra, CA. Football 1940-41.

BAILEY, DON, Birmingham, AL. Halfback 1940-41. Navy.

BALLARD, IRA C. (IKE), Gadsden, AL. Lineman 1926. ROTC and Scabbard and Blade. Civilian Conservation Corps camp commander as Army lieutenant prior to WWII. Provost Marshal at several German POW camps in U.S. and Europe during and after the war. Discharged as captain December 1945. Served as sheriff of Etowah County.

BARKER, TROY, Lineville, AL. Lineman 1930-32. Army captain.

BATY, WILLIAM. C. Jr., Bessemer, AL. Halfback 1920-23. Played professional football while in medical school. Career Navy surgeon assigned to the Fourth Marine Division in the Pacific Theater during WWII. Served aboard battleships Arkansas and New Mexico and destroyers Gilmer and Berry. As division surgeon, Baty was responsible for the care and treatment of 17,000 casualties during WWII. Retired rear admiral with Bronze Star, Legion of Merit, Asiatic-Pacific Campaign Medal, Presidential Unit Citation, American Campaign Medal, American Defense Service Medal and National Defense Service Medal. Alabama football team physician 1959-71 and Tuscaloosa County Health Officer for ten years. (See story page 192)

BAUGHMAN, WILLIAM H., Jeannette, PA. Center 1941-42, 1946. Navy.

BEARD, HERMAN, Guntersville, AL. Fullback 1941. Army corporal.

BEARD, SILAS A., Birmingham, AL. Halfback 1936-38. Army.

BEASLEY, JIM. Quarterback 1934-35. Army corporal.

BENNETT, WILDON H., Huntsville, AL. End 1941-42. Enlisted in the Army Air Forces on September 18, 1942. Served 40 months of active duty, most of it training P-47 and P-51 fighter pilots at Page Field in Fort Myers, Florida. Attained rank of staff sergeant. Operated a refrigeration and air conditioning business in Huntsville for 50 years.

BEST, MITCHELL C., Bowling Green, OH. Back 1935-36. Captain in Army Air Forces.

BIJUR, ROBERT D., New York, NY. Football 1939-40. Left school to join the Royal Air Force. Killed in Europe August 1943.

BIRES, ANDREW P., Ambridge, PA. End 1941-42. Army Air Forces bomber pilot and flight instructor.

BLACK, HOY D., Collinsville, AL. Guard 1926-27. Army sergeant.

BLACKMON, SUMPTER, Columbus, GA. Quarterback 1940-41. Also played baseball. Army officer in 101st Airborne Division. Twice parachuted behind enemy lines, the first on D-Day, June 6, 1944. Earned Silver Star and Purple Heart. High school coach and principal in Columbus, GA, after the war. (See story page 12)

BLUDWORTH, JOHN FRANK, DeFuniak Springs, FL. Fullback 1934-36. Army PFC with 106th Infantry Division. Taken prisoner during the Battle of the Bulge in December 1944 and liberated from Stalag IV B by Russian troops at the end of the war in May 1945. High school coach, principal and county schools superintendent for 35 years in DeFuniak Springs, FL. Died on the eve of his election to a fourth term as mayor. (See story page 16)

BOOZER, YOUNG J. Jr., Dothan, AL. Halfback 1933-36. President of the A Club Alumni 1962-64. Served 28 months in the Pacific as a Navy ensign, including service aboard attack transport ship USS Monrovia during assault landings at Guam, Saipan, Tarawa and Luzon. His brother, Lt. Wilmer H. Boozer, was killed in a plane crash at Robins Field, GA, during the war. (See story page 196)

Bart Avery

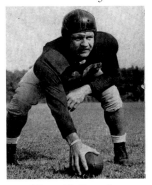

William H. Baughman

Wildon H. Bennett

Young J. Boozer Jr.

Thomas H. Borders

Lewis T. Bostick

Jack Vincent Brown

Paul W. Bryant

BORDERS, THOMAS H., Birmingham, AL. Tackle 1937-39. First lieutenant with the Army Air Forces. Piloted a B-17 bomber named "Birmingham Blitzkrieg" as it shot down the first German fighter of the war by a U.S. crew over occupied France in August 1942. Later died with his crew as their plane's bomb load was struck by enemy flak over Tunisia. (See story page 94)

BOSTICK, LEWIS T., Birmingham, AL. Guard 1936-38. Captain of the 1938 team. Played professional football with Cleveland Rams. Coached at Howard College and University of Alabama. Served as a fitness instructor in the Navy during WWII.

BOSWELL, CHARLES A., Birmingham, AL. Halfback 1937-39. Played 44 of 60 minutes in 7-0 win over Vanderbilt in 1938. Punted 10 times for 46-yard average and gained 33 yards in a 72-yard drive for the winning score. Also on Alabama track team. Blinded by enemy gunfire as an Army infantry captain in Germany. Won 17 national and 11 international blind golf championships. Featured on "This is Your Life" television show. Received the Sports Illustrated Silver Anniversary All-America Award in 1964. Inducted into the Alabama Sports Hall of Fame in 1972 and the Alabama Academy of Honor in 1983. Received the University of Alabama National Alumni Association's Paul W. Bryant Alumni-Athlete Award in 1990 in recognition of his accomplishments and contributions to society after leaving the University. (See story page 19)

BOWEN, ROBERT A. (BOB), East Point, GA. Quarterback 1940-41. Navy ensign. Wrote a novel (*The Islands*) about his wartime experiences in the Pacific.

BRADFORD, FRANK, Memphis, TN. Fullback 1939. Marines.

BRADFORD, HENRY VICTOR, Memphis, TN. Quarterback 1936-38. Also played baseball and basketball. Kicked the winning field goal in 3-0 win over Tulane in 1938. Alternate captain, second team All-SEC and All-South in 1938. Navy lieutenant.

BRANTMAN, WILLIAM T., Mt. Vernon, NY. Freshman football 1936. Navy lieutenant.

BRINKERHOFF, LESTER A., Hackensack, NJ. Center 1938-39. Lieutenant in Army Air Forces.

BROWN, BOB, Blytheville, AR. End/guard 1938-40. Army captain.

BROWN, DAVID A., Birmingham, AL. Halfback 1940-42. Navy seaman first class. Played professional football with the New York Giants. Head coach at Dothan High School. Banker, sheriff and businessman in Keystone Heights, FL.

BROWN, JACK VINCENT, Selma, AL. Back 1948-51. Team captain 1951. Also played basketball. Averaged 39 yards per kick on 64 punts in 1948. Army sergeant with occupation forces in Japan. Became president of Liberty National Life Insurance Company. Received the University of Alabama National Alumni Association's Paul W. Bryant Alumni-Athlete Award in 2009 for professional accomplishments and contributions to society after leaving the University. (See story page 26)

BROWN, LEROY, Blytheville, AR. Guard 1938-39. Army.

BRYANT, PAUL W., Fordyce, AR. End 1933-35. A-Club president 1936. Navy lieutenant for 42 months, including 14 months in North Africa. Coached Georgia and North Carolina Navy Pre-Flight football teams. Coached college football at Maryland, Kentucky, Texas A&M and Alabama. Won six national championships in 25 seasons at Alabama, averaging 9.3 wins per season. Had a career coaching record of 323-85-17, with an average of 8.5 wins per season over 38 years. Elected to Alabama Sports Hall of Fame 1969 and College Football Hall of Fame 1986. (See story page 198)

BUCKALEW, GEORGE, Thomasville, AL. Tackle 1934. Army.

BURKENHEIMER, LOUIS, Rochester, NY. Quarterback 1942. Army.

CADENHEAD, JOHN, Greenville, MS. End 1939. Army Air Forces pilot in Europe. Shot down by German flak but survived to return to duty. Career Air Force officer. Brother of Bill Cadenhead.

CADENHEAD, WILLIAM R. (BILL), Greenville, MS. Halfback 1946-49. Four-year letterman. Chosen team's most valuable player 1948 and team co-captain in 1949. Navy seaman first class in the submarine service. Head football coach at Coffee High of Florence before going into insurance. Brother of John Cadenhead. (See story page 206)

CAIN, JOHN L., Montgomery, AL. Fullback 1930-32. Team captain 1932. All-America 1931 and 1932, All-Southern Conference 1930-31-32. Punted 21 times for a 48-yard average in a 7-3 loss to Tennessee in the rain in 1932. Navy lieutenant. Coached at Georgia Navy Pre-Flight School. Head football coach at Southwest Louisiana before and after WWII. Assistant coach at Alabama 1934 and at Ole Miss 1947-72. Elected to the Alabama Sports Hall of Fame and College Football Hall of Fame.

CAIN, SAM, Bessemer, AL. Quarterback 1942, 46-47. Army.

CALDWELL, HERMAN "BLACKIE," Tallassee, AL. Halfback 1935-36. Also played basketball. Army Air Forces captain.

CALVIN, TOM, Athens, AL. Fullback 1948-50. Led Alabama in rushing in 1949 with 339 yards. Played professional football with the Pittsburgh Steelers 1952-54. Coached high school football 33 years at Baldwin County, Austin and Sylacauga, posting a 204-129-11 record. Member of the Alabama High School Athletic Association Hall of Fame. Served in the Army during WWII.

CAMPBELL, TILDEN (HAPPY), Pine Bluff, AR. Quarterback 1931-34. Served as assistant football coach and head baseball coach at Alabama. Crimson Tide baseball coach for 25 seasons (1935-42 and 1947-63). His teams won nine Southeastern Conference championships and two SEC Western Division titles. As a navy lieutenant during World War II, Campbell coached the Georgia Navy Pre-Flight baseball team and served as athletic director at the Corpus Christi, TX, Naval Station.

CASHIO, GREGORY R. (GRI), Gadsden, AL. Guard 1942, 46-47. Served as president of the A Club. Saw action with the Marines in four Pacific assault landings,

including Guam and Okinawa, during 26 months overseas. High school coach and businessman. (See story page 175)

CAUSEY, JOE, Douglas, AZ. Halfback 1929-31. Also on basketball and track teams. Navy captain.

CHAMBERS, BILL, Los Angeles, CA. Tackle 1942. Earned All-SEC honors while playing for Georgia Tech as a member of the Navy's V-12 program in 1943.

CHAMBLISS, BYRON, Birmingham, AL. End, 1946-48. Army corporal. Saw duty in Germany and the Pacific. High school football coach and insurance executive. (See story page 29)

CHAPMAN, JOEL HERBERT (HERB), Elmore, AL. Center 1942, 1946-47. Led Tide baseball teams of 1946-47 in hitting (.368 and .322); hits (32 and 31); home runs (3 and 3) and runs batted in (29 and 17). Also led team in runs scored (22) in 1946 and in doubles in 1947 (6). Saw duty with the Army's 82nd Airborne Division in France, Belgium and Holland during WWII. Minor league baseball player, high school coach and business executive after college. Hit .303 with 24 home runs in 477 minor league baseball games 1949-52. (See story page 31)

CHAPPELL, HOWARD, Sylacauga, AL. Halfback 1931-33. Navy lieutenant fitness instructor during WWII. Coach at Deshler High School in Tuscumbia, AL, 1934-42 and 1949-60, posting a 110-50-2 record with three undefeated seasons. Elementary school principal 1961-76. City Commissioner 10 years. Deshler High football stadium is named in his honor. Elected to the Alabama High School Athletic Association Hall of Fame. He died in 2006 at age 96.

CHORBA, JOE, Follansbee, WV. Guard 1941-42. Army lieutenant. Head coach at Guntersville High School.

CHRISTIAN, CHARLES, Tuscaloosa, AL. Freshman football 1938. Army Air Forces lieutenant.

CHRISTIE, JOHN, Talladega, AL. Guard 1948. Navy.

CLARY, MURPHY (RED), Tuscaloosa, AL. Army private with the 232nd Field Artillery Battalion.

John L. Cain

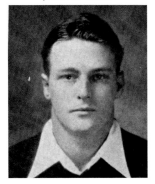

Tilden Campbell

Gregory R. Cashio

Howard Chappell

David M. Cochran

Ben Compton

Ted Cook

Russ Craft

CLARK, EDWARD W., Alexandria, AL. Halfback 1936-38. Army major with the 42nd Infantry Division in Germany. Won the Silver Star and Bronze Star for heroism. Participated in the liberation of the Nazi concentration camp at Dachau. Also served in the Army during the Korean War. (See story page 35)

COCHRAN, RALPH GRAHAM, Hueytown, AL. Quarterback 1948-49. Navy.

COCHRAN, ROBERT ELLIS, Hueytown, AL. Halfback 1947-49. Navy. Coach at Andalusia High School.

COCHRANE, DAVID M. (PAL), Tuscaloosa, AL. Back, 1929-32. Army mess sergeant aboard the Army transport ship *USS Grant.* Later a Tuscaloosa attorney and county probate judge.

COCHRAN, HENRY, Paducah, KY. Quarterback 1936-37. Navy.

COLLIER, JOHN E., Wetumpka, AL. Back 1926. Army lieutenant.

COFFMAN, ROLAND. Back / tackle 1924. Navy ensign.

COHEN, DAVE, Chicago, IL. End 1941. Army Air Forces lieutenant.

COHEN, HERB, Middletown, NY. Guard 1944. Army.

COLLINS, ROBERT, Morgantown, WV. Tackle/center 1944-46. Army.

COMPTON, BEN, Greensboro, AL. Lineman 1921-24. All-Southern Conference 1924. Army Air Forces major assigned to Air Force training bases at Tuscaloosa and Tuskegee. A former highway patrolman in Tuscaloosa, Compton died of a heart attack at the Tuskegee Army Air Forces Base on October 18, 1946.

COMPTON, CHARLES E., Sylacauga, AL. Tackle 1942, 46-47. Spent 15 months in combat with the 100th Infantry Division in Germany. Earned the Distinguished Service Cross for heroism in action, two Purple Hearts, Bronze Star and other medals. Recommended for the Congressional Medal of Honor. A daring machine gunner, Compton became the subject of several news and magazine articles. Spent more

than 20 years as a Southern Baptist missionary in Brazil before being killed in an automobile accident in 1972 at age 52. (See story page 40)

CONWAY, BILLY, Birmingham, AL. Guard 1944-46. Served in the Navy at Guantanamo Bay and aboard the *USS Princeton.*

COOK, TED, Birmingham, AL. End 1941-42, 1946. Army Air Forces June 1942-February 1946. Received the American Campaign Medal, Victory Medal and Good Conduct Medal and attained the rank of sergeant. Athletic instructor and player on the 3rd Air Force football team. Named to the 1945 All-Service football team while playing for the MacDill Field Gremlins in Tampa, FL. Played in the 1945 College All-Star game. A Club president 1946-47. Played professional football with Detroit (1947) and Green Bay (1948-50). Played in 46 professional games, 14 as a starter, with 61 receptions for 891 yards and five touchdowns. Long-time Birmingham automobile dealer.

COX, RAYMOND F., Lincoln, AL. Fullback 1941-42. Army lieutenant.

COX, WILLIAM CARY, Bainbridge, GA. Center 1937-39. All-America and team captain 1939. Reached the rank of colonel while serving with the Army in North Africa, Sicily, Tunisia, France, Belgium and Germany. Earned Silver Star and Bronze Star. Commanded an infantry battalion which helped break the Siegfried Line. Later an automobile dealer in Sylacauga. Elected to the Alabama Sports Hall of Fame. (See story page 47)

CRAFT, RUSS, Beach Bottom, WV. Halfback 1940-42. Star player on the baseball team. Second-team All-SEC in 1942 while gaining 394 yards on 68 carries. Hit .346 on 1941 baseball team. Served as Army lieutenant in graves registration in Germany. Played professional football for Philadelphia (1946-53) and Pittsburgh (1954). Later operated a business and served as sheriff of Brooke County, WV. (See story page 54)

CRIGLER, PHILLIP. Football 1941. Army captain during WWII. Retired Air Force lieutenant colonel. Coached at Elba High School.

CRISMAN, RUDY. Football 1938-39. As B-26 pilot, flew 68 missions over Europe with the 9th Air Force.

CRISP, HENRY (HANK), Tuscaloosa, AL. Served as assistant football coach, head basketball coach, athletic director and intramural sports director 1921-42, 1945 and 1950-67. Served as civilian physical fitness instructor, football coach and head trainer with Georgia Navy Pre-Flight School June 1942-January 1945. Elected to the Alabama Sports Hall of Fame. (See story page 148)

DABBS, BILLY, Hueytown, AL. End 1942. Played football at Howard College in 1943 while enrolled in Navy V-12 program.

DANIEL, CECIL, Andalusia, AL. Football 1926-27. Army captain. Served with 26th Infantry Division in the Battle of the Bulge. First coach at Straughn High School.

DAVIS, ALVIN (PIG), Green Forest, AR. Fullback/end 1936-38. The first player signed by former Alabama head coach Paul "Bear" Bryant when he was an assistant coach for the Crimson Tide (1936-39). Averaged six yards per carry in 1938 with 335 yards on 56 rushes. Davis served four years in the Navy during World War II as a chief petty officer, including service aboard a destroyer in the Atlantic. High school coach for 40 years. Sons Tim, Steve, Bill and Mike were all kicking specialists at Alabama and the Davis family is said to have collectively scored more than 500 points for the Crimson Tide. The Davis clan played in one Rose Bowl, three Orange Bowls, five Sugar Bowls and two Cotton Bowls and helped win three national championships for Alabama.

DAVIS, CHARLES D., Uniontown, PA. Halfback 1947-49. Davis was offered a scholarship to Alabama by Tide head coach Frank Thomas after a high school game near Pittsburgh. "I was a poor kid; I had no money; my parents were divorced, and I was living with another family. He offered me a scholarship with everything paid, so I took it," Davis said. Davis was at Alabama only a short time before being drafted into the Army in October 1945 as a freshman. "Coach Thomas said he could get me a deferment but I refused, so I listened to the January 1, 1946, Rose Bowl game while on KP at Fort Sill, Oklahoma,"

Davis said. He served as a private in the U.S. and East Africa with Army intelligence as a message decoder for 15 months before returning to school in the spring of 1947. He played 1947-49 before sitting out his senior season due to an injury. He graduated from University in 1951 with a degree in marketing and worked 35 years for General Electric. His late wife of 57 years, Lorraine McGovern Davis, played in a "Honey Bowl" game (girl's football) in Denny Stadium in the late 1940s. The teams were coached by members of the men's football team.

DAVIS, FRED L., Louisville, KY. Tackle 1937-40. All-SEC and alternate team captain 1940. Named MVP in the 1940 East-West College All-Star Game. Earned Rookie of the Year honors in 1940 while helping the Washington Redskins win the NFL championship. Played in the 1941 Pro Bowl. Earned All-Pro honors two years with the Chicago Bears, helping the team win the 1946 NFL title. All-State in football, basketball and track in high school. Elected to the Alabama Sports Hall of Fame in 1981. Davis was the first Alabama football player to be drafted into military service. He served two years as a lieutenant in the Army Air Forces. Son Fred Jr. played football at Alabama in the mid-1960s.

DAVIS, PAUL, Tuscaloosa, AL. End 1944-45. Marines.

DENDY, EMMETT, Luverne, AL. Halfback 1946. Army Air Forces. Turret gunner on a B-24 bomber during 22 missions over Germany. (See story page 98)

DEVECCHIS, GUIDO, Weirton, WV. Halfback 1942. Army. Played at West Virginia 1946.

DEWITT, BILL. End 1942. Army.

DILDY, JAMES A., Nashville, AR. Tackle 1931-33. Army Air Forces lieutenant. Taught physical fitness in Florida and California. Worked for Arkansas Power & Light for many years as industrial recruiter and worked closely with many Arkansas governors, including Nelson Rockefeller and Bill Clinton. Is said to have urged UA coaches to recruit Paul "Bear" Bryant, against whom he had played in high school. Died in 2001.

DILDY, JOSEPH L., Nashville, AR. Center 1932-34.

Henry Crisp

Alvin Davis

Charles D. Davis

Joseph Dildy

Harold Drew

Albert B. Elmore Sr.

Ben M. Ennis

Charles Erwin

Army Air Forces lieutenant. Head football coach at Blytheville, AR, and later line coach at Ole Miss.

DILL, RICHARD, Football 1940-41. Airman first class in Army Air Forces.

DIMITRO, MIKE, Weirton, WV. Guard 1942. Navy.

DIORIO, AL, Mingo Junction, OH. Tackle 1948-49. Army.

DISMUKES, ROY, Boyles, AL. Guard 1925-27. Army Air Forces lieutenant.

DOMNANOVICH, JOSEPH J., South Bend, IN. Center 1940-42. Three-year starter. All-America, All-SEC and team captain in 1942. Received Army commission in 1943 and served as a physical fitness instructor and special services officer in the states and in Europe. Played six years of professional football then spent 30 years with U.S. Steel in Birmingham. Served as president of the A Club Alumni 1976-77. Elected to the Alabama Sports Hall of Fame. (See story page 56)

DONALDSON, WILLIAM C. (BILL). Center 1939. Served in the Royal Canadian Air Force.

DREW, HAROLD (RED), Tuscaloosa, AL. Head football coach 1947-53. Assistant football coach 1931-42 and 1945. Track coach 23 years. Served as pilot in WWI and became the first American flyer to bail out of a plane during training. Served as a fitness instructor in WWII. Was fleet recreation officer on Saipan when war ended in 1945. Head football coach at Ole Miss 1946 and at Alabama 1947-53. Elected to the Alabama Sports Hall of Fame. (See story page 151)

ELLIS, ERNEST RAIFORD, Birmingham, AL. Member of 1935 Rose Bowl team. Army captain.

ELMORE, ALBERT B. SR., Gordo, AL. End 1928-30. President of the A Club while in college and president of the A Club Alumni 1964-65. Head coach and athletic director at Troy State 1931-37. Assistant coach at VMI and Alabama. Brothers James F. (1941) and Eugene (1944) also played football and baseball at Alabama. Son Albert Jr. played quarterback at Alabama 1953-55. Nephews Dudley Kerr (1966-67) and Grady Elmore Jr. (1962-64) also played for the

Crimson Tide. Served as a captain in the Army Air Forces teaching physical fitness and coaching football during WWII.

ELMORE, EUGENE, Reform, AL. Tackle 1944. Army.

ELMORE, FERMAN, Reform, AL. Center/guard 1941, 1946. Also played baseball. Army. Spent 30 years as a high school coach and teacher, including 17 years as a head coach. Had a record of 99-51-12. Member of the Alabama High School Athletic Association Hall of Fame.

ENNIS, BEN M., Fayette, AL. End/guard 1923-26. Played on Alabama's first two Rose Bowl teams. As Navy lieutenant, coached Georgia Navy Pre-Flight football. Assistant coach under Dixie Howell at Idaho, Pooley Hubert at VMI and Frank Thomas at Alabama. Also coached at LSU and Sidney Lanier High School.

ERWIN, CHARLES, Athens, GA. End 1941-42. Also basketball player. Served in the Marines during WWII. Earned the Bronze Star as flame thrower operator on Iwo Jima and saw duty at Nagasaki, Japan, after the war ended.

FARR, HOSMER, Tuscaloosa, AL. Halfback 1938. Army private first class.

FELD, BERNARD D. JR., Birmingham, AL. Freshman football 1931. Army Air Forces sergeant.

FELD, PHILLIP H., Birmingham, AL. Awarded letter as manager 1932. Captain in Army Air Forces.

FICHMAN, LEON, Los Angeles, CA. Tackle 1941-42. Army officer. Played professional football with Detroit Lions. High school coach and teacher in Tulsa, OK.

FISHER, CHARLES J., Tampa, FL. End 1944. Maritime Service.

FITZGERALD, JOSEPH T., Los Angeles, CA. Guard 1942. Army.

FLEMING, ROBERT H., Pensacola, FL. Freshman football 1929. Navy lieutenant.

FLETCHER, MAURICE W., Clarksdale, MS. Quarterback 1935-37. Served in Navy Medical Corps.

FLOWERS, CHARLES, Bainbridge, GA. Quarterback 1941. Marines.

FORNEY, JOHN M. SR., Tuscaloosa, AL. Center 1920. Served three years in the Pacific as a Navy surgeon, including duty as chief surgeon aboard the hospital ship *USS Bountiful* and during assault landings at Mindoro, Lingayen, Leyte and Corregidor. Physician in Tuscaloosa before the war and later in Birmingham and New York City. Forney earned the Bronze Star and other decorations and attained the rank of commander. (See story page 209)

FOSHEE, JESSE F., Clanton, AL. Guard 1937-38. Army lieutenant. Assistant coach at Alabama and head coach at Tuscaloosa, Talladega and Columbus, GA, high schools.

FRANCIS, WILLIAM KAVANAUGH, Timpson, TX. Center 1933-35. Army.

FRANKO, JAMES A., Yorkville, OH. Guard 1947-49. Spent 33 months as Army infantry rifleman in Europe.

FREY, CALVIN C., Arkadelphia, AR. Guard 1930-33. Long-time assistant coach at East Tennessee State University. Died November 25, 1969 at age 59. Also coached at Union College and Tennessee Tech. Army corporal during WWII.

FULLER, BEN S., Tuscaloosa, AL. Football 1937. Army captain.

GAMBRELL, DANIEL JOSEPH, Talladega, AL. Center 1942, 1945-46. Star catcher on the baseball team. Served 21 months with Marines in the Pacific. Head coach at Walker County High School 1952-66.

GAMMON, GEORGE, Cullman, AL. Back 1940-42. Also on track team. As a B-17 bomber pilot, Gammon flew 33 missions over Germany, many of them in a plane he christened the "Alabama Gal" in honor of his wife. Saw action in five campaigns with the 15th Air Force. (See story page 100)

GANDY, RALPH FULTON, Birmingham, AL. Quarterback 1932-34. Army captain.

GELLERSTEDT, SAM ERIC, Dothan, AL. Tackle 1946. Awarded three Purple Hearts while serving as a machine gunner with Army infantry in Europe. Son Sammy earned All-America honors as nose guard at Alabama in 1968.

GERBER, ELWOOD G., Naperville, IL. Guard 1939-40. Played professional football with the Philadelphia Eagles 1941-42. Navy sea duty and football player with Bainbridge (MD) Navy Training Station, where he was captain of the 1943 unbeaten team which outscored opponents 313-7.

GIBSON, RICHARD D., Mobile, AL. End 1945. Marines.

GODFREE, NEWT, Alexander City, AL. Tackle 1930-32. All-Southern in 1932. Army captain with Special Services in Japan. Coached high school football at Bridgeport and Oxford, AL, and Tifton, GA. Produced a 10-0 team at Tifton in 1940.

GOLDBERG, LEROY A., Pine Bluff, AR. Quarterback 1933-35. Army private first class.

GRANTHAM, HUBERT, Llano, TX. Tackle 1946. Served with the Army in Europe after going ashore at Normandy on June 9, 1944. High school coach and principal at Greenville and Phenix City, AL, for over 30 years. His Greenville team went 10-0 in 1955. Mrs. Grantham was a war bride from England, and although her husband played and coached the sport, she said she never liked American football. "They ran about a bit, struggled, stopped, and ran a bit more. They kept stopping and whispering. I didn't know what they were up to. I was bored so I didn't go very often," she said.

GRANTHAM, JAMES MORRIS (JIM), Llano, TX. End 1942, 1945-46. Army Air Forces. Head football coach at Troy State 1951-54. Successful high school coach in New York and New Jersey for 30 years.

GRAY, LECIL D., Jasper, AL. Freshman football 1932. Army lieutenant.

Jesse F. Foshee

Daniel Joseph Gambrell

George Gammon

James Morris Grantham

James V. Gunnin

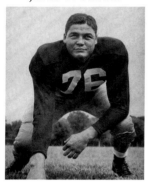

Herbert Hannah

Cliff W. Hansen

Billy Harrell

GREEN, JACK P., Centre, AL. Guard 1942, 1944-46. Lieutenant Army Air Forces.

GRESHAM, JOHN S., Millbrook, AL. End 1941-42. Army Lieutenant.

GRIFFIN, CLYDE, Union Springs, AL. Guard 1942. Army.

GIFFIN, G. W., Timpson, TX. Football and track 1935-36. Army Private.

GUNNIN, JAMES V., Bessemer, AL. Tackle 1942, 1946. Marine private. Saw action on Iwo Jima and served in occupied Japan. Received Purple Heart. Graduated 1948. Coached high school sports at Brookwood and Boaz in Alabama and at Palmetto and St. Petersburg, FL, until 1965. Died in 1966 at age 44.

GUNTER, SAMUEL M., Walker County, AL. Halfback 1936. Army Air Forces staff sergeant.

HAGAN, JAMES H., Mobile, AL. Quarterback 1912-1916. Also played baseball and basketball. Served on UA ROTC staff and as an assistant football coach during the 1920s. Spent 33 years in the Army, including service during World War I and World War II. Retired as a colonel.

HANNAH, HERBERT (HERB), Athens, AL. Lineman 1948-50. Spent five years as a Navy pilot, including flying patrols along the East Coast of the U.S. His brother Bill and sons John, Charles and David also played football at Alabama. (See story page 211)

HANSEN, CLIFF W. (SWEDE), Gary, Indiana. Tackle 1939-40. Army lieutenant. Killed in a plane crash in Tennessee in 1942.

HANSON, JOHN L., Roanoke, AL. Fullback 1939-40. Elected captain for the 1941 season but passed up his senior season to join the Army Air Forces. Buzzed the Alabama practice field once in 1941 after getting his wings and commission as a lieutenant.

HARGROVE, THOMAS. Football 1944. Army.

HARRELL, WILLIAM E. SR., Bainbridge, GA. Halfback/quarterback 1938-41. Also on the track team. A Club president 1941. As a Navy lieutenant, Harrell played football for the Great Lakes Naval Station in 1942 and served as a physical fitness instructor. Long-time educator and civic leader in Columbus, GA.

HARKINS, GROVER, Gadsden, AL. Guard 1936-38. Sergeant in Army Air Forces.

HARMON, LESTER G., Bainbridge, GA. Guard 1941. Enlisted in the Marines in 1942 and served in WWII, Korea and Vietnam before retiring in 1968 as a colonel. A graduate of the University of Maryland, Harmon died in Slidell, LA, in 2006.

HAUSE, ORVIL R., Piedmont, AL. Quarterback 1946. Earned Bronze Star and Purple Heart as infantry platoon leader in Europe 1941-45. Among the assault troops who landed at Normandy on D-Day June 6, 1944. He fought in France and Germany until the war's end in May 1945. After earning post-war degrees from Alabama, served as commandant of cadets, physical education teacher and head baseball coach at North Georgia College, Dahlonega, GA, 1950-1986. His son, O. R. Hause Jr., served in the Air Force for 25 years and earned the Distinguished Flying Cross as a fighter pilot in Vietnam.

HEARN, FRED, Albertville, AL. Guard 1931-32. Army lieutenant.

HECHT, GEORGE A., Chicago Heights, IL. Guard and drop-kicking specialist 1940-42. Army lieutenant. Played for Fort Benning Doughboys during training with the 131st Infantry Regiment.

HENDERSON, WILLIAM (BILLY), Tuscaloosa, AL. Guard spring 1946. Also played baseball 1946. All-Service with Charleston Coast Guard in 1943. Scored 33 points, including three touchdowns via blocked kicks, a field goal, six PATs and a rushing touchdown. Earned All-Southern Conference honors at The Citadel 1949. Coached at Tuscaloosa High School for 20 years, winning state titles in football and basketball. Officiated SEC football for 28 years. Was UA football practice official for many years. Member of the Alabama High School Athletic Association Hall of Fame. His son Bill played football at Alabama.

HEWES, WILLIS DONALD, Russellville, AR. Center 1931-32. Navy lieutenant. Head coach at Dothan High School and city recreation director.

HICKERSON, J. EDWARD (ED), Ventura, CA. Guard, 1938-40. Second-team All-SEC 1940. Coached Georgia Navy Pre-Flight team 1942 and served as a sub chaser in Miami 1943. Navy lieutenant. Later served as an assistant coach at Alabama.

HITE, JOHN EDWIN, Nashville, TN. Halfback 1944, 1946. Also played basketball. Army Air Forces. Played for Keesler AFB against Alabama in 1945.

HOLLEY, HILMON D., Tuscaloosa, AL. Back 1930-32. Army training instructor.

HOLLIS, DANIEL L. JR., New York, NY. Football 1935-36. Navy midshipman.

HOLM, BERNARD P. (TONY), Ensley, AL. Fullback 1927-29. All-America and All-Southern Conference 1929. Played professional football with Providence, Portsmouth, Chicago and Pittsburgh. Was the first quarterback for Pittsburgh. Head coach of the Charlotte (NC) team in the American Professional Football League. Physical fitness instructor as a Navy lieutenant during WWII.

HOLM, CHARLES HAROLD, Ensley, AL. Fullback 1936-38. Chosen All-SEC and team MVP 1938. All-Scandian-American 1938. Averaged over five yards per carry 1938 as team's second-leading rusher with 390 yards. Navy ensign. Pilot and flight instructor during the war.

HOOD, ROBERT A. (BOB), Gadsden, AL. End 1946-48. Army Air Forces.

HOUSTON, ELLIS (RED), Bessemer, AL. Center 1930-32.

HOWELL, MILLARD F. (DIXIE), Hartford, AL. Halfback 1932-34. All-SEC triple-threat halfback in 1933 and 1934. All-America 1934. Star of 1935 Rose Bowl win over Stanford (29-13) with 313 all-purpose yards and three touchdowns. Voted the game's outstanding player and named to the All-Time Rose Bowl Team. Set an SEC record with an 89-yard punt against Tennessee in 1933. Played in five games with NFL's

Washington Redskins in 1937. Head coach at University of Mexico 1935. Head coach at Arizona State 1938-41, posting a 23-15-4 record. Won conference titles in 1939 and 1940 and took ASU to its first two bowl games. Joined the Navy as a lieutenant in 1942 and served as a physical fitness instructor and coach at North Carolina Pre-Flight, Georgia Pre-Flight and in the Marshall Islands. Following military duty, served as an assistant football coach at Alabama then as head coach at Idaho 1947-50, posting a 13-20-1 record. Had a non-credited role as a football player in the 1936 movie *The Adventures of Frank Merriwell* and was mentioned in the book *To Kill A Mockingbird.* Inducted into the College Football Hall of Fame in 1970 and the Alabama Sports Hall of Fame in 1971. The most valuable player award for the University of Alabama spring game is called the Dixie Howell Award in his honor. Former Alabama coach Frank Thomas once called Howell the "greatest player he ever coached," comparing him to the immortal George Gipp of Notre Dame, with whom Thomas had played. "Dixie was as near faultless as a player can be. He had that thing called a touch of genius," Thomas said of Howell. Howell married stage and screen actress Peggy Waters of Birmingham, AL, in 1935. He died of cancer in 1971 at age 58.

HUDSON, BEN AUSTIN, Montgomery, AL. End 1923-25. Army lieutenant colonel with 31st Division.

HUDSON, EDGAR. Football 1939-40. Physical fitness instructor and coach as Army Air Forces lieutenant. Coach at Tuscaloosa High School.

HUGHES, HALBERT ELTON, Pine Bluff, AR. Quarterback 1938-39. Army captain.

HUGHES, HOWARD, Little Rock, AR. Halfback 1941. Also played baseball. Served as a sergeant with the Army Air Forces in the 57th Troop Carrier Squadron in the Pacific.

HUGHES, LARRY G. (BUCK), Tuscaloosa, AL. Back 1931-33. Earned All-State and All-Southern honors as a fullback on the undefeated Tuscaloosa High School teams of 1927-29 under Coach Paul Burnum. Navy lieutenant during WWII. Saw duty on a tanker ship and as a fitness instructor. Head coach at Tuscaloosa, Russellville and Huntsville high schools and assis-

J. Edward Hickerson

Hillman Holley

Tony Holm

Dixie Howell

Roy M. Johnson Jr.

Crawford H. Jones

Henry "Red" Jones

Eli Kaluger

tant coach at Howard College and the University of Alabama. Retired from Naval Reserve as lieutenant commander.

HURT, CECIL A., Chattanooga, TN. End 1926-29. Also on basketball and track teams. Army lieutenant colonel with service in India.

HUTSON, RAY, Pine Bluff, AR. Halfback 1940 and spring 1941. Also played basketball. As an Army Air Forces pilot, lieutenant Hutson flew 77 missions over the "Hump" in Asia. His twin brother Robert, also a pilot, was killed in the Pacific. Younger brother of Alabama All-America end Don Hutson. (See story page 110)

HUTSON, ROBERT, Pine Bluff, AR. Halfback 1940 and spring 1941. Also played basketball. Army Air Forces pilot. Died in a crash in the South Pacific August 27, 1943. Twin brother of Ray Hutson and younger brother of Alabama All-America end Don Hutson. (See story page 110)

JACKIMCZYK, WILLIAM STANLEY, Northampton, MA. Football 1940. Army Air Forces lieutenant.

JANNETT, ANTHONY V., Birmingham, AL. Freshman football 1928. Army lieutenant.

JENKINS, ROBERT THOMAS, Talladega, AL. Fullback 1942. Joined the Navy in 1943 after outstanding sophomore season at Alabama. Played football for the Naval Academy 1943-44, earning All-America honors in 1944. Later a Birmingham businessman. Elected to Alabama Sports Hall of Fame. (See story page 215)

JOHNSON, ROY M. JR., Birmingham, AL. Left halfback 1940-42. Also played baseball 1941-42 and 1946-47. At only 5-2 and 137 pounds, Johnson was a fan favorite as a football player. Completed 13 of 21 passes for 170 yards in a "B-team" game against Mississippi State in 1942. Rejected by ROTC and pilot training because he was too short, Johnson later became a B-24 bombardier with the Army Air Forces and flew 35 missions over Burma with the 9th Bomb Squadron, 7th Bomb Group in the 5th Air Force, earning the Distinguished Flying Cross and Air Medal. Returned to UA after the war and earned a law degree

while playing on the baseball team. He practiced law in Birmingham for 58 years and died in 2006. One of Johnson's hobbies was researching and speaking on the trial of Jesus Christ. (See story page 102)

JONES, BRUCE, Jasper, AL. Guard 1923-25. Captain of Alabama's first Rose Bowl team. Professional football 1927-34. Army lieutenant colonel. Served 16 months in North Africa and Italy. Served as president of the A Club Alumni 1955-56.

JONES, CRAWFORD H. (HAL), Tuscaloosa, AL. Quarterback 1941-42. Army captain. Killed by an enemy sniper in Germany on April 19, 1945. His father Henry Heard Jones (1901) and brother Harwell Jones (1928) also played football at Alabama. Hal Jones is buried in France. (See story page 114)

JONES, HARWELL H., Tuscaloosa, AL. Football 1928. Also on track team. A-Club member. Army Air Forces. Also served during Korean War. Retired lieutenant colonel. Father Henry (1901) and brother Hal (1941-42) also played football at Alabama. Grandson Robert Eubank was a 1996 UA football walk-on. (See story page 114)

JONES, HENRY EDWARD (RED) JR., Laurel, MS. End 1942. Army sergeant. Killed in action in Luxembourg on January 2, 1945.

JONES, RALPH C., Florence, AL. End 1944. Military duty 1941-44.

KALUGER, ELI, Shadyside, OH. End 1941-42. A Marine corporal, Kaluger served in a number of assault landings in the Pacific, including Guadalcanal, Guam and Okinawa. He received the Purple Heart for wounds on Guadalcanal. Played in the infamous "Mosquito Bowl" game played by the Marines on Guadalcanal in December 1944. One of five brothers who served in the military during WWII. (See story page 177)

KASER, BILL, Los Angeles, CA. Football 1940. Army private first class.

KELLY, WILLIAM M., Jacksonville, FL. End 1920-21. Army lieutenant colonel.

KENDALL, FRANK (SWEDE), Tuscaloosa, AL. End 1928-30. Member of 1930 national championship team under Wallace Wade. His sister was married to Tide assistant coach Hank Crisp. Served as a captain in the Army's Coast Artillery in New York 1943-45. High school coach for more than 25 years, 18 of them at Tuscaloosa High School, where he had played on unbeaten Black Bear football teams. Elected to the Alabama Sports Hall of Fame. Sons Frank Jr. and Tommy played varsity tennis at Alabama. (See story page 59)

KILGROW, JOE, Montgomery, AL. Halfback 1934-37. All-America and All-Southeastern Conference in 1937. All-SEC baseball 1938-39. Led Alabama in passing and scoring during an undefeated regular season (9-0) in 1937 before a 13-0 loss to California in the Rose Bowl. Assistant coach at Mercer College. Hit .295 in minor league baseball 1939-40. Called to active duty with National Guard 1940. Received a battlefield commission for leadership during 38 months of front-line duty in the Pacific theater. Alabama assistant coach 1945-57. University golf course superintendent 1957-67. Elected to the Alabama Sports Hall of Fame. (See story page 118)

KILGROW, BENNY, Montgomery, AL. Fullback 1938-40. Joined Army Air Forces December 12, 1941. Bombardier on a B-17 Flying Fortress that was shot down over France on July 4, 1943. Spent remainder of the war as POW. Younger brother of Joe Kilgrow. (See story page 118)

KILLIAN, FRANK, Ambridge, PA. Guard 1942. Marines.

KIMBALL, MORTON W., South Bend, IN. Guard 1939-41. Saw duty as an Army major with the Quartermaster Corps in Europe starting at Omaha Beach on June 9, 1944. Served throughout France and Belgium. Career Army officer with service during the Korean War. Retired in 1969 at rank of lieutenant colonel. Earned Legion of Merit, Bronze Star, Army Occupation Medal. European-African-Middle Eastern Campaign Medal, American Campaign Medal, National Defense Service Medal with oak leaf cluster, Korean Service Medal, United Nations National Service Medal, World War II Victory Medal, Distinguished Unit Citation, Meritorious Unit Citation and Distinguished Unit Badge. Married Andree LeRoy in Binche, Bel-gium, making Mrs. Kimball one of the thousands of European war brides who followed their husbands back to the United States after the end of the war.

KING, GEORGE, Townley, AL. Guard 1936-37. Army medical corps lieutenant.

KIZZIRE, DOYLE M., Birmingham, AL. Fullback 1946-49. Army Air Forces first lieutenant. Earned his wings in March 1944 and piloted B-24 bombers in the European theater of war from July 1944-May 1945. Earned Air Medal and Distinguished Flying Cross among other decorations while assigned to the 15th Air Force near Foggia, Italy, Kizzire flew 50 bombing sorties on European targets, including the heavily protected oil refineries of Ploesti, Romania. Kizzire escaped injury although his plane ("Ice Cold Katie") was riddled by enemy flak and gunfire. Was a high school coach at Slocomb and Hartford before becoming a civilian helicopter flight instructor at Fort Rucker, AL, and Fort Walters, TX. "There was nothing heroic about it," Kizzire said of his service during World War II. "It was just the thing to do at the time---a fact of life."

KOSLASKY, ALBERT, Fayette, PA. Guard 1944. Navy. Worked for Pennsylvania DOT after military service.

KRAUTWALD, WILLIAM F. (BILL), Peoria, IL. Tackle 1940. Enlisted in the Army in 1941. Sergeant Krautwald was killed in action in Asia on January 18, 1944.

LANE, HARRY, Dothan, AL. Freshman football 1938. Army Air Forces lieutenant.

LANGDALE, NOAH, Valdosta, GA. Tackle 1938-41. Phi Beta Kappa 1941. Played on Georgia Navy Pre-Flight team against Alabama 1942. Coached North Carolina Navy Pre-Flight and served in the Pacific during WWII. Earned MBA and law degrees from Harvard. Served as president of Georgia State University 1957-88 as the campus grew from two buildings and 5,200 students to 20 buildings and 22,000 students. Widely known as an eloquent orator. Received the University of Alabama National Alumni Association's Paul W. Bryant Alumni-Athlete Award in 2005 for his professional accomplishments and contributions to society after leaving the University. Died at age 87 in February 2008.

Morton W. Kimball

Joe Kilgrow

George King

Noah Langdale

Carney G. Laslie

William E. Lee

Vaughn Mancha

Charlie Marr

LASLIE, CARNEY G., Charlotte, NC. Tackle 1930-32. Navy lieutenant. Physical fitness instructor and coach at Navy Pre-Flight schools. Assistant coach under Paul "Bear" Bryant at Maryland (1945), Kentucky (1946-51), Texas A&M (1957) and at Alabama (1958-69). Also assistant coach at West Point 1952-56. Died at age 61.

LAWLEY, GEORGE B., Bessemer, AL. Fullback 1940-41. Army Air Forces lieutenant. Pilot with 450th Bombardment Group in the 15th Air Force. Flew combat missions over enemy territory throughout Europe.

LEACH, FOY ALVIN, Siloam Springs, AR. End 1931-33. Team captain 1933. Army.

LEE, J. D. (BUTCH), Birmingham, AL. End 1942, 1946-48. Navy.

LEE, WILLIAM E. (BILL), Eutaw, AL. Tackle 1932-34. All-America, All-SEC and team captain in 1934. Alabama teams went 25-3-1 during Lee's playing days, including winning the 1934 national championship with a 10-0 record that included a 29-13 victory over Stanford in the Rose Bowl. Saw duty as a navy captain in the Pacific during WWII. Played professional football with the Brooklyn Dodgers 1935-40 and with Green Bay 1941 and 1946. Wrestled professionally as "Alabama Bill." Elected to Alabama Sports Hall of Fame. Followed in the footsteps of his father and brother by serving as sheriff of Greene County (16 years). Son Bill also played football at Alabama.

LEETH, WHEELER BOOKER, Boaz, AL. End 1940-42. All-SEC basketball player. Served as a captain in the Army's 508th Parachute Infantry Regiment in Europe and with the occupation forces in Germany. Jumped behind enemy lines at Normandy on D-Day June 6, 1944, and again on Sept. 17, 1944, in Operation Market Garden. Also fought in the Battle of the Bulge. Spent 35 years as a coach, educator and administrator in Bradenton, FL. Had an 85-30-7 record as head coach. Elected to the Florida High School Athletic Hall of Fame.

LEON, ANTHONY (TONY) DAVID, Follansbee, WV. Guard 1940-42. Army. Played professional football with Washington, Brooklyn and Boston.

LOCKRIDGE, DOYLE, Gadsden, AL. Alabama football 1940. Served as an Army training instructor 1941-45. Later worked for the Postal Service and served as assistant baseball coach at Gadsden State Community College, where his son Bill has been head coach for almost 30 years.

LUMPKIN, C. R. Marine private first class.

LYON, SAMUEL (HAMP), Meridian, MS. Tackle 1934-36. Also on track team. Army major during the war. Long-time coach at Benjamin Russell High School in Alexander City, AL, when the football stadium was named in his honor.

MacCALLUM, JOHN NELSON, Monroe, NY. Football 1946. Navy.

MACHTOLFF, ALBERT (JACK), Sheffield, AL. Center 1935-37. Also played baseball at Alabama. Played professional minor league baseball and served as athletic director for a company in Georgia prior to joining the Navy in 1942. Served in the Pacific theater, where he received a Purple Heart when his ship was struck by a Japanese torpedo. Spent 10 years in the Navy, reaching the rank of petty officer. Served with the occupation forces in Europe aboard the *USS Spokane* 1947-48 and at Guantanamo Bay 1949-50. Received a medical discharge in 1951. Served as head baseball coach at Arizona State 1952-53. Died January 3, 1958, of complications from his war injuries. His brother Francis also served in the Navy during WWII.

MANCHA, VAUGHN, Birmingham, AL. Center, 1944-47. All-SEC and All-America 1945. Four-year letterman. No. 5 overall pick in 1948 NFL draft. Played one season with Boston Yanks. Head coach Livingston University 1949-51 with 18-10-2 record. Assistant coach at Florida State 1952-56 and at Columbia 1957-58. Athletic director at Florida State 1959-70. Rode a freight train to California and worked as a welder in the shipyards repairing damaged U.S. warships 1942-44 after being rejected for military service due to blindness in one eye from a childhood accident. Reclassified eligible for limited service in 1944, but never called to duty. Elected to the Alabama Sports Hall of Fame, College Football Hall of Fame (1990) and to Alabama's Team of the Century.

MARR, CHARLES, Pine Bluff, AR. Guard 1932-34. All-SEC 1934. Played professional football and baseball after college.Army Air Forces colonel. Served in U.S. and India as recreation director. Head football coach at University of Mexico 1936-37. Marr worked in business and law after WWII.

MARTIN, FRANK HAYES, Columbiana, AL. Halfback 1940-41. Army lieutenant.

MARCUS, GEORGE, Burgettstown, PA. Tackle 1942. Army sergeant.

MARX, NATHAN, Birmingham, AL. Football manager, 1937. A Club member. Navy lieutenant. Flight instructor. Killed April 28, 1945, in a plane crash at Los Alamitos, CA.

MAXWELL, TOM, Tuscaloosa, AL. End 1940. Army lieutenant.

MAY, WALTER T. JR., Mobile, AL. Guard 1946-49. Served as Army private first class infantry rifleman in France, Germany and Austria with 67th Armored Infantry Battalion, 13th Armored Division after joining the fighting shortly after the Battle of the Bulge in January 1945. Joined the Army with friend and teammate Bill Theris on the day they graduated from Murphy High School on June 1, 1944. Both returned from military service to play football at Alabama. May earned a degree in business and was an accountant in Vicksburg, MS, for 30 years. He lived in Gulf Breeze, FL, in May 2010.

McALLISTER, JAKE, Oakmulgee, OK. Tackle 1941. Army. Served 24 months overseas with combat engineers. Played at Oklahoma after WWII.

McCOY, MACKEY, Birmingham, AL. Halfback 1941. Army Air Forces sergeant. Played with Randolph Field service champions in 1944.

McDONALD, CHARLES E. JR., Mandeville, LA. Football 1941. Navy ensign.

McKEWEN, JACK LEARD JR., Birmingham, AL. Tackle 1940-42. Army lieutenant. Earned All-Southeast honors as a player with the 124th Infantry at Fort Benning, GA. Served 18 months patrolling the Panama Canal. Son Jack III also played football at Alabama. Insurance executive for 50 years. President of Million Dollar Round Table. Received the 2001 University of Alabama National Alumni Association's Paul W. Bryant Alumni-Athlete Award for professional accomplishments and contributions to society after leaving the University. He died April 10, 2010, at age 90. (See story page 62)

McKOSKY, THEODORE S., Monessen, PA. Guard 1940-42, 1946. Spent four years in the Army during World War II, rising to the rank of captain and serving as a company commander with the Corps of Engineers in the South Pacific. Spent 35 years as an engineer with Bethlehem Steel before retiring in 1983.

McLEOD, BENJAMIN W. JR., Leakesville, MS. Halfback 1934-36. Also played baseball and basketball, earning eight letters at Alabama. Played in the 1935 Rose Bowl with Dixie Howell, Don Hutson and Paul "Bear" Bryant. Named UA's athlete of the year in 1935. Saw military duty as a Navy physical fitness instructor at Pensacola Naval Air Station and at sea in the North Atlantic. Retired from the Navy reserve as a full commander. Son Ben III also played football at Alabama. Received the University of Alabama National Alumni Association's Paul W. Bryant Alumni-Athlete Award in 2008 in recognition of his accomplishments and contributions to society after leaving the University. McLeod was also recognized in 2008 as the oldest (95) living A-Club member. (See story page 217)

McMURRAY, WILLIAM, Roanoke, AL. Quarterback 1938-39. Army Air Forces master sergeant.

McRIGHT, RALPH C., Russellville, AL. Halfback 1928-30. Starter on the 1930 Alabama national championship team that went 10-0, including a 24-0 win over Washington State in the Rose Bowl. Also played baseball and basketball. Coached at North Carolina Pre-Flight School as a Navy lieutenant during World War II. Coached high school football 27 years at Paducah and Hopkinsville, KY, and college football at the University of Kentucky one season.

McWHORTER, JAMES P. (RED), Athens, GA. Quarterback 1942, 1946. Army Air Forces lieutenant. Served 30 months as a B-29 bomber pilot. Worked for the

Walter T. May Jr.

Jack L. McKewen Jr.

Benjamin W. McLeod Jr.

Ralph McRight

Walter O. Merrill

Floyd Dean Miller

Hugh Barr Miller

Mike Mizerany

Coca Cola Company many years. His brother Hamilton "Mac" McWhorter won five Distinguished Flying Crosses and recorded 12 kills as one of the most famous fighter pilots in the Pacific Theater during WWII.

MERRILL, WALTER O., Andalusia, AL. Tackle 1937-39. Alternate captain 1939. Third team All-SEC 1938 and 1939. Voted most valuable player by teammates 1938. Played in the Shrine East-West All-Star game 1940. Named first-team All-Southeastern by sports writers in 1939. Chosen 34th overall in 1940 NFL draft by Brooklyn Dodgers. Started 22 of 28 games with the Dodgers as a 6-2, 217-pound tackle 1940-42 even though he was blind in one eye. Served as a master sergeant in the Army Air Forces during WWI, playing football and coaching at Randolph Field and Keesler Air Field. Died in March 1953 at age 35 of a service-connected disability. Grandson Seth Moates also played football at Alabama. (See story page 64)

MILES, WALTER M. JR., Powderly, AL. Tackle 1942. Served 27 months in the Pacific as a seaman first class aboard the Navy minelayer *USS Terror.*

MILLER, FLOYD DEAN (KO), Oneonta, AL. Tackle 1946-49. Army sergeant. Served as an infantryman and rehabilitation instructor in the Pacific. Prominent Blount County educator and youth leader. Son Noah Dean and grandsons Marc and Matt also played football at Alabama. (See story page 66)

MILLER, HUGH BARR, Hazlehurst, MS. Quarterback 1928-30. Drop-kicked a field goal from the 40-yard-line against Howard College in 1930. Served as gunnery officer on the destroyer *USS Strong* in the Pacific until the ship was sunk by Japanese bombers. Survived 39 days on a Japanese-held island before being rescued. Killed 15 enemy soldiers while collecting valuable military intelligence information. Nominated for the Congressional Medal of Honor. Received the Navy Cross for heroism from Eleanor Roosevelt and Admiral W. F. "Bull" Halsey. Later featured on the "This is Your Life" television show. Retired as a Navy captain. His son Landon also played football at Alabama and served in the Navy. (See story page 219)

MIMS, CARL EDWARD SR., Sylacauga, AL. Halfback 1941, 1946.. Averaged 6.1 yards a carry as a sophomore at Alabama in 1941. Led nation in scoring as high school senior at B. B. Comer High with 179 points. Went into the Army immediately after the Cotton Bowl game of January 1, 1942, and served at Fort Dix, NJ, and Fort Benning, GA. Attained the rank of sergeant as a training and recreation NCO. Returned to Alabama to play briefly after the war. Ran a construction company after college.

MIZERANY, MIKE, Birmingham, AL. Guard 1948-50. Team captain and All-SEC 1950. Led Alabama's baseball team in fielding percentage in 1951 (.994). Served as an Army military policeman in Italy after the war. Operated Big Mike's Restaurant in Birmingham 1952-1982.

MONSKY, LEROY G. SR., Montgomery, AL. Guard 1935-37. All-America, All-SEC and team captain 1937. Won the Jacobs Trophy as the best blocker in SEC 1937. As an Army captain, Monsky commanded an artillery company in Italy. Later an insurance agent in Birmingham.

MORROW, BOB ED, Selma, AL. Guard 1932-34. Army major. Served in transportation at the Boston port of embarkation.

MOSELEY, FRANK O. (CHESTY), Montgomery, AL. Fullback 1931-33. Alternate team captain and All-Southern in 1933. Navy lieutenant. Served as an assistant coach with Georgia Pre-Flight and as a gunnery officer aboard the aircraft carrier *USS Lexington.* The *Lexington* spent 21 months in combat in the Pacific and its planes were credited with sinking 300,000 tons of enemy cargo and destroying 372 enemy planes. Moseley served as an assistant coach at Maryland (1945) and Kentucky (1946-50) under Paul "Bear" Bryant. He was head football coach and athletic director at Virginia Tech 1951-60 and athletic director 1961-1978. Had a 54-42-4 record as head coach. Elected to the Virginia Tech Hall of Fame. Moseley once said "Fighting is just like playing football. Every man has an assignment and through proper cooperation the objective is met." Moseley also said "For sheer courage and daring you can't beat the American sailor, soldier, Marine or pilot. I have seen some mighty fine examples of raw courage when the chips were down and I have yet to see a man fail to do his duty."

MOSLEY, HERSCHEL E. (HERKY), Blytheville, AR. Halfback 1937-39. Alabama's leading passer in 1938 and 1939. Gained 465 yards on 78 carries, completed 28 of 63 passes and averaged 40.6 yards punting in 1939. Played professional football with the Long Island Indians. As an Army Air Forces lieutenant, Mosley served as a B-17 bomber pilot in Europe. His brothers Russ and Norman (Monk) also played at Alabama and served in the military during WWII. (See story page 123)

MOSLEY, NORMAN S. (MONK), Blytheville, AR. Halfback 1942, 1946-47. Army master sergeant. Served 31 months in the South Pacific, including the Solomon and Philippine islands. His brothers Herschel and Russ also played football at Alabama and served in the military during World War II. (See story page 123)

MOSLEY, RUSSELL C., Blytheville, AR. Halfback 1940-42. Led team in passing in 1942 with 352 yards and two touchdowns on 24 completions in 48 attempts. Also the team's top punter and kick returner in 1942. Army Air Forces B-24 bomber pilot. Flew 26 combat missions over Germany. Coached high school football 27 years, including 12 at Blytheville, where his team won state titles in 1949 and 1954. (See story page 123)

NELSON, JIMMY, Live Oak, FL. Halfback 1939-41. All-SEC 1940 and 1941. Led Alabama in rushing in 1941 with 361 yards and led the team in passing in 1940 (231 yards) and 1941 (394 yards). Second in rushing in 1940 with 332 yards and led the team in punting with a 40.9 average on 47 kicks. Army Air Forces private. Played on the Western Army All-Star team coached by Wallace Wade in 1942.

NEWMAN, HAROLD L. (HAL), Birmingham, AL. End 1937-40. Named UA's best all-around athlete 1939-40. Second-team All-America 1939. Third-team All-SEC 1939 and 1940. Team captain 1940. Played in 1941 Blue-Gray Game. Served in Europe as Army lieutenant. Second Alabama football player to be drafted into military service.

NEWTON, JAMES C., Birmingham, AL. Guard 1926. Army lieutenant.

NISBET, JAMES L. (BUBBER), Bainbridge, GA. Fullback 1933-36. All-America and team captain 1936. Navy lieutenant. Coach with North Carolina and Iowa Navy Pre-Flight. Won three state championships as a high school coach in Greenville, SC. Also coached at El Dorado, AR, and Pascagoula, MS.

NOONAN, LIONEL W. (RED), Mobile, AL. Fullback 1946-49. Navy physical fitness and judo instructor. Attorney and Probate Judge in Mobile, AL. (See story page 226)

O'SULLIVAN, IGNATIOS L. (PAT), New Orleans, LA. Center/linebacker 1947-50. All-SEC 1950. Ran away from home to join the Marines at 15 but was rejected. Joined the Merchant Marines but his family located him in San Francisco and brought him home. Drafted into the Army three years later (1945) and was in boot camp when the war ended. Served as an MP with the occupation forces in Japan. Selected to "Betty Grable's Most Handsome All-America Football Team" in 1950. Ran a construction business in Birmingham. Received the University of Alabama National Alumni Association's Paul W. Bryant Alumni-Athlete Award in 2002 in recognition of his professional accomplishments and contributions to society after leaving the University.

OLENSKI, MITCHELL JOSEPH, Vestal, NY. Tackle 1941-42. Played in Cotton and Orange Bowl games. Army lieutenant. Served as physical fitness director at Fort Warren, Wyoming. Played service football 1944-45, earning All-Service and All-Rocky Mountain honors. Played in the 1946 College All-Star game. Played professional football with the Miami Seahawks in 1946 and the Detroit Lions in 1947. High school official 1951-93. Insurance agent 1947-58. Owned and operated a restaurant and bar in Binghamton, NY, from 1958 until his death in 2000.

PAPAIS, JULIUS, Hammond, IN. Halfback 1939-41. Assistant coach at Alabama 1942. Army lieutenant during WWII. Coached swimming at Hammond High School 1951-72, winning three state championships and producing 17 individual champions. Inducted into the Indiana High School Swimming and Diving Hall of Fame and Hammond Sports Hall of Fame.

Frank O. Moseley

Jimmy Nelson

Harold L. Newman

Ignatios L. O'Sullivan

Howard Pierson

James Radford

Holt Rast

George Wallace Richeson

PARTLOW, WILLIAM D., Tuscaloosa, AL. Football 1928. Also on the track team. Army colonel.

PATTON, DAVID B., Tuscaloosa, AL. Freshman football 1937. Navy lieutenant.

PATTON, NEAL, Decherd, TN. Guard 1941. U.S. Coast Guard. Killed December 14, 1942, when two patrol bombers collided off the coast of California. Played football with Western Coast Guard team in 1942.

PERRY, CLAUDE, Jasper, AL. Tackle 1923-26. Served as a corporal in the Marines.

PIERSON, HOWARD, Succasunna, NJ. End 1946-49. Left high school early to join the Navy. As an apprentice seaman with an antiaircraft gun battery aboard the battleship *USS Iowa* Pierson was eye witness to the Japanese kamikaze attacks on the U.S. Navy fleet during the invasion of Okinawa. Completed high school after the war and earned a scholarship to Alabama. Received Air Force ROTC commission in 1951. Flew B-29 bombers during Korean War and B-47 and B-52 bombers with the Strategic Air Command during the Cold War. Saw four years of combat duty in Vietnam and Southeast Asia as a command pilot with U.S., Vietnamese and Thai air force units. His last assignment in Southeast Asia was as commander of the Forward Air Controllers. He was the last man to fly out of Cambodia on August 15, 1973. Combat decorations include three Distinguished Flying Crosses, 39 Air Medals, three Bronze Stars, Meritorious Service Medal, Medal of Valor and the Vietnamese Gallantry Cross. Accumulated over 10,000 flight hours. Flew military fighters, bombers and trainers with one, two, four, six, eight and sometimes no engines. Retired as lieutenant colonel. Lived in Grass Valley, CA, in June 2010. (See story page 229)

POLIZZI, IGNATIUS (IGGY), Indianola, MS. Halfback 1940-41. Served as non-commissioned officer at Army Air Forces bases in Colorado and California during the war. Played one year of football at UCLA after the war and remained in California throughout his life.

POURCHOT, RAY, Phoenix, AZ. Freshman end 1946. Served in the Navy assigned to the Marines during WWII. Saw duty in Germany at the Nuremberg Trials. Played at Southern Cal 1947-48.

RADFORD, JAMES S., Hartford, AL. Tackle 1934-36. Navy ensign. Coached at Georgia Pre-Flight and led a gun crew while on sea duty. Coached at Elba and Murphy high schools.

RADOSEVICH, BILL, Midland, PA. Tackle 1947-48. Served with the Army Corps of Engineers in Europe and the Pacific.

RANEY, WILLIAM B. Football trainer and track coach. Served as a major in the Army Air Forces in the China-Burma-India Theater of war.

RAST, HOLT, Birmingham, AL. End 1938-41. All-SEC 1940 and 1941. All-America 1941. Played on the Army's Western All-Star team coached by Wallace Wade in 1942. Reached the rank of major while serving as a combat engineer with the Ninth Infantry Division in North Africa, Sicily, France and Germany. Earned the Silver Star, Bronze Star and Purple Heart with oak leaf cluster. Elected to the Alabama Sports Hall of Fame in 1977 and the Alabama Academy of Honor in 1989. Received the SEC Living Legends Award in 1998 (posthumously) and shared the University of Alabama National Alumni Association's Paul W. Bryant Alumni-Athlete Award with his brother Tom in 1993. The Bryant Award is presented in recognition of a former athlete's professional accomplishments and contributions to society after leaving the University. Rast was a business and civic leader in Birmingham. (See story page 68)

REDDEN, JAKE M., Vernon, AL. Tackle 1935-38. Served in the Navy in the Pacific.

REESE, KENNETH E. (KENNY), El Dorado, AR. Halfback 1942. Saw overseas duty as a corporal in the Marines. Returned to Alabama in 1946 but never returned to pre-war form due to an illness contracted in the Pacific. Played for the Detroit Lions in 1947.

RICHESON, GEORGE WALLACE, Russellville, AL. Tackle 1939-41. Lieutenant with Army Air Forces. Navigator on B-17 bombers during 36 missions over Europe with the 8th Air Force. Younger brother Ray also played football at Alabama and served in the Army Air Forces. (See story page 130)

RICHESON, THOMAS RAY, Russellville, AL. Guard, 1946-48. Team captain 1948. Played professional football with Chicago and Pittsburgh. Head coach at Meridian High School and Livingston State College. Pilot with 15th Air Force, flying B-24 bombers over Tunisia and Italy. His brother Wallace also played football at Alabama and served in the Army Air Forces during WWII. (See story page 130)

RILEY, JOSEPH R., Dothan, AL. Halfback 1934-36. Played on Alabama's 1934 national championship team Rose Bowl team. A 60-minute player, Riley averaged 5.6 yards per carry in 1936 as the Tide's right halfback and was among the SEC's top punters. Named to the 1937 College All-Star team which upset NFL champion Green Bay 6-0. Also a sprinter on the Alabama track team with a time of 9.8 seconds in the 100-yard dash. Served as head coach at Sidney Lanier High School and as golf coach at The Citadel. As a captain serving as personnel and recreation officer in the Army Air Forces on the Pacific island of Tinian during WWII, Riley witnessed the takeoff of the B-29 bomber Enola Gay on its way to drop the first atomic bomb on Hiroshima, Japan, on August 5, 1945. Retired as lieutenant colonel after 28 years of service in the Air Force. Received the Legion of Merit among many other military decorations. Started the Air Force Junior ROTC programs at Lee High School in Montgomery, AL, and Bay High School in Panama City, FL. Served as the first president of the Emerald Coast Red Elephant Club in 1992. Born April 28, 1914, Riley was one of the oldest living Alabama A Club members in May 2010 at age 96.

ROBERTS, JAMES L. (BABS), Blytheville, AR. End 1940-42. Football co-captain 1942. Captain of the UA boxing team. Army sergeant. Killed in a rifle range training accident at Fort Campbell, Kentucky, December 22, 1944.

ROBERTS, JOHN QUINCY (JOHNNY), Birmingham, AL. Fullback 1936-38. Also on baseball and boxing teams at UA. President of the A Club. Assistant coach of UA freshmen 1940. As a Navy ensign, Roberts served as a pilot on the aircraft carrier *USS Enterprise.* Killed June 4, 1942, when he purposely flew his dive bomber into the deck of the Japanese carrier *Kaga* during the Battle of Midway. Received the Navy Cross and had a Navy ship named in his honor. (See story page 234)

RODGERS, HOSEA W., Brewton, AL. Fullback 1942. The only freshman to play for Alabama in the January 1, 1943, Orange Bowl game. Joined the Marines in 1943 and played football at North Carolina in the V-12 program in 1943. Attained the rank of captain while serving in the Pacific and occupied Japan. Returned to North Carolina after the war and played 1946-48, earning All-Southern Conference honors.

ROGERS, LEE OTIS, Holt, AL. Quarterback 1931-33. Also played basketball and baseball at Alabama. Navy lieutenant during the war. Played professional baseball, helping pitch Little Rock (AR) to the Southern Association pennant in 1937. Played with Boston and Brooklyn in 1938, appearing in 26 games as a relief pitcher and posting a 1-3 record with four saves. Later a sporting goods dealer and game official in Little Rock. Inducted into the Arkansas Sports Hall of Fame.

ROGERS, VICTOR L., Tuscaloosa, AL. End 1934-35. Army captain. Operated Moon Winx Court in Tuscaloosa.

ROHRDANZ, CLARENCE W., East Chicago, IN. Fullback 1932-35. Navy.

RUPICH, JIM, Wheeling, WV. End 1946. Army.

RYBA, JAMES JOHN, Cicero, IL. Tackle 1934-37. All-America 1937. Played in the Tide's January 1, 1938, Rose Bowl game. Also played in the 1938 College All-Star game, where he blocked a punt by Washington Redskins punter Sammy Baugh that led to a touchdown and helped the All-Stars win 28-16. Coached basketball and led physical fitness programs as a lieutenant with North Carolina Navy Pre-Flight 1943-45. Athletic director and head football and basketball coach at Sidney Lanier High School in Montgomery before and after the war. Died February 16, 1950, at age 42 after falling from a tree while installing a swing for his children.

SABO, ALBERT RALPH, Los Angeles, CA. Quarterback 1940-42. Two-year starter and 60-minute player. Rated one of the top blocking backs in the SEC. Also played baseball at Alabama. Saw overseas duty as an Army officer during WWII. Head coach at Bay High School in Panama City, FL. President of the A Club Alumni 1978-81.

Thomas Ray Richeson

Joseph R. Riley

James L. Roberts

James John Ryba

Albert Ralph Sabo

Donald Joseph Salls

Louie Scales

Sam Sharpe

SALLS, DONALD JOSEPH, White Plains, NY. Fullback 1940-42. Although only 170 pounds, Salls was known as a power runner and hard-hitting linebacker. Returned an interception 76 yards for a touchdown in his first game as a sophomore. Commissioned an Army lieutenant through ROTC. Received the Bronze Star for heroism and a Purple Heart for wounds received in Germany. Became head coach at Jacksonville State in 1946 and holds school record with 95 wins in 19 seasons. Taught at JSU an additional 18 years. Elected to the Alabama Sports Hall of Fame. Salls received the University of Alabama National Alumni Association's Paul W. Bryant Alumni-Athlete Award in 2005 in recognition of his professional accomplishments and contributions to society after leaving the University. (See story page 74)

SANDERS, WILLIAM E., Fayette, AL. Tackle 1930-32. Army private.

SANFORD, HAYWARD A. (SANDY), Adona, AR. End/kicker 1937-39. Kicked field goals to win two games for Alabama in 1938. Played professional football with the Washington Redskins in 1940 before joining the Navy. As a Navy lieutenant, Sanford served two tours of duty overseas. He kicked a field goal to give St. Mary's Pre-Flight a 3-0 win in the Northern California Service Football championship game.

SESSIONS, PAUL T. (TRAM) JR., Birmingham, AL. Center 1941-42. Served in the Navy. His father played center at Alabama in the 1920s.

SCALES, LOUIE, Glencoe, AL. Fullback 1941-42, 1945. A Club president. Played professional football with Detroit. Served three years in the Army, including duty as a drill sergeant. Awarded Purple Heart for injury received in grenade explosion. Coached high school sports for 38 years, 37 of them at Alexandria. Had a record of 224-145-15 in football. Elected to the Alabama High School Athletic Association Hall of Fame. The Alexandria High School football stadium is named in his honor.

SHARP, SAM HOUSTON, Birmingham, AL. End 1940-42. Played center on the basketball team and batted .410 as the first baseman on the 1941 baseball team. Chosen school's best all-around athlete 1941. Bomber pilot in the Pacific theater during WWII. Retired Air Force colonel.

SHARPE, JOSEPH F., Mobile, AL. Center 1929-31. Team captain 1931. Head football coach at Pearl River (MS) Community College and at Tuscumbia, AL, and Panama City, FL, high schools. Enlisted in the Army Air Forces in 1941. Received a field commission while serving in Egypt in 1943. Served with the Ninth Air Force in Africa, Middle East and France. Attained the rank of lieutenant colonel.

SHEPHERD, JOE RUFUS, Tuscaloosa, AL. Guard 1934-36. Assistant coach with UA freshmen 1939. Led UA military department's "Fit to Fight" program for ROTC cadets. Earned ROTC commission and served in WWII, Korea and Vietnam. Retired as an Army colonel after heading University of Tennessee ROTC staff.

SHOEMAKER, SAMUEL PERRON JR., Birmingham, AL. End 1937-39. Third-team All-SEC 1938. Also lettered in baseball and basketball at Alabama. Head baseball coach and assistant football coach at Chattanooga 1939-42 and 1946. Assistant coach under Dixie Howell at Idaho 1947-48, at Florida 1949-50 and at Georgia 1951-56. Played professional baseball in the minor leagues, batting .290 in 463 games 1939-42. Served in the Army as a private first class with the 36th Infantry Division in Germany, earning the Combat Infantryman's Badge with four battle stars.

SHOUSE, WILLIAM BANKS JR., Nashville, TN. End 1946-48. Served 37 months with Marines during WWII, including duty as a crew chief on a night-fighter plane on the Pacific island of Bougainville. (See story page 179)

SIBEN, AARON, Central Islip, NY. Guard 1940. Served with the Army in Italy after enlisting November 16, 1942. Captured by Germans but escaped by pushing an enemy solider off a cliff. Returned to New York after the war and worked in law and real estate.

SINGTON, FRED, Birmingham, AL. Tackle 1928-30. All-America and All-Southern Conference 1929 and 1930. Phi Beta Kappa student. Also baseball All-America. Leader of Alabama's 1930 defensive unit that shut out eight of 10 opponents, allowing only 13 points during the season. Hailed as the nation's best lineman after the Tide's 24-0 win over Washington State in January 1, 1931, Rose Bowl. Named to both football and baseball All-Century teams at Alabama. Assistant coach at Duke under Wallace Wade four years. Played major league baseball with the Washington Senators and Brooklyn Dodgers. Named the Southern Association most valuable player in 1936 with a .384 batting average for Chattanooga. A Navy lieutenant during WWII, Sington served as a fitness instructor, executive officer, coach and athletic director of Navy training programs. He was head coach of the Oklahoma Zoomers, one of the top service teams during the war. SEC football official 1935-55. Received the University of Alabama Distinguished Alumnus Award in 1967 and the University of Alabama National Alumni Association's Paul W. Bryant Alumni-Athlete Award in 1991 in recognition of his professional accomplishments and contributions to society after leaving the University. Served as president of the National Alumni Association. Long-time prominent Birmingham business and civic leader. Elected to the Alabama Sports Hall of Fame, the Helms Hall of Fame, College Football Hall of Fame, National Football Hall of Fame, the Alabama Academy of Honor and the Alabama Business Hall of Fame.

SMALLEY, ROY B. JR., Birmingham, AL. Guard 1948-50. Navy.

SMITH, RILEY H., Columbus, MS. Quarterback 1933-35. All-America and All-SEC 1935. Won the Jacobs Trophy as the best blocker in SEC 1935. Also on track team. Second player chosen in first-ever NFL draft in 1936. Missed only three minutes in 26 games with Redskins (1936-38) before an injury ended his playing career. Assistant coach at Washington and Lee University 1939 then head coach 1940-42 before joining the Navy for World War II. Served as a lieutenant commander physical fitness instructor at Jacksonville and Miami Navy schools before discharge in 1945. Real estate developer in Mobile, AL, after the war. Elected to Alabama Sports Hall of Fame, Mississippi Sports Hall of Fame and the College Football Hall of Fame.

SPENCER, PAUL B., Hampton, VA. Fullback 1938-40. Team's leading rusher and scorer in 1940 with 503 yards rushing and 48 points. Navy pilot stationed at Lakehurst, NJ, during WWII.

SPURRELL, DONALD W., Brentwood, NY. Halfback 1948. Navy fireman on the destroyer escort *USS Daniel A. Joy* in the Pacific 1944-45. Earned UA law degree 1954. Noted patent attorney in Johnson City, TN.

ST. JOHN, BUELL A., Aliceville, AL. Halfback 1939. Served in the Navy during WWII. Earned UA degree 1944 and worked at Cape Canaveral, FL, for many years.

STAPLES, JOHN S. (STUDIE), Owensboro, KY. Guard 1942, 1946. Ordnance officer with the Marines in the Pacific and Japan. Earned the Bronze Star on Iwo Jima. Also served on active duty during the Korean War. Long-time coach and educator in the state of Florida. (See story page 181)

STAPP, CHARLES D., Birmingham, AL. Halfback, 1932-35. Assistant coach in track and football at Alabama. Navy lieutenant 1944-45. Served as superintendent of physical education for the state of Alabama.

STEINER, REBEL ROY SR., Birmingham, AL. End 1945, 1947-49. Played on Alabama's Rose Bowl team of January 1, 1946. Also played basketball. Served with Army occupational forces in Japan. Played professional football with Green Bay 1950-51, intercepting 10 passes in 24 games and returning one for a 94-yard touchdown. Once said "for a man who lives in Alabama, having played football for Alabama gives you a head start in other things and with other people."

STEWART, VAUGHN M., Anniston, AL. Center 1941. Member of 1941 national championship team at only 165 pounds. Saw Army duty on the East Coast 1943-45. Played professional football with Chicago and Brooklyn for two years after the war. Insurance agent and well-known cartoonist. Co-chairman of the board for the Huntsville-Madison County Athletic Hall of Fame and a 1990 inductee.

STRANGE, JACK B., Russellville, AL. Fullback 1940-41. Drafted into the Army in July 1942. Contracted malaria while serving in the South Pacific. Played minor league baseball.

Fred Sington

Riley H. Smith

John S. Staples

Rebel Roy Steiner Sr.

Joseph Cullen Sugg

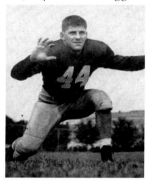

Nicholas J. Terlizzi

James Baird Tipton

William T. Van der Graaff

SUDDUTH, JOSEPH E., Birmingham, AL. Tackle 1940-41. Served as a lieutenant in the Marines.

SUGG, JOSEPH CULLEN, Russellville, AL. Guard 1936-39. A Club president 1939. Served with General George Patton's Third Army in Normandy, Belgium and Germany, reaching the rank of captain as an Army artillery officer. Returned to North Alabama and farmed until retirement. (See story page 78)

SUTHER, JOHN HENRY (FLASH), Tuscaloosa, AL. Half-back 1927-30. All-America and All-Southern Conference 1930. High school coach at Hopkinsville, KY, Gadsden and Hueytown prior to WWII. Called to active military duty as a National Guard first lieutenant March 5, 1942. Served with 305th Military Police, reaching rank of lieutenant colonel. Later served as sheriff of Tuscaloosa County.

SWAIM, MOSES M. SR., Tuscaloosa, AL. End/guard 1931-32. Army captain.

TAYLOR, JOHN. Halfback, 1933-34. Army sergeant.

TERLIZZI, NICHOLAS J., Upper Montclair, NJ. Tackle 1945-46. Organized and played on Alabama's 1943 "Informals" football team, which had a 2-1 record. Joined the Navy in early 1944 and played service football in 1944. (See story page 239)

THERIS, WILLIAM (BILL), Mobile, AL. Tackle 1948-49. Army paratrooper with the 82nd Airborne Division in France, Belgium and Germany. Joined the Army on the day he graduated from Murphy High School, June 1, 1944. Returned from military duty to play football at Alabama.

TINSLEY, PHIL, Bessemer, AL. End 1942. Joined the Navy in 1943. Played at Georgia Tech 1943 in the Navy V-12 program, earning All-SEC honors. Earned All-America honors in 1944 while helping Tech win the SEC championship. Captain of the 1945 Georgia Tech team and inducted into the school's Hall of Fame in 1970.

TIPTON, JAMES BAIRD, Blytheville, AR. End/tackle 1935-37. Graduated from Alabama in 1938 with a degree in aeronautical engineering. Received his wings and commission in the Army Air Forces in 1939. Served as pilot instructor until 1943, when he was sent overseas as a pilot with the Ninth Air Force. Flew 93 combat missions in P-47 and P-51 aircraft against German targets in Europe. He retired from the Air Force as a major general. Flew 38 combat missions over North Korea in F-80 and F-84 jet fighters during the Korean War (1951-52). His decorations included the Distinguished Flying Cross; Legion of Merit with two oak leaf clusters; Air Medal with 15 oak leaf clusters; British Distinguished Flying Cross; Belgium Croix de Guerre with Palm; French Croix de Guerre with Palm; World War II Victory Medal; Korean Service Medal; United Nations Service Medal, and Korean Eulchi Distinguished Military Service Medal with silver star. Received the Sports Illustrated Silver Anniversary All-America Award in December 1962 in recognition of his achievements in athletics and in his chosen profession. Died March 29, 1995.

TOLLETT, VAUGHN H., Nashville, AR. Halfback 1938-41. Still holds Arkansas high school record for most all-purpose yards in a single game (551) in 1935. Set a world record as a high school freshman by winning first place in nine individual events and running the anchor leg on two winning relay teams at a junior high track meet in 1934. High scorer in 1937 Arkansas high school track meet as state's top athlete. Recruited by Alabama assistant coach Paul "Bear" Bryant. Played on Alabama's 1941 national championship team and won numerous track and field events on Tide track teams. Army lieutenant during WWII. Earned a degree from Southern Baptist Theological Seminary in Louisville, KY, in 1946. Served 27 years as a military chaplain with the Air Force before retiring as a lieutenant colonel in 1976. Died March 16, 2007.

TUCKER, CALVERT, Round Mountain, AL. End 1941-42. Army.

VAN DE GRAAFF, WILLIAM T. (BULLY), Tuscaloosa, AL. Tackle/fullback 1912-1915. Alabama's first football America (1915) and first All-Southern player 1914-15. Had an 80-yard punt against Sewanee in 1915 for a school record that stood until Dixie Howell's 82-yard kick in 1933. Served as fitness instructor and coach with 8th Army Special Services in U.S. and Japan during WWII. Coached the winning team in the

8th Army Bowl game in Yokohama, Japan, on New Year's Day 1947. Oldest known UA football player to take part in WWII. Alabama freshman football coach in 1922-24 while on UA ROTC staff. Served as head coach and athletic director at Colorado College. ROTC instructor at UCLA 1951-53. Brothers Adrian, Hargrove and Robert also played football at Alabama. Robert became a physicist and invented the Van de Graaff Generator, which was critical to the development of the atomic bombs that were dropped on Japan to help end World War II. Elected to the Alabama Sports Hall of Fame. (See story page 82)

WADE, WALLACE, Trenton, TN. Head football coach 1923-30. Posted overall record of 61-13-3 at Alabama with four conference titles and three national championships (1925, 1926 and 1930). Head coach at Duke 16 seasons with 110-36-7 overall record. Southern Conference Commissioner 1950-60. Served as cavalry officer in WWI and artillery officer in Europe during WWII. Elected to College Football Hall of Fame in 1955. Also elected to the Alabama Sports Hall of Fame, the Tennessee Sports Hall of Fame and the North Carolina Sports Hall of Fame. (See story page 153)

WADSWORTH, JAMES L., Jacksonville, FL. Football 1925. Army sergeant.

WAITES, W. L. (BUD), Tuscaloosa, AL. Halfback 1937-39. Army lieutenant.

WALDING, MALCOLM, Opp, AL. Football 1926. Also on baseball and track teams. Army lieutenant colonel. Commander of 4th Regiment at Camp Siebert (AL) Training Center.

WALDROP, MORRIS, Tifton, GA. End 1940-42. Army lieutenant.

WALKER, DAVID WAYNE, Nashville, TN. Tackle 1944. Army Air Forces.

WALKER, HILMAN B., Hattiesburg, MS. End 1933-35. Played professional baseball 1936-37 in the Brooklyn Dodgers organization. Assistant football coach at Arizona State under Dixie Howell and head coach in 1942 after Howell went into service. Had a 2-8 record as head coach. Navy lieutenant during WWII.

WALKER, JAMES E. (JIMMY), Holt, AL. End 1933-35. Football captain 1935. All-SEC basketball player two seasons and captain of the basketball team 1934-35. Head basketball coach and assistant football coach at Virginia Military Institute prior to joining the Navy during WWII. As a Navy lieutenant, Walker served as an assistant coach of the Georgia Navy pre-Flight football team in 1942 along with former Alabama teammate Paul "Bear" Bryant and former UA coaches Hank Crisp and Tilden "Happy" Campbell. Walker was killed in an automobile accident while on duty in Brazil in 1943. (See story page 241)

WALLACE, CLAUDE D. JR. Quarterback 1938. Army captain.

WALLACE, JIM. Tackle 1942. Army private.

WARREN, ERWIN THOMAS (TUT), Montgomery, AL. End 1935-38. Also basketball letterman. Navy lieutenant. Served as physical fitness instructor at Great Lakes Naval Station during the war. High school coach at Gadsden, AL, and Crestview, FL.

WEBSTER, JOE, Pasadena, CA. Guard 1942. Army.

WEEKS, GEORGE E., Dothan, AL. End 1940-42. Army lieutenant. Assistant coach at Florence State.

WELDON, HOWARD, Birmingham, AL. Tackle 1942, 1946. Marine Corps private.

WELSH, CLEMENT JOSEPH, Winchester, IL. Halfback 46-48. Also on track team. Played with Navy's Oklahoma Zoomers 1944-45. Noted aerospace engineer.

WESLEY, NORMAN RAY, Talladega, AL. Center 1938-41. Also played baseball. Navy lieutenant. Saw combat duty in the South Pacific. High school coach at Talladega.

WHATLEY, JAMES W., Alexander City, AL. Center/tackle 1932-35. Also lettered in baseball (1934-36), basketball (1934-36) and track (1936). All-SEC in football and basketball. Played professional football three years with the Brooklyn Dodgers and minor league baseball two years, batting .273 in 149 games. Athletic director and head football, basketball and baseball coach at West Carolina State Teachers College 1939-

Wade Wallace

W. L. Waites

James E. Walker

James W. Whatley

Arthur P. White

Don Whitmire

Temple Williamson

41. Joined the Navy during World War II and served as a physical fitness instructor and coach at the U.S. Naval Station in San Diego, California. He served as head basketball coach and assistant football coach at Ole Miss 1946-49 then moved to the University of Georgia, where he was head baseball coach for 25 years. He also served as head basketball coach at Georgia 1949-50, and his 1950 team upset SEC champion Kentucky. Whatley had a 27-year record of 360-339-4 in baseball and was elected to the College Baseball Hall of Fame. He served as president of the American Association of College Baseball Coaches in 1964 and was inducted into the Alabama Sports Hall of Fame in 1987.

WHITE, ARTHUR P. (TARZAN), Atmore, AL. Guard 1933-36. All-SEC sophomore on the 1934 national championship Rose Bowl team. All-America 1936. First pick of the New York Giants in 1937 NFL draft and played four seasons with the team, making the All-Pro rookie team and helping the Giants win the NFL championship in 1938. Named to the Pro Bowl team in 1938. Also played two years with the Chicago Cardinals. As a professional wrestler using the name "Tarzan," White was recognized as the world heavyweight champion twice (1939 and 1947). Coached high school sports four years in Cherokee County. Elected to the Alabama Sports Hall of Fame in 1981. Served as an Army lieutenant during World War II. Retired from Air Force Reserve as lieutenant colonel.

WHITE, EDWARD P., Anniston, AL. End/halfback 1947-49. Served in Army's 82nd Airborne Division in Europe during WWII. Played minor league baseball 1950-57, including six years with the Memphis Chicks, batting .307 with 77 home runs for his career. Played in three games with Chicago White Sox 1955, getting two hits in four at bats as a 29-year-old rookie.

WHITLEY, THOMAS L., Birmingham, AL. Tackle 1944-47. Army Air Forces.

WHITMIRE, DON, Decatur, AL. Tackle 1940-42. All-SEC as a sophomore. All-SEC and NEA All-America as junior in 1942, although only 5-11, 215 pounds. Joined the Navy in 1943 and played football at the Naval Academy, earning All-America honors in 1943 and 1944. Received Knute Rockne Memorial Award as nation's best lineman in 1944 and finished fourth in Heisman Trophy balloting. At the Naval Academy, Whitmire became brigade commander, the highest rank a Midshipman can attain. Selected to the All-Time All-SEC team in 1968. Elected to the Alabama Sports Hall of Fame (1979), the Helms Hall of Fame and College Football Hall of Fame (1956). Career Navy officer. Served two tours of duty in Vietnamese waters. Directed the evacuation of Cambodia and Saigon at the end of the Vietnam War, helping 82,000 men, women and children escape to freedom. Once said that football taught him the virtue of team play and enhanced his leadership qualities. "Football taught me to take hard knocks and come up fighting," Whitmire said, adding that traits learned in football had proven valuable in his Navy career. Retired as a rear admiral after 32 years of service. Received patriotism award from President Ronald Reagan in 1984. Also received the Audie Murphy Patriotism Award given at the Spirit of America Festival in his home town of Decatur, AL. Died May 4, 1991. Buried at Arlington National Cemetery.

WILLIAMSON, TEMPLE, Tuscaloosa, AL. Halfback 1933-36. Played on the 1934 SEC and national championship football team that defeated Stanford 29-13 in the Jan. 1, 1935, Rose Bowl game. Fought in five major campaigns in Europe with the Army's 5th Armored Division. Discharged as a lieutenant colonel in 1946. Operated Town & Campus Men's Wear on University Boulevard for 25 years.

WISE, LLOYD, Blytheville, AR. Tackle 1939-41. Drafted into the Army prior to his senior season. Earned a commission through OCS and served as a combat engineer in the Pacific. His company cleared the beach for General MacArthur's return to the Philippines at Leyte in October 1944. Earned the Bronze Star. Returned to the University of Alabama to complete his degree after the war. Called to service during the Korean War and remained in the Army until retirement as a full colonel. (See story page 85)

WOOD, ROBERT H., McComb, MS. Tackle 1936-39. Army lieutenant.

WICKE, HERMAN DALLAS, Pensacola, FL. End/back 1937-39. Army lieutenant.

WOODALL, HENRY IRBY, Centre, AL. Guard 1940. Army Air Forces lieutenant.

WYHONIC, JOHN, Lima, OH. Guard 1938-41. Team captain and All-SEC in 1941. Served as a Navy chief petty officer aboard the USS Chauncey and as a physical fitness instructor during the war. Played professional football with the Philadelphia Eagles and Buffalo Bills.

YOUNG, MONCER L., Mishawaka, IN. Football 1937. Army.

YOUNG, WILLIAM A. JR., Pine Bluff, AR. Tackle 1933-36. Army lieutenant. Was a prisoner of war in Germany.

ZIVICH, GEORGE J., East Chicago, IN. Halfback 1935-38. Rushed for 207 yards on 47 carries in 1938. Played minor league baseball and coached high sports 1939-40. Served as an Army captain in the China-Burma-India Theater. Received the Bronze Star and Purple Heart. Coached at Gadsden, AL, and Rockmart, GA, after WWII. Recalled to service for the Korean War and remained on duty through 1967. Retired as a full colonel. (See story page 87)

Lloyd Wise

George J. Zivich

VICTORY AT LAST!

General Douglas MacArthur signs the surrender treaty with Japan (below right) on September 2, 1945 to officially end World War II. Other phhotos show Allied troops celebrating the victory in various displays of celebration.

Fans cheer Crimson Tide heroes of 1935 Rose Bowl fame.

EPILOGUE

by Delbert Reed

They remain the heroes of our youth

My earliest childhood memory is of my father's departure for induction into the Army in the spring of 1944. I was three years old at the time, and it must have been a traumatic experience for me to have remembered it for so long.

Daddy's only sister, her husband and their children spent the night at our house the night before Daddy left. The children slept on pallets on the floor. Daddy was gone when I awoke the next morning; my uncle had driven him the 20 miles to the bus station before dawn for his trip to Fort McClellan, Alabama.

Daddy was gone only a few days before being classified 4-F and sent back home because of stomach ulcers. The Army doctor was right, too. A few months later Daddy's stomach ruptured, perforated by the ulcers, and he spent 29 days in Druid City Hospital in Tuscaloosa and months longer recovering from the life-threatening ordeal.

Another of my World War II-era memories includes seeing airplanes for the first time as pilots flew area skies while training at Tuscaloosa's Van de Graaff Field.

I remember well the veterans coming home from the war, some missing arms or legs, some blind or scarred from battle, some with tattoos on their arms. Some were relatives, and many of them had been not much more than boys themselves when they left. They were different when they came home from the war, though. They were no longer the shy farm boys they had been before. They smoked Lucky Strike cigarettes and spoke with confidence. They had been to war and won and they were proud.

They were my heroes then and they are my heroes still.

The men who fought in World War II have been the subjects of hundreds of inspiring movies and books, yet only a few of their millions of stories have been told.

Writing about many of the men I admired on the football field and in wartime has been an honor. I have met, known and written about many of them before and during this project, and it is a good feeling to know that they will not be forgotten.

One thing I know for certain: We were fortunate as boys to have these men as our heroes.

ACKNOWLEDGEMENTS

We are sincerely grateful to the military veterans and their families for their assistance in the research efforts for this book. It would not have been possible without them.

Thanks also to the Paul W. Bryant Museum staff of director Ken Gaddy, who coordinated the project; Brad Green, who collected and compiled the photographs; Jan Scurlock, who assisted with research; Olivia Arnold, who assisted with proofreading, and to Taylor Watson, David Mize, Kenny Denton, Debra LeGrone, Lynn Bobo and Coach Clem Gryska (who played with many of the veterans) for their support and assistance during the research, writing and production of this book.

Additional thanks go to Laura Lineberry for book design and to Janice Fink and the staff of the *Alabama Alumni Magazine* for their research assistance.

Special recognition is due Paul W. Bryant Jr., who provided the original idea and material support for the entire project, making this book possible.

PHOTO CREDITS

National Archives, University of Alabama Archives, Paul W. Bryant Museum, Department of Defense, Associated Press (page 188), *Life* Magazine paintings by Peter Hurd (pages 138 and 141), University of Alabama Alumni Magazine, Getty Images (page 210), Arlington National Cemetery, United States Holocaust Memorial Museum (pages 37 and 39). (The views or opinions expressed in this book and the context in which images from the Holocaust Museum are used do not necessarily reflect the views or policy of nor imply approval or endorsement by the United States Holocaust Memorial Museum.)

Special thanks to the veterans and their families for sharing their personal photographs and memorabilia.

Maps produced by the University of Alabama Cartographic Research Laboratory.

MISSION

The mission of the Paul W. Bryant Museum is to collect, preserve and exhibit items and to disseminate information relating to the sports history of the University of Alabama.